Gender and Fatherhood in the Nineteenth

Gender and History
Series editors: Amanda Capern and Louella McCarthy

Published

Trev Lynn Broughton and Helen Rogers (eds)   *Gender and Fatherhood in the Nineteenth Century*

Rachel G. Fuchs and Victoria E. Thompson   *Women in Nineteenth-Century Europe*

Angela Woollacott   *Gender and Empire*

Forthcoming

Shani D'Cruze and Louise A. Jackson   *Women and Crime since 1660*
William Foster   *Gender, Slavery and Servitude in the Atlantic World*
Perry Wilson   *Women in Twentieth-Century Italy*

Gender and Fatherhood in the Nineteenth Century

Edited by

TREV LYNN BROUGHTON

and

HELEN ROGERS

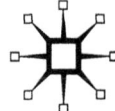

© Selection, editorial matter and Introduction © Trev Lynn Broughton and Helen Rogers 2007. Individual chapters (in order) © Megan Doolittle; Matthew McCormack; Valerie Sanders; Terri Sabatos; Margaret Markwick; Neil Armstrong; Andrew Walker; Helen Rogers; Julie-Marie Strange; Alison Twells; Claudia Nelson; Elizabeth Buettner 2007

All rights reserved. No reproduction, copy or transmission of this publication may be made without written permission.

No paragraph of this publication may be reproduced, copied or transmitted save with written permission or in accordance with the provisions of the Copyright, Designs and Patents Act 1988, or under the terms of any licence permitting limited copying issued by the Copyright Licensing Agency, 90 Tottenham Court Road, London W1T 4LP.

Any person who does any unauthorized act in relation to this publication may be liable to criminal prosecution and civil claims for damages.

The authors have asserted their rights to be identified as the authors of this work in accordance with the Copyright, Designs and Patents Act 1988.

First published 2007 by
PALGRAVE MACMILLAN
Houndmills, Basingstoke, Hampshire RG21 6XS and
175 Fifth Avenue, New York, N.Y. 10010
Companies and representatives throughout the world

PALGRAVE MACMILLAN is the global academic imprint of the Palgrave Macmillan division of St. Martin's Press, LLC and of Palgrave Macmillan Ltd. Macmillan® is a registered trademark in the United States, United Kingdom and other countries. Palgrave is a registered trademark in the European Union and other countries.

ISBN-13: 978-1-4039-9514-8 hardback
ISBN-10: 1-4039-9514-1 hardback
ISBN-13: 978-1-4039-95155 paperback
ISBN-10: 1-4039-9515-X paperback

This book is printed on paper suitable for recycling and made from fully managed and sustained forest sources.

A catalogue record for this book is available from the British Library.

A catalog record for this book is available from the Library of Congress.

10 9 8 7 6 5 4 3 2 1
16 15 14 13 12 11 10 09 08 07

Transferred to Digital Printing 2012

Gender and Fatherhood is dedicated to
Phil Davies and Ellen Rachel Hart

Contents

List of Illustrations and Tables — ix
Acknowledgements — xi
List of Contributors — xiii

Introduction: The Empire of the Father — 1
Trev Lynn Broughton and *Helen Rogers*

Part 1 Rights and Responsibilities

1. Fatherhood, Religious Belief and the Protection of Children in Nineteenth-Century English Families — 31
   Megan Doolittle

2. 'Married Men and the Fathers of Families': Fatherhood and Franchise Reform in Britain — 43
   Matthew McCormack

3. 'What do you want to know about next?' Charles Kingsley's Model of Educational Fatherhood — 55
   Valerie Sanders

Part 2 Patterns of Involvement

4. Father as Mother: The Image of the Widower with Children in Victorian Art — 71
   Terri Sabatos

5. Hands-on Fatherhood in Trollope's Novels — 85
   Margaret Markwick

6. Father(ing) Christmas: Fatherhood, Gender and Modernity in Victorian and Edwardian England — 96
   Neil Armstrong

Part 3 A Different Class?

7. Father's Pride? Fatherhood in Industrializing Communities — 113
   Andrew Walker

8. 'First in the House': Daughters on Working-Class Fathers and Fatherhood — 126
   Helen Rogers

9   'Speechless with Grief': Bereavement and the Working-Class
    Father, c. 1880–1914   138
    Julie-Marie Strange

Part 4 Frontiers of Fatherhood

10 Missionary 'Fathers' and Wayward 'Sons' in the South Pacific,
    1797–1825   153
    Alison Twells

11 A Wealth of Fatherhood: Paternity in American Adoption
    Narratives   165
    Claudia Nelson

12 Fatherhood Real, Imagined, Denied: British Men in Imperial
    India   178
    Elizabeth Buettner

Select Bibliography   190
Index   193

Illustrations and Tables

Illustrations

1	Frederick Daniel Hardy, *The Volunteers*, 1860	2
2	Sir Luke Fildes, *The Widower* [1874], 1902	72
3	Thomas Faed, *Worn Out*, 1868	74
4	Arthur Stocks, *Motherless*, 1883	77
5	S.J. Cash, 'Why Santa Claus Was Late', in *Partridge's Children's Annual*, 1904	103
6	Charles Crombie, 'Santa Crashing an Airship', *London Magazine*, Vol. 36, 1907	104
7	Williams' Shaving Soap, *Illustrated London News*, Christmas Number, 1901	105

Tables

7.1	Household familial employment in colliery settlements	118
7.2	Family groupings in signing-on books: Mitchell Main colliery	119
7.3	Familial colliery employment links discerned from marriage records where the bridegroom is an underground mining worker, 1850–85	120
7.4	Familial colliery employment links discerned from marriage records where the bridegroom is a surface worker at a coal mine, 1850–85	121

Acknowledgements

Many of the chapters in this book were first presented at the interdisciplinary conference 'Father Figures: Gender and Paternity in the Modern Age' held at Liverpool John Moores University, 2003. The editors would like to thank all the participants at the conference and in particular David Morgan, John Tosh and Jacky Eden for their support for the event and this publication. The Centre for Women's Studies at the University of York and the Research Centre for Literature and Cultural History at Liverpool John Moores University made generous financial contributions towards the conference and the making of this book for which the editors are very grateful, as well as for the unflagging interest and suggestions of colleagues.

The editors would like to thank Andrew G. Wallis of the Guards Museum, Wellington Barracks, Birdcage Walk, Westminster, London; Caroline Worthington of York City Art Gallery; Captain Alan Henshall of the Regimental Museum of the Royal Dragoon Guards and the Prince of Wales's own Regiment of Yorkshire, Tower Street, York. This project has benefited from the patience and support of the editorial team at Palgrave and from the insightful comments of unnamed readers and the series editors. Above all, the editors would like to thank the contributors for their unfailingly enthusiastic, energetic and good-humoured commitment to the book.

Abbreviations

As elsewhere in the Gender and History series, frequently cited texts are given in shortened form after the first citation. Full titles can be found in the Select Bibliography on p. 190.

Contributors

Neil Armstrong is Lecturer in Modern British History at the University of Gloucestershire. He completed his doctorate at the University of York in 2004, and is currently revising his thesis for publication as a monograph and series of journal articles.

Trev Lynn Broughton is Senior Lecturer in English and Related Literature at the University of York, where she is also a member of the Centre for Women's Studies. She has published widely on Victorian auto/biography, including *Men of Letters, Writing Lives* (Routledge, 1999), and is currently editing a four-volume collection of autobiographical theory and criticism, also for Routledge.

Elizabeth Buettner is Lecturer in Modern British and Imperial History at the University of York. Her book *Empire Families: Britons and Late Imperial India* (Oxford University Press, 2004) was joint winner of the Women's History Network Annual Book Prize, and in 2005 she was shortlisted for Young Academic Author of the Year by the *Times Higher Education Supplement*. She has published essays in *History and Memory, Women's History Review, Scottish Historical Review* and in several edited collections.

Megan Doolittle is Senior Lecturer in Social Policy at The Open University. Her research interests include the history of the family, fatherhood and masculinity, contemporary families and their alternatives, and relationships between law, social policy and the family. Her publications include 'Sexuality, Parenthood and Population: Explaining Fertility Decline in Britain 1860s to 1920s', in J. Carabine (ed.), *Sexuality* (Policy Press, 2004); *The Family Story: Blood, Contract and Intimacy in Modern England, 1840–1960* (Longman, 1998), with Leonore Davidoff, Janet Fink and Katherine Holden (1999).

Margaret Markwick, of Exeter University, has been writing about Trollope for more than ten years. She published *Trollope and Women* in 1997, introduced *The Small House at Allington* for the Folio Society in the same year, and wrote entries for *The Oxford Reader's Companion to Trollope* in 1999. *New Men in Trollope: Rewriting the Victorian Male* will be published by Ashgate in 2007.

Matthew McCormack is Lecturer in History at the University of Northampton. He is interested in the links between masculinity and political culture in Georgian Britain, and his published works in these areas include an article in the *British Journal for Eighteenth-Century Studies*. His book *The Independent Man: Citizenship and Gender Politics in Georgian England* is published by Manchester University Press.

Claudia Nelson is Professor of English and Director of Women's Studies at Texas A&M University. She is the author or coeditor of six books and numerous articles on matters relating to family, gender roles and sexuality in nineteenth-century Britain and America, including *Invisible Men: Fatherhood in Victorian Periodicals, 1850–1910* (University of Georgia Press, 1995).

Helen Rogers is Senior Lecturer in Literature and Cultural History at Liverpool John Moores University. She has published extensively on Victorian political representation and life-writing and is the author of *Women and the People: Authority, Authorship and the Radical Tradition in Nineteenth-Century England* (Ashgate 2000). Currently, she is working on the prison visitor Sarah Martin and a project on 'Domesticity and Working-Class Women in Nineteenth-Century Britain'.

Terri Sabatos is currently Assistant Professor of Art History at the United States Military Academy, West Point, New York. Current research involves work on death and mourning in Victorian visual culture, specifically images of widows, widowers and the dead and dying child.

Valerie Sanders is Professor of English at the University of Hull. She has written on anti-feminist women novelists, Victorian women's autobiography and Victorian family relations, and has edited a selection of Harriet Martineau's letters. Her most recent book is *The Brother–Sister Culture in Nineteenth-Century Literature from Austen to Woolf* (Palgrave, 2002); her next project is a study of father–child relations in writing families, and their representations of each other in auto/biography.

Julie-Marie Strange is Senior Lecturer in Nineteenth-Century British History at the University of Manchester. She has published in *Women's History Review*, *Journal of Contemporary History*, *Social History of Medicine*, *Social History* and *Past and Present*. She has just published *Death, Grief and Poverty in Britain, 1870–1914* (Cambridge University Press) and is currently working on a cultural history of menstruation.

Alison Twells is Lecturer in Social and Cultural History at Sheffield Hallam University. She has published in *Women's History Review*, in *Women's Studies International Forum* and in Eileen Janes Yeo (ed.), *Radical Femininity: Women's Self-Representation in the Public Sphere, 1800–1914* (Manchester University Press, 1998). She has recently completed *British Women's History* (I. B. Tauris). Her monograph *The Civilizing Mission and the English Middle Class, 1792–1857* is to be published by Palgrave in 2008.

Andrew Walker is Head of the Department of Humanities at the University of Lincoln where he teaches on history and journalism degree programmes. His research interests, which focus upon local and regional societies, also include the history of the English provincial press in the nineteenth and early twentieth centuries. He is currently undertaking work on the social and cultural history of nineteenth- and twentieth-century Lincolnshire.

Introduction:
The Empire of the Father

Trev Lynn Broughton and Helen Rogers

In his *Commentaries on the Laws of England* (1765–9), William Blackstone described the father's absolute legal power within his family as 'the empire of the father'. The mother, by comparison, was 'entitled to no power, but only to reverence and respect'.[1] This construction of fatherhood proved remarkably resilient and continued to underwrite family law. Despite this, the 'empire of the father' was assailed over the nineteenth century, as the home and family were, to a significant extent, annexed to the moral dominion of the mother. In this book, the first full-length study of paternity in Britain and its colonies to encompass the long nineteenth century, we begin to investigate the ideological work of the father figure – the construction and effects of fatherhood as discourse – and the very different experiences of being a father at a time when middle-class ideals of motherhood and domesticity held unprecedented sway, and when paternal status, authority and credibility were sharply inflected by family shape and social position.

John Tosh claims that 'Of all the qualifications for full masculine status, fatherhood was the least talked about by the Victorians.'[2] We argue, by contrast, that the characterization of fathers in art, literature and public debate was more extensive and nuanced than has hitherto been acknowledged. Investigating legal cases, census documents, missionary memoirs, correspondence, employment records, fiction, autobiography, educational writing, political rhetoric and painting, the contributors to this volume reveal the diversity of paternal roles from protector and provider to playmate and guide, nurturer and teacher. We explore what it might have meant to occupy the position of paterfamilias when the relationships of masculinity to family, class and nation were under scrutiny.

This introduction sketches some of the interpretive frameworks within which surviving evidence about nineteenth-century paternity has been evaluated. Far from being an object of consensus or indifference, fatherhood, we contend, mattered a great deal to the Victorians, though in different ways within different social and cultural contexts. We then map out those contexts, asking how changing institutional practices and priorities, material conditions and demographic shifts worked to reshape the family and, within it, the paternal role. To what extent and in what guises did cultural commentary consolidate or challenge 'the empire of the father'? What was the spiritual significance of fatherhood and how did it respond to the pressures of secularization? How far were individual experiences of fathering and being fathered contingent on the shape, structure and size of particular families?

For now, our point of entry into this complex field is Frederick Daniel Hardy's canvas of 1860: *The Volunteers* (see Illustration 1). Uniting both commonplace and more unfamiliar discourses of fatherhood, the painting opens up many of our larger themes and concerns.

I. Putting fathers in the picture

There's no place like the humble cottage interior in a mid-Victorian genre painting. Cosily crowded, picturesquely disordered, sparsely yet comfortably appointed, *The Volunteers* offers us a vigorously sentimental version of the Victorian happy family, playing out in miniature a moment of national triumph. Rosy-cheeked, neatly shod children play a joyful game of soldiers – the skittles on the floor representing the tumbling of territories in the face of British military prowess – while father and grandfather preside benignantly, and mother churns out love and apple pies in the corner. Hardy's work often centres on tableaux of children at play, acting out precocious fantasies of adult life, while bemused but indulgent adults observe from the sidelines. The picture is relatively unusual in Hardy's oeuvre, however, in that it places the children's father within the action. At first glance the painting seems to emit reassuring messages about divisions of labour and lines of command: grandfather, smoking the comfortable pipe of retirement, yields centre stage to his son, home from service in the Guards, who watches protectively over the youngsters. There is something touching in the contrast between the father's formal, almost regal demeanour

Illustration 1 Frederick Daniel Hardy, *The Volunteers*, 1860.
Courtesy of the York Museums Trust © York Museums Trust (York Art Gallery)

(reminiscent, along with the moustache and hairstyle, of the glamorous figure of Prince Albert) and his lowly position in the action: seated, and therefore at eye level with the youngsters – part of the furniture of their game rather than domineering over it. The finery of his uniform suggests that he is a recruiting sergeant, possibly on leave from the Crimea.[3] The ease with which he has recruited his little 'volunteers' implies that his sons will sign up only too gaily for the version of authority, citizenship and patriotism which their father embodies. His daughters gawp admiringly, clutching their dolls. The canvas works hard to present a spectacularly unalienated vision of labour and its reproduction within the family.

At the same time, there is something incongruous about the figure of the father in Hardy's picture: in a sense, his endearing qualities are inextricable from his slight air of awkwardness. That he sits while his wife stands, reversing the conventions of Victorian family portraiture, is only part of the anomaly. His upright bearing, his rigid posture and even the lines of buttons on his pristine jacket have more in common with the exacting geometry of the window than with the rollicking curves of the domestic interior and its inhabitants: he is home, but only just. His liminality is reinforced by the gesture of the toddler on his lap, tugging at a medal to pull him more fully into the intimacy of the family. A dissonant note in the chorus of welcome is suggested by the figure of the grandmother, whose categorically turned back hints at regretful anticipation of the departure into danger each visit may herald; she, too, must be coaxed back into the throng.

The carefully distinguished heights of the children imply that, though intermittent, this father's returns to the bosom of his family have been consistent enough to produce regular and abundant progeny. (Hardy himself fathered five sons and a daughter.) It may be relevant to our understanding of the picture that the number of married soldiers per company allowed living quarters and other benefits for their families was strictly curtailed: soldiers who married 'off strength' found their ability to support a family severely compromised.[4] Attempts to boost recruitment at around this time by admitting into the company a number of boys from the age of 15, often as drummer boys, may suggest a more urgent material injunction behind these apparently carefree romps.[5]

Reformist rhetoric in the mid-century was reconfiguring the 'respectable' working-class male as eligible for the franchise by representing him not only as a sober, independent householder, but also, crucially, as responsible for a wife and children.[6] And in so far as the state could intervene in the life of the household by calling him to serve his queen and country, it had a duty, the rhetoric held, to recognize him as a full citizen. Serious in the midst of jubilation, oriented in the field of action by the moral compass of home, the ambiguous figure of Hardy's soldier-father thus speaks to the countervailing interests being brought to bear in the middle of the century on paternity as a political discourse.

The moral gravity invested in Hardy's father figure points to his position in another debate, for 1860 was also a moment of national soul-searching over the future of Britain's colonial aspirations, and the role the forces might play in realizing them. The squalid administrative shambles of the Crimean War (1854–6) had exposed as contingent and insufficient the model of valour and self-sacrifice that underpinned Britain's sense of itself as a righteous military power, a model further shaken by the so-called Indian Mutiny of 1857. The Crimean War marked a watershed in the thinking about the physical and moral health of military personnel serving the state overseas, and many argued for the imperative of strengthening domestic ties and making family life – in an appropriately respectable, white, British family – a realistic affiliation for the servants of empire. Questions of entitlement to furlough, pensions, retirement and holidays, which became increasingly insistent, were thus more than simply matters of 'pay and conditions': they were seen as fundamental to the precarious integrity of the nation as family.[7] Hence *The Volunteers* can be read as participating in the complex choreography of presences and absences that, as this volume will show, characterises contemporaneous debates about paternal conduct. The father must be absent enough to provide, to represent his family in public settings, to support his country's mission abroad, and to afford the mother her ascribed role as primary influence and educator, but present enough to participate in, and benefit from, the domestic rituals, duties and pleasures that were understood as formative of personal, civic – and civilian – virtue.

But to participate how? In a domestic sphere properly shaped by a wife and mother, what did the office of father consist of, and how did it relate to his other, primary office of breadwinner?[8] One element was the duty to chastise and discipline, though this role, like breadwinning itself, overlapped with and sometimes countervailed against other practices and ideals through which the Victorians sought to carve out a role for the father figure in public and private life. The emphatic uniform of the 'guardsman' in the painting suggests another: the need to shield the children – as he would shield the nation – from harm. As well as having the legal right to punish members of his household, he was expected to protect them from danger, though what 'danger' meant, and equally what fatherly protection meant, were ideologically circumscribed and contested. The duty to educate – in particular to prepare older sons to survive, command respect and prosper in the world outside the home – was also part of the picture, though again the claims of mothers, and the inducements offered by formal education in a competitive market-place, rendered this paternal function open to question. The Christian responsibility of the father as moral and spiritual head of household still seemed unassailable to many, but, as we see below, what it meant to represent the Fatherhood of God in the home was not necessarily a given. Finally, there was the question of intimate interactions with children. Should a father, regardless of class, play with, dress, feed, nurse his offspring? Or was his role, like that of Father Christmas or Hardy's sergeant, to appear intermittently and distribute good cheer and largesse? To what extent was the dignity invested in these other paternal roles compatible with the day-to-day burdens, joys and provocations of close contact with children? Even Hardy's picture, for all its playfulness, labours to reconcile the two.

In order to tease out the kinds of ideological work performed by representations of domesticity such as Hardy's, we should consider their intended audience. The consumers of such images were primarily the middle-class visitors to the exhibition halls, for whom, as we shall see, the role of the paterfamilias in the home did not necessarily go without saying. It is significant, however, that in an era when open criticism and attempts to regulate the behaviour of drunken, abusive or irresponsible fathers were largely focused on the working classes, Hardy should have chosen a relatively humble *mise-en-scène* for his canvas.[9] Was he attempting to rebut such stereotypes, to claim the upper stratum of the working classes for the bourgeois hegemony by suggesting a commonality of familial values and priorities, implicitly to critique fatherhood as practised in affluent households by celebrating the comforts and easy affections of a home without servants, or to project, and thereby manage, middle-class anxieties about an increasingly etiolated paternal role on to the awkward but exotic figure of the soldier on leave? Whichever interpretation we might seek to fix on Hardy's painting, we need to remember that middle-class constructions of good or bad fathers did not take place in a vacuum. As we see in section III of this introduction, the rights and responsibilities of fathers were routinely and sometimes vociferously interrogated in debates over the poor laws and in political and social campaigns. Nor should the ideal of domestic manliness be seen as a middle-class invention to be imposed on other classes, for working-class constructions of the 'good father' were shaped by distinctive cultural traditions and patterns of labour.

In exploring the possible meanings of Hardy's soldier-father, a range of approaches and types of evidence prove useful: biographical information, military, political and social history, the conventions of Victorian genre painting, and so on. One of the premises of this volume is that perspectives drawn from a multitude of disciplines will enable us to reanimate what might otherwise remain flat, static representations of the nineteenth-century father.

II. Histories of fatherhood

Hardy's engaged and playful father is very different from the caricature of the Victorian paterfamilias whose cold and forbidding presence still touches the popular imagination. The earliest efforts to historicize the Victorian father have proved the most enduring. In their fictional and autobiographical accounts of Victorian family dynamics, the 'moderns' turned their backs on what they saw as their stuffy, sanctimonious forefathers by representing the paterfamilias as domineering, judgemental and austere. Dissecting the antagonisms of the father–child relationship, Samuel Butler, Edmund Gosse, John Galsworthy and Virginia Woolf set the paterfamilias in amber, preserving him as an antediluvian specimen of Victorianism.[10]

Psychoanalytically, these authors are 'storytelling sons and daughters', using the resources of narrative to work toward a 'kernel of childhood material', an 'explanatory origin' which will make sense of themselves as subjects.[11] Fathers function within these critical narratives rather as they do in Freud's case studies: as the focus of attachment, hatred or fear, but always, by definition, as *objects* rather than *subjects*. This negative portrayal of the Victorian father persists in contemporary psychoanalytic readings of the nineteenth-century novel, which have tended to theorize fictional fathers mainly as symbolic figures around whom 'configurations of desire organize themselves'. Such analyses fix upon fathers as embodiments of 'relentless paternal will', as the 'law' or 'Word', against whom women attempt to forge an identity beyond daughterhood, or against whom sons can pit themselves as rivals.[12] Echoing the preoccupation of psychoanalysis with the father as the locus of 'paternal agency' within the Oedipal triangle, literary history as a discipline has, by default, helped to maintain the myth of the Victorian paterfamilias as the incarnation of unqualified and often unrestrained power.

To suggest that the despotism of Victorian fathers has been subject to a kind of cultural amplification is not of course to argue that they lacked power *vis-à-vis* their dependants, both before the law and within Judaeo–Christian rhetoric, nor to deny that some fathers abused that power. It is simply to suggest that we know more about how this authority was played out in stories of the emergent literary subject – the author as child – than we do about the micropolitics of everyday life when many competing forces were reshaping households, families and communities.[13] Compounding the problem is the fact that most of the classic accounts of the Victorian filial relationship are upper middle-class in provenance and, outside of that class or beyond the imperial metropole, we know very little about the experiences and expectations of being or having a father.

Despite the efflorescence of histories of the family and gender since the 1970s[14] and the more recent interest in the history of masculinity,[15] little attention has been paid to the changing meanings and experiences of fatherhood in Britain.[16] On-going and furious debate in the media and academia over the 'new man' and the 'crisis in masculinity' is thus largely ignorant of earlier formations of fatherhood. Investigating the ideological construction of the family has been central to feminist historiography, but the project of recovering and re-evaluating the hidden history of women's reproductive labour has understandably involved highlighting women's role in the family and household at the expense of that of men.[17] More recently, historians of gender have problematized the too-easy equation of nineteenth-century women with the home and men with the paid workplace, pointing to the multitude of ways in which concepts such as the 'separate spheres' fail to do justice to differences between, as well as experiences within, households.[18] However, despite the reconceptualization of masculinity as at least in part dependent on domestic attachments and power relations, few have pursued the implications of this insight for fatherhood.[19]

In the 1990s, Claudia Nelson and Megan Doolittle took up this challenge, looking beyond the familiar territory of conduct literature for evidence of attitudes to and experiences of fathering.[20] A narrative has subsequently emerged of Victorian fatherhood in flux, though it is still uncertain precisely what the changes consisted of or meant. The consensus among historians is that, until the mid-eighteenth century, fathers were expected to be actively involved in the nurturing and training of their children and to lead familial celebrations and rituals.[21] With the rise of domestic ideology in the late eighteenth century, gender relationships underwent profound changes. As male labour moved away from the household with the development of industrialized manufacture, men's primary identity became associated with the shop, the office or the factory, and with the role of provider. Where hitherto advice on the running of the house had been aimed principally at men, women now became the target audience of household literature and guides to parenting. John Gillis has argued that, though the male householder was still regarded as the legal head and representative of the family, motherhood and fatherhood effectively 'switched places in [the] symbolic universe', with Victorian mothers occupying the central position of homemaker and the more intimate parental role.[22] Tosh has modified this narrative by suggesting that, for much of the nineteenth century, the 'cult of the home', underpinned by evangelical beliefs and practices, was a key component of the bourgeois family ideal, and as such was as central to hegemonic understandings of masculinity as it was to femininity and childhood.

However, domesticity was 'beset by serious inner contradictions', not least around the proper role of the patriarch within the feminine – and potentially feminizing – sphere of the home.[23] Forced into second place in the oversight of the household by the imperative of economic activity outside it, their power gradually curtailed, fathers, it has been suggested, found themselves correspondingly short-changed in the cultural market-place in favour of ideologies and discourses of motherhood.[24] As the cultural resonance of the paternal role declined, and as feminist challenges to male power increased, the custom of automatically yielding to the paterfamilias as the head of the household waned.

To pursue this narrative for a moment, from the 1870s onwards, both the fantasy of imperial adventure and the exigencies of colonial rule and administration were subtending a gradual drift away from the home as a secure site of masculine identity and identification. Suffocated by the oppressiveness of the suburban home, many middle-class men, Tosh suggests, embarked on a 'flight from domesticity', opting for prolonged bachelorhood and the freedoms afforded by the burgeoning homosocial worlds of city club-life and imperial culture. Simultaneously, the 'new woman's' challenge to patriarchalism in public, civic and private spheres heralded 'the end of paternal deference'.[25]

While most scholars see fatherly involvement and authority as ebbing in the Victorian period, this narrative has been neither universally accepted nor uniformly understood. It is possible to argue, for instance, that, faced with the uncertainties of the competitive market-place and the anxieties and pessimisms engendered by the new sciences and secularism, Victorian fathers, by way of compensation, renewed their efforts to instil virtues of self-control and deference in their children, especially sons. Intensified paternal surveillance and intervention provoked a corresponding ratcheting-up of filial rebellion. Another possibility, explored in this volume, is that the combined force of an insistent 'cult of motherhood' and a sustained and trenchant feminist critique of the damaging effects of abusive and neglectful masculine behaviour on the family generated a discourse of paternal accountability to supplement the more aggressive language of patriarchal rights.

Moreover, the masculine withdrawal from domesticity detected by Tosh represents, as he acknowledges, a move within middle-class culture away from a particular experience and ideal of family life. A very different pattern emerges when we examine the organization of domestic life in working-class settings. If the domestic ideal was at its apex in middle-class culture in the 1830s and

1840s, at the same time the working-class family was perceived to be in crisis. Wally Seccombe argues that working-class families had 'weathered the storm' of industrialization, urbanization and migration by drawing on the support of neighbourhood and kinship ties beyond the immediate biological family. By the 1840s, however, workers were claiming that the prevalence of child and female labour in the factories was jeopardizing the integrity of the working-class home and family. Meanwhile, commentators and reformers both sympathetic to and critical of working-class communities asserted that proletarianization was threatening to undermine traditional order and authority within the family. Working-class people were urged from all sides to conform to new standards of respectability hinging on marriage and the male breadwinner norm.[26]

While the ideal of the male head of household as primary wage-earner proved attractive to many working-class people, it was not until the 1870s, argues Seccombe, that it became commonplace (and even then was often dependent on women taking in some paid work).[27] For Seccombe, therefore, the 1870s see the partial consolidation of the nuclear family at the very moment when, for Tosh, middle-class companionate domesticity is beginning to unravel. At the very least, this should alert us to the possibility of multiple, even divergent, histories of fatherhood in the period.[28]

III. Framing fatherhood

The 'empire of the father' is, of course, a metaphor, but one whose embeddedness in legal discourses and practices rendered it profoundly consequential for day-to-day relationships. Such metaphors worked not only to establish a man's relationships within his own family, but, importantly, to distinguish relationships of responsibility, power and subordination outside it. This section explores some of the sites on which the symbolic resonances and social realities of fatherhood intersected: namely, law and legislation, employer–employee relationships and religious belief. In pursuing the fortunes of the 'empire of the father', the Fatherhood of God, and the trope of industrial paternalism, we outline some of the key nineteenth-century interventions in the construction and social regulation of fatherhood, and offer salient contexts, not only for our contributors' case studies, but, we hope, for our readers' own research.

Law and the father: paternity and parenting

Until the mid-eighteenth century, the male head of household was regarded as a father figure for all its members, whether or not he was their biological parent, and his paternal responsibilities extended to servants and apprentices who were deemed part of his 'family'. Parenting itself was considered independent of the fact of biological parenthood: in the higher classes the intimate and day-to-day practices of nursing, nurturing and education were contracted to others – wet-nurses, tutors, governesses – at no cost to the respectability or status of the parents, even when the child was placed away from home. Likewise, in the lower classes, older children often undertook much of the care of younger siblings or, as servants, worked in the homes of others where their master was *in loco parentis.*²⁹ Gradually, however, parental rights and responsibilities were associated more and more with biological paternity within legally formalized marriage, as non-legalized unions were culturally proscribed. It was overwhelmingly within the context of marriage, therefore, that the Victorians debated the authority and the meanings of fatherhood. The rights and duties of the father were considered synonymous and co-extensive with those of the husband, while the legal powerlessness of the mother was the corollary of her lack of separate legal identity as a spouse: both she and her children were the property of her husband.

The first incursion on the legal sovereignty of the father was the Infant Custody Act of 1839. This followed a series of high-profile cases in which violent and philandering fathers had succeeded in depriving devoted mothers of any contact with their children.³⁰ As the architect of the bill pointed out, the Court of Chancery could 'interfere with the father's power' only in the most exceptional circumstances; it had no jurisdiction to 'act on behalf of the mother' and 'no power to compel a father to perform his duty'.³¹ The new Act empowered the courts to award the mother access to, or custody of, her children under the age of seven in the event of divorce or separation if she was deemed the innocent party in the marital breakdown.

The protestations of aggrieved women and their lawyers suggest that many people were unaware how absolute the legal supremacy of the father was. Even opponents of reform acknowledged that there were gendered differences in parental attachment and 'that men had very little notion of the intensity of a mother's affection for her children'.³² Reform of the law on custody and guardianship was contested principally on the grounds that it would undermine the institution of marriage by bringing disharmony into the home and dividing parental authority, so that filial esteem for both parents would be diminished: 'The children will be brought up in that unnatural and most deplorable state of want or confidence in their parents.'³³ Parental authority, thus invoked, meant the rule of the father. Furthermore, the awarding of custody rights to the mother necessarily involved reform of the laws on coverture and separate maintenance, in order to enable her to provide for her children. Thus parental obligations were an important point of dispute in the successive revisions of the laws on married women's property rights, eventually fully installed in 1882.³⁴ Though further amendments enabled the courts to award mothers greater rights of custody and maintenance in cases of cruelty, the principle of equal rights was rejected repeatedly by parliamentarians until 1923, on the grounds that it would weaken the authority of the father within his family.³⁵

The developments in civil law relating to marriage were paralleled by changes in the criminal justice system which sought to discipline men's (and particularly working-class men's) conduct towards women and children. While male legislators in Britain were reluctant to impede the paternal rights of their own class, they proved much readier to intervene in the family affairs of lower-class men.³⁶ Male violence became a major subject of concern in the 1840s and was widely publicized in the press, in literature, on the stage, and in social surveys and official reports on the labouring classes, which disseminated new standards of male domesticity.³⁷ Advocates of temperance highlighted the problem of domestic violence, representing drunkenness as a major source of social delinquency. This movement, perhaps more than any other, was responsible for the promotion of two dichotomous father figures: one sober, industrious and affectionate who spent his leisure time predominantly with his family; the other drunken, negligent and brutal who wasted his time in the alehouse, returning only to wreck his home.

In his recent examination of the criminal justice system, Martin Wiener contends that over the century domestic manliness was encoded within a legal discipline aimed at policing 'excessive' violence against women and children.[38] We propose that, at a time when explicit positive recommendations about fatherly conduct seemed lacking, they were sometimes available by default in the proscriptive mechanisms of the law and the state and, significantly, were directed, in the main, to men of the lower classes. Despite misgivings about interfering in the home, Parliament passed the first statute specifically aimed at the protection of wives in 1853, and in 1857 the Society for the Protection of Women and Children began actively to pursue the prosecution of abusive husbands and fathers through the police courts.[39] As Wiener argues, lawyers and judges, in an *ad hoc* manner and often in the face of intransigence from juries, sought to impose new standards for marital relations on the lower classes.[40]

The cases cited by Wiener, however, were concerned primarily with wife-beating: it seems that cruelty towards spouses became a focus of popular and official opprobrium before cruelty towards children. The authorities proved even more loath than in marital relations to meddle with the parental right to discipline children and, even after the formation of the National Society for the Prevention of Cruelty to Children in 1884, it was overwhelmingly the children of the poor who came under the surveillance and protection of the police, social workers and the courts.[41] Although the emergence of a child welfare movement points to a growing awareness of the plight of orphaned, abandoned and neglected children, agreement was lacking as to who was best fitted to act as a substitute parent. Uncertainties about the qualities required for fatherhood thus extended to questions about the appropriate structure of surrogate institutions or agencies, or indeed the credentials of foster or adoptive fathers. So far, there has been no history of the provision for adoption in Britain. Given the tardy implementation of adoption policies, the comparison with the United States is striking. Over the nineteenth century, American courts and legislative bodies began to recognize the principle of the child's 'best interests' and the equal claims of mothers and fathers. This led to the much earlier equalization of laws on custody in many American states and to the first modern adoption law in history passed in Massachusetts in 1851. It was not until 1926 that the British parliament gave legal protection for adoption, despite almost a century of demands from foundling societies.[42]

In the absence of other agencies and safety nets, the prospect of the workhouse loomed large, not only for orphaned or fatherless children but also for men who were unable to support their family. If the ability to provide for a family could be construed as qualifying a man for citizenship, so failure to maintain his household could strip him of social status. The Poor Law Amendment

Act of 1834 stipulated that outdoor relief should no longer be given to the able-bodied poor since monetary or food supplements were held to encourage indigence and dependence. For the proponents of this Act, a man who could not or would not provide for his family had failed the first test of manhood: independence – a virtue that was to be instilled negatively by the removal of his parental authority. A father who was incapable of supporting his household would have to enter the workhouse, where families were generally separated into male, female and children's wards. This break-up of working-class families was decried by the Anti-Poor Law movement as an unchristian and inhumane measure designed to criminalize the poor. Fury with this 'class legislation' fuelled the Chartist movement's demand for manhood suffrage to enable men better to defend their families, living standards and working conditions, and thus to fulfil their responsibilities as providers and protectors. In championing their menfolk's right to representation as husbands, fathers and brothers, Chartist women overwhelmingly endorsed the model of the husband and father as breadwinner able to maintain his wife and his children at home. Henceforward, the emergent labour movement tended to emphasize the paternalist duties of men as fathers, both to argue for the breadwinner wage and for the 'protection' and even exclusion of female and child workers, a strategy that, as feminist historians have claimed, gave working-class institutions a distinctively patriarchal character.[43]

Another change within Poor Law administration with implications for family ideology and practice concerned the maintenance of illegitimate offspring. In common law, a bastard child was defined as a '*filius nullius*' or 'son of nobody', had no rights of inheritance, and could only be made legitimate by Act of Parliament. Where legitimate children had to apply for poor relief to the same parish as their father, the bastard was settled on the parish where he was born, 'for he hath no father'.[44] Under the Elizabethan Poor Law, if a mother applied for relief for her illegitimate child, the parish could seek weekly payments from the putative father on pain of imprisonment if he failed. One of the frequent objections of Poor Law reformers and rate-payers (echoed in recent debates about lone mothers) was that this practice undermined marriage and encouraged profligacy, precipitating soaring illegitimacy rates and the false naming of innocent men by malicious women seeking to profit from debauchery. The Poor Law commissioners proposed giving entire responsibility for her illegitimate child to the mother, or, where she could not support it, to her parents. Otherwise, both mother and child would be confined in the workhouse. A bastard would thus be 'what Providence appears to have ordained that it should be, a burthen on its mother'. The parish could pursue the father for maintenance, but to reimburse the parish, not to support the mother and child.[45] The proposals met with fierce opposition from working-class activists who challenged the inequitable burden placed on unmarried mothers and the exemption of men from paternal obligation. Opposition also came from Anglicans and Tory paternalists in Parliament who argued that the measures would prove a licence to seducers and who cited biblical authority for mutual parental responsibility. While the commissioners largely won the day, this controversy reveals the depth of popular belief, evident across the classes, in the 'natural' paternal obligation of maintenance and protection.

We turn finally to two seemingly anomalous areas of legislation in which the interests and status of men as fathers appear to have been overridden. First, at the very moment when working-class men who failed to support their family were being punished under the provisions of the New Poor Law, one subset of working men were being released from any such obligation. The responsibilities of enlisted men for their families were held by the military to jeopardize their allegiance to their regiment and queen. In order to shore up the ideal of a 'bachelor army', the Mutiny Act of 1837 exempted soldiers from the obligation to support their wives and their children, whether of legitimate or illegitimate unions. When, in the 1860s and 1870s, the government sought to diminish the spread of venereal disease by introducing compulsory medical examination and treatment of suspected prostitutes, social purity and feminist campaigners were quick to attack the Mutiny Act as part of the institutionalization of double standards in respect of parenthood as well as sexual conduct. The exemption was seen by many civilians as a major contributor to high levels of breach of promise and desertion in garrison towns, forcing destitute women into prostitution. Attacking servicemen who neglected their 'natural' paternal duties, they called on fathers across the country to defend their daughters from the iniquitous legislation and from seducers. Fathers as much as mothers, they insisted, had a duty with regard to the moral protection of their daughters.[46]

The second dissonant intervention concerned the conditions within which a widowed father might remarry. The ideological priority ceded to maternal influence and care, combined with high rates of maternal mortality, rendered the predicament of the widowed father of minors a matter of cultural pathos and social concern. Under what circumstances, if any, was a father capable of responding to the daily exigencies of child care and nurture? Second marriage seemed the obvious solution for many, providing a substitute mother whose maternal instincts would be 'naturally' quickened by the plight of the motherless young. That this apparently straightforward expedient aroused almost as many anxieties as it solved problems is witnessed by the strange career of the law, passed in 1835, invalidating marriages to the deceased wife's sister. Known as Lord Lyndhurst's Act, it effectively proscribed as incestuous (i.e. within forbidden degrees of affinity) the very remarriages most convenient to many widowers. For the whole of the Victorian period, this Act was virtually exceptional in actively delimiting the privileges of middle- and upper-class men as fathers. Despite mounting evidence that the law was being flouted, that it discriminated against poorer families, that it lacked scriptural authority and that it was internationally and historically anomalous, vigorous and repeated attempts to legalize marriage to a deceased wife's sister failed until 1907.[47] The intensity and persistence of the debate can be read as speaking – codedly, but volubly – to concerns about the adequacy, competence and needs of lone fathers as parents and, by extension, to uncertainty about the paternal role *per se*.[48]

The paternal metaphor and industrial society

The 'empire of the father', so impervious to assault in the courts, seemed from another point of view quite hollow, its notional ruler dispossessed of his throne and in a state of almost perpetual exile. Many cultural commentators were perplexed by the declining cultural and symbolic status of fathers, and they struggled to find a language to articulate a satisfactory role for the paterfamilias. In her survey of the construction of fatherhood in Victorian middle-class, 'general interest' periodicals, Nelson draws attention to the consistent, albeit shadowy, ways in which such publications sought to theorize male parentage:

> They could treat fathers as lesser mothers attempting with indifferent success to give the child what he or she was already receiving from another source; they could claim fathers as the obverse of mothers, brutes or martinets yoked to angels in human form; they could argue that fathers served a function complementing rather than duplicating that of mothers; they could discuss fathers metaphorically, explicating the parental role as it related to such surrogates as headmasters, judges, or even state programs. But each strategy forced an acknowledgment of mothers' superior influence and fathers' dwindling role within the family.[49]

Much energy, therefore, was devoted to forging a plausible role for fathers at the heart of the domestic project. Mrs Sarah Stickney Ellis, the popular author of conduct guides and a central figure in the dissemination of 'separate spheres' ideology, wrote effusively on women's duty to preside over the comfort of the hearth, but fretted over men's marginalization within the domestic sphere. Her fears were for men's confinement in the workplace, rather than women's incarceration in the home; in other words, she considered that men, rather than women, were reduced to 'relative creatures'. For her, the symbolic authority of the father was compromised by the separation of home and work that characterized industrial and manufacturing society. In the middling classes, with whom she was principally concerned, husbands and fathers were compelled to work relentlessly in comfortless offices while their wives and daughters, no longer deigning to help the master in his shop or share in the care of apprentices and assistants, frittered away hard-earned money on luxuries, without regard for their men's ease and well-being:

> We cannot believe of the fathers who watched over our childhood, of the husbands who shared our intellectual pursuits, of the brothers who went hand in hand with us in our love of poetry and nature, that they are all gone over to the side of mammon, that there does not lurk in some corner of their hearts a secret longing to return; yet every morning brings the same hurried and indifferent parting, every evening the same jaded, speechless, welcomeless return – until we almost fail to recognize the man, in the machine.

It was a woman's Christian and national duty, Ellis instructed, to call the man back to the home, to enable him to spend more than the Sabbath with his children, that he might 'keep as it were a separate soul for his family, his social duty, and his God'.[50]

For Ellis, men's alienation from the home was precipitated by 'the system' of remorseless competition in commerce and trade which required women to provide men with a domestic haven from the heartless world.[51] It was in the novel, however, that the effects of this system on fathers and their relationships with others could be emplotted, its contradictions imaginatively played out and even resolved. In contrast to Ellis's view, in the social fiction of the mid-century that explicitly addressed the problems of the new industrial and class society, it was the man of business – who turned his back on the world of sentiment – who was frequently cast as the chief perpetrator of family and community disintegration. No writer contributed more to the stereotype of the stern, unbending, Victorian paterfamilias than Charles Dickens, whose misguided and unfeeling fathers – Pecksniff, Dombey, Gradgrind – had to learn (largely from women) the cost of paternal neglect, the joys of intimate parenting and their paternalist obligations to workers and the poor.

Tellingly, nurturing fathers are found most often among the working classes in mid-Victorian literature. In *Mary Barton* (1848), Elizabeth Gaskell repeatedly shows male factory workers in domestic activities: nursing the sick, holding babies, making gruel. As in Hardy's *The Volunteers*, the depiction of the homely and affectionate lower-class father might be read as a defence of working men's virtues at a time when they faced intensive scrutiny from above, a reflection of the more fluid allocation of gender roles in working-class families, or as an implicit critique of men's neglect of paternal feeling in the privileged classes.

In *Mary Barton* and in Gaskell's *North and South* (1854–5), working men's care for their own families and those of others is contrasted with the indifference of employers towards their workers.[52] Like other industrial fictions, Gaskell's novels participate in debates over the respective rights and obligations of masters and men, interrogating the paternalist responsibilities of both employers and the state for the welfare of workers and the maintenance of social order.[53] In this context, the language of paternalism – or social fatherhood – was a means of articulating and mediating relationships between men of different social status. In *North and South*, Margaret Hale, expounding the philanthropic position, condemns masters who treat their workers as 'merely tall, large children' and insists on their religious duty to guide and advise their workers. The paternal metaphor is dismissed by the industrialist Thornton. As 'in our infancy we require a wise despotism', so in his factory his hands are 'in the condition of children' and despotism is the best form of government. Beyond its walls he has no responsibility towards them, in either 'making' or 'keeping' them as children; to do so would be to undermine the very independence he cherishes for himself. The danger of such despotism, suggests the benevolent tutor Mr Hale, is that the masses, already growing towards 'the troublesome stage that exists between childhood and manhood', will, without wise paternal guidance, become rebellious and destructive adolescents.[54]

The debate between the Hales and Thornton enacted the contradictions inherent in the rhetoric of paternalism and reflected broader ambivalences about what it meant to be a good father. As Donald Reid points out in relation to debates over paternalism in nineteenth-century France, it 'threw into question the employer's identity – contractor or confidant; disciplinarian or doting parent'.[55] The paternal metaphor held only limited appeal for male workers, whose claims for industrial and political citizenship rested so heavily on their sense of themselves as rational adults and independent family men, or for entrepreneurs, such as Thornton, committed to the idea that autonomy could only be fostered in a free market. In their own organizations, working men rejected paternalist affiliations and identified with each other as 'brothers'. The gentleman leaders who won the endorsement of popular movements did so by styling themselves as 'friends' rather than 'fathers' of the people. Even more problematic was the idea of protection. As Robert Gray argues, the discourse of the 'family firm' recast employer–employee relations as domestic and therefore private, and thus was a means by which employers could refute the right of the state to intervene in the workplace. During the industrial crises of the 1830s and 1840s, workers rejected employer paternalism precisely because most industrialists opposed the introduction of protective legislation, as in the limitation of working hours.[56]

Paternalist management appears to have been most effective in periods of relative social stability – as in the mid-century decades – when, through the provision of schools, chapels and good housing, industrialists could demonstrate materially their fatherly guidance and benevolence towards their workers. By evoking the affective and reassuring rhetoric of familial reciprocity and deference, paternalist rhetoric offered the possibility of humanizing capitalist relationships. Stressing his responsibility for the moral welfare and development of his workers, a Manchester spinner claimed, 'they should be regarded as part of my own family' and, in return, he was fêted by his workforce for his 'kind and paternal affection' and 'fatherly solicitude'.[57] As Sonya Rose has indicated, paternalist management was underpinned by a model of family relationships as 'hierarchical, gendered, harmonious, and co-operative'. In order to appreciate its workings, industrialists have to be viewed 'not just as employers but as men, who with their wives, shaped bourgeois culture'. The manufacturer's authority as head of the 'family firm' rested on his status as a family man. Company excursions or dinners designed to foster intimacy and community were often occasioned, for instance, by the birth of a son or his entry into his father's business. Such rituals, according to Rose, 'reinforced and celebrated male authority' and helped to diffuse the ideology of 'separate spheres' among workers.[58]

However, while many workers enjoyed such 'treats' and welcomed employer benevolence, this does not mean that they readily adopted the position of children grateful to their industrial father. Rather, company events were occasions for symbolic negotiation in which the terms of the responsible employer as well as the dutiful worker were defined and recognized on both sides, and this involved a very public presentation of paternity. For workers, the good master was one who acknowledged them as men and women, not slaves, who realized that poverty was the major bar to a comfortable home and the fulfilment of family obligations and who, by fair wages and a respectable division of labour between the sexes, enabled the maintenance of respectability in the workplace and in the home. At such events, employers and workers participated on the same terms as family men and women, and it was less the paternalist authority of the employer that was fêted, than the shared commitment to a familial ideal in which men were held to be the chief breadwinners and heads of household.[59]

It has been suggested that in France, and towards the end of the century, the 'language of paternity gave way to one of masculinity'; that fraternity replaced paternalism but at the cost of a highly gendered discourse in which women were ideologically contained in the domestic sphere.[60] In Britain, however, the discourse of paternalism had long jostled with, and generally taken second place to, that of manhood. The controversy over the role of the employer in *North and South*, for instance, is finally resolved when Thornton agrees to experiment in 'personal intercourse' with the men, but the paternal metaphor has been dropped; they will speak to each other as individual men in the bonds of 'common interest'.[61] Likewise *Mary Barton*, for all its exploration of employer responsibility, ultimately resists a paternalist ending. It is in their recognition of each other as suffering fathers and brothers in Christ that the Chartist John Barton and the industrialist Mr Carson become reconciled to each other as men. If, as we have argued, spiritual and moral guidance was constructed as one of the duties of paternalism, then the tensions between Christian conceptions of paternity and brotherhood mark another area of debate and uncertainty over the meanings of fatherhood, to which we now turn.

Our Father: family and religion

Leonore Davidoff and Catherine Hall have demonstrated the importance of 'serious' Christianity to the emergence of middle-class culture in the late eighteenth and early nineteenth centuries, to the extent that 'by mid century adherence to evangelical protestant forms had become an accepted part of respectability'.[62] From their earnest forebears the Victorians inherited a highly moralized understanding of the family as a microcosm of God's kingdom, and a concomitant reverence and deference toward the position of head of household as representing God's authority within the family. The popularity of family prayers, led where practicable by the father, cast a spiritual aura over his leadership within the home. Other elements of the evangelical legacy, however, were more paradoxical for the paternal role.

Answerable before God for his children's safety, maintenance, education and conduct, a father might find his task exorbitant, might wonder who was judging whom: 'Parents may well tremble as they feel God watching them through the loophole of a child's eye.'[63] As the romantic idealization of childhood gained purchase in the cultural imagination, philanthropists, novelists and policy-makers could legitimately suggest that fatherhood was a *sensibility* to be learned from experience with children, rather than a God-given prerogative. If the evangelical emphasis on religious and emotional expressiveness waned in favour of more reserved models of masculinity, the ideal of the tender-hearted, benevolent paterfamilias survived alongside that of the preacher, ruler and judge. In the early century, it was widely assumed that Christian piety was sufficient to reconcile these divergent characteristics of the godly father: '[It] will strengthen *and* soften every domestic tie', as the Revd John Angell James advised young men.[64] God was a loving Father, hence a father could be loving and yet godlike. There is evidence, however, that religious belief and perceptions of fatherhood gradually became less harmonious and more mutually interrogative.

The sphere of theology and Christian praxis was a site where fatherhood was explicitly and regularly discussed. From 1850 until the First World War, the

Fatherhood of God was a topic of prayers, hymns, sermons, tracts and even political debate.[65] This concern crossed denominational boundaries and touched Sunday school teachers as nearly as learned biblical exegetes. At stake was a sense that, in an increasingly secular age, God must be made knowable and familiar: his fatherly relation to Christ and to humankind might be a cipher for that knowledge. At the same time, however, there was less consensus about what that fatherly relation might consist of. In order to teach the spiritual lessons to be learned from the Fatherhood of God, its exponent would have to outline the ideal 'paternal relation and character', a practice as constructive as it was descriptive: 'He should stand up before his family consciously as a model; and should rejoice in nothing so much as in seeing his well-regulated life and dignified bearing, and benevolent feelings, insensibly imbibed by, and gradually appearing in, his children.'[66]

In sermons and tracts, therefore, we find an attempt positively to identify core elements of the father's role. Christ's description of Heaven as 'My Father's house' entitled commentators to ascribe to the afterlife all the qualities of idealized domesticity. This will be no cold and comfortless dwelling, 'lacking beauty and arrangement, where no lovelinks bind the heart; and no feeling dances to the music of homejoy'. On the contrary, this house will be a *home*, 'where hearts throb, and the fountains of feeling play and sparkle in the light of the paternal smile'. It will be spacious, stable, and full of the 'charm of novelty': indeed there will be 'room and rest and real family life for all the faithful'.[67] Such detailed fantasies of the paradisal home tell us much about Victorian ideals of domesticity and the responsibilities of fathers in attempting to bring them about.

In days of doubt and darkness, the 'paternal idea of God' offered a rallying point to the embattled churches,[68] as well as a personal source of security and support that was partly spiritual, partly practical: 'Do you want advice? Consult your Father. Do you need supplies? Ask them of your Father. [. . .] Do your difficulties appear insurmountable? Appeal to your Father. God is not merely a Father in name – He has a Father's nature.'[69]

The growing sense that the universe was driven by relentless impersonal forces threatened to supersede the idea of a single, 'designing, regulating, actuating WILL' in the person of God the Father. At the same time, however, this conception of a mechanistic, exclusively material world, and its corollary, the spectre of universal orphanhood, lent urgency and appeal to the notion of a 'vast system of paternal administration in pursuance of one purpose of eternal good'.[70] Further, to the idea of God the Designer could be added the element of a personal relationship: 'Reptiles, laws, forces, protoplasm, and cells, may have meanings that are deep enough', wrote evangelical pastor Robert Mitchell in 1879, 'but they are not *The Father*.'[71]

In one sense such debates were simply the expression of doctrinal differences in the accessible language of the family: fatherhood was a symbol of divine authority. Conversely, in its condensation and malleability, the metaphor encapsulated a distinctively Victorian uncertainty about what fatherhood was *for*: what it consisted of, how its established rights related to its practical responsibilities, and how both related to those of other family members. It could mean the right to protect children from danger, specifically from infidelity and spiritual error: 'He uses the rod of a father, that he may not use the sword of a Judge.'[72] Yet, as commentators' frequent recourse to the parable of the prodigal son suggests, it could connote the right to waive the rod in favour, if not of spoiling, at least of cherishing and nurturing the child.

There were, none the less, fault lines within the idea of God the Father as the source of unconditional love and forgiveness. Hence, while there was a considerable degree of consensus across denominations (and even occasionally across faiths) over God's primary role as Father, theologians differed widely over what this fatherhood might mean in the context of human frailty and sin. Struggling to reconcile the apparently antagonistic principles of justice and mercy, some delegated the merciful aspect of the divine to the Christ figure, or to the figure of Mary, while others firmly prioritised the exacting doctrines of atonement or satisfaction. For believers of a Unitarian bent, the emphasis was on fatherly guidance, tenderness and pity, on a love that knew no bounds and required no satisfaction.[73] Those, however, who preached and practised within a more austere Calvinist tradition were more likely to stress the boundaries of forgiveness. Rewarding good conduct was the best way of ensuring obedience, but what if the 'child' persisted in disobedience? To 'pardon him at once without terms' 'would destroy the law and order of his family, and shatter the integrity of his character'. For Presbyterian minister George Gilfillan, the fatherly love of God had distinct frontiers: if chastisement failed, if the scheme of redemption also failed, then the divine Father must drive his erring child from his house 'emphatically and forever'. Otherwise, 'he might remain a parent but would cease to be a man'.[74]

At a theological level, then, the idea of God's Fatherhood provided a language and imagery with which to delineate relationships of accountability and responsibility both within the system of divine governance and within earthly familial networks. The paternal metaphor could be extended to include men's Christian responsibilities for the spiritual development of others beyond the household. And yet, as a rhetorical means of negotiating social relationships beyond the home, the paternal metaphor proved much less flexible than the discourse of 'woman's mission', which was widely invoked to justify female philanthropy and political action on the grounds of women's 'natural' maternal inclinations and responsibilities for others. By contrast, the implicit hierarchalism in paternalist discourse associated uneasily with other idealized forms of masculine identification, such as those of brotherhood or fellowship, thereby generating conflict rather than resolution. As Catherine Hall has shown, for instance, in the aftermath of emancipation in Jamaica, the abolitionist ideal of Christian brotherhood and universalism – 'Am I not a man and a brother?' – began to fracture as former slaves resisted the paternalist leadership of Baptist missionaries, who, in turn, found it difficult to view former slaves as full and equal adults.[75] Incursions into the home or community of institutional paternalism in the person of the father (as spiritual teacher, citizen or employer, for instance) did not necessarily meet passive acquiescence on the part of its objects, nor even whole-hearted or unequivocal acceptance on the part of the father himself, but involved a renegotiation of family relationships on the one hand,

and a reformulation of the interface between private and public patriarchies on the other. Indeed, national and international contexts shaped by migration and emigration, missionary impulse and colonization could complicate even the most taken-for-granted assumptions about paternal power.

Fatherhood, fertility and family shape

In their pioneering work on Victorian fatherhood, both Nelson and Doolittle pointed out the methodological challenge posed by what then seemed a barely visible dimension of family history.[76] The contributors to this volume take up this challenge, pointing to the ways in which the historical record can be remapped to disclose the hitherto elusive figure of the Victorian father and to discriminate the often complex and contradictory meanings with which he was invested. More difficult to discern are the ways in which these meanings may have been appropriated, reconfigured or revised at the level of individual paternal subjectivity.

Cultural historians have noted the role of Freud's experience of a particular mode of bourgeois childhood – with its complement of servants and nannies – in shaping both the insights and the aporias in his theories of sexuality and consciousness.[77] However, as Barbara Caine observes in her biography of the Strachey family, there is still no adequate theoretical framework, psychoanalytic or psychological, with which to comprehend the psychic consequences of living within the complex, sprawling family networks fostered by the contingencies of Victorian life. Maternal mortality rates, coupled with higher rates of infant survival, left many fathers managing their households as single parents, however temporarily or partially.[78] Such factors as the exigencies of colonial service and the obligation of older children to take responsibility for, or even effectively to adopt, their younger siblings necessarily complicate any application of Freud's model to the actuality of Victorian family life. To pursue Caine's point for a moment, Richard Strachey, father of ten, was a very different parent in the eyes of those of his children born in the 1860s, when he was in his forties and consolidating his role in the government of India, than he appeared to those who were born when he was in his fifties when he settled back in England, or to those born in the 1880s, to whom he was a kindly but distant grandfatherly figure. Such a pattern not only suggests the importance of historical specificity across our period, but also that an individual father – or mother for that matter – could *simultaneously* be a very different kinds of parent to different cohorts of offspring. Such factors need to be taken into account if we are to come closer to understanding how a particular father, overseeing an apparently continuous parental regime, could raise children who had such widely differing approaches to authority, tradition, duty, and so on.[79]

In the late nineteenth and early twentieth centuries the shape and life-cycle of families underwent a dramatic transformation. Family size began to shrink in the 1870s, long before the emergence of an elaborated public discourse associating small families with respectability.[80] Whereas couples married in the years 1861–9 went on, like Hardy's sergeant, to conceive an average of 6.12 children, those married between 1920 and 1924 would conceive only 2.31.[81] How and why this 'great fertility decline' took place across Europe is difficult to explain. In Britain, as in most countries, there was no official sanctioning of family limitation, and dissemination of birth control advice was banned.[82] In the face of official prohibition and silence, men and women voted in their beds, turning to informal and illicit sources of knowledge that nurtured the emergence of the 'modern' family: coded advertisements; techniques gleaned from pornographic literature and prostitution; 'quack' medicine; and, perhaps above all, hints and tips whispered by family members, friends, workmates, masters, mistresses and servants. Though facilitated by public policies such as compulsory education and restrictions on child labour, what has been fittingly described as 'the quiet revolution' was conducted at the most intimate level. It must have involved, in most cases at least, discussion and agreement between partners about the kind of family they wanted and could afford, with profound implications for the experience and meaning of parenting and sexual relations.

This cultural change would seem to challenge recent scholarship that has emphasized the agency of institutional structures in the production of familial norms – medicine, psychiatry, the law, and so on. One of the recurrent themes of this volume, and one of its significant innovations, is the attempt to investigate the reciprocal dynamics between macroeconomic and macropolitical change and the day-to-day negotiations shaping fatherly identity and practice. Our contributors point to aspects of the paternal role – often barely spoken – that are either ignored or only hinted at in the sources hitherto used to track the vicissitudes of nineteenth-century fatherhood.

IV. Gender and fatherhood: an overview

The assumption behind the 'empire of the father' was, as we have seen, that the rights of fathers prevailed over those of mothers. Part I demonstrates that along with these privileges and entitlements came a more tacit expectation of duty. A father should provide for his family and for their protection and education. As Megan Doolittle observes, there were few sanctions against fathers who failed to meet these obligations. In the following studies, however, we find an emergent discourse of accountability in which the responsibilities as well as the rights of fathers were spelled out.

Paradoxically, however, men's obligations as fathers can be understood as inextricable from a move to extend masculine authority. From the 1780s onwards, middling and working men challenged the existing property qualifications for the vote and began to frame their entitlement to political enfranchisement on the basis of their status as married men, fathers and heads of household. By doing so, contends Matthew McCormack, they took literally 'the rule of the father' central to the patriarchal model of early modern political theory. This would be the basis of a new democratic order in which gender, rather than property, would be the primary category of inclusion and exclusion: the 1832 Reform Act explicitly defined the elector as male for the first time. However, the new formulation of manhood suffrage rested, at least in theory, on a man's duty 'virtually to represent' the interests of his family rather than simply his own individual needs and aspirations. Understanding how ideas about fatherhood and domestic responsibility were mobilized politically thus requires us to interrogate the 'separate spheres' model and to think beyond binary categories such as 'public' and 'private'.

Although, as we have seen, both Parliament and the Court of Chancery that handled family law proved remarkably reluctant to impinge on paternal rights, there were limits to this entitlement. The rights of the father were contingent on marriage, not merely on biological paternity. As Doolittle illustrates, challenges to conventional understandings of marriage and equality were often related to, and perceived as, attacks on Christianity itself. This could have severe repercussions, because the provision of religious instruction was held by the courts to be a crucial element of protection. Focusing on two of the most notorious custody battles of the nineteenth century, involving the radical freethinkers Percy Bysshe Shelley and Annie Besant, Doolittle explores the gendered ideology of protection as it was rehearsed and contested in the courts.

While few fathers were called to account in such explicit terms as Shelley or Frank Besant, the responsibilities of fathers for the moral and intellectual development of children was of concern not only to those few who, like workingclass radical Chester Armstrong, questioned traditional understandings of marriage, but also to the many who, like author and cleric Charles Kingsley, subscribed to more conventional views of the family. An involved and controlling father, as Valerie Sanders shows, Kingsley worked hard in his day-to-day interactions with his family, and in his fiction for children, to define the different pedagogical purposes and styles of motherly and fatherly figures and to assert the superiority of paternal authority.

That the Victorians did not care to teach or learn about fatherhood through the medium of an explicit conduct literature should not blind us to the existence of lessons in and messages about paternity in other media, from fiction to advertising. The contributors to Part 2 suggest that, far from assuming male absence or disconnection from the affective life of the home, such representations enjoin men to participate in its joys and trials. Margaret Markwick's study of the novels of Anthony Trollope and Terri Sabatos's discussion of the widower in narrative painting show that father figures from the poorest to the most powerful classes were mobilized (significantly here by men) in support of an engaged, tender, child-centred mode of male parenting. Neil Armstrong's examination of the Victorian Christmas suggests that, with the gradual commercialization of domesticity and family life, breadwinning itself could be construed as an eloquent expression of care (pointing up, by the by, another of the blind spots of the 'separate spheres' concept). But Part 2 reveals that the range of permissible ways in which fathers could be involved in child care was extensive, from seasonal rituals and gift-giving to the offices of nurse, adviser and sympathizer. When one attends to the indirect suggestions levied at nineteenth-century audiences, a new theme emerges: fatherhood envisioned as a process. This adds a further dimension to Tosh's influential typology of Victorian fatherhood (absent, tyrannical, distant and intimate) by drawing attention to the possibility that men could be all four over the course of a lifetime (and in relation to children of different ages).[83] Moreover, the discourse of fatherhood as process implies that men could and should be socialized, humanized, by the on-going adventure of bringing up a family. Fatherhood, in other words, could be an education in emotional literacy.

This possibility is most vividly dramatized in the person of the widower. Lone fatherhood, usually precipitated by the death of a spouse, was a common predicament in the nineteenth century, one that highlighted the structural fragility of divisions of labour within the household, and forced individuals and communities to reconsider the role of father as caregiver. While the challenge of lone fatherhood could, to some degree, be mitigated by the assistance of servants in better-off homes, the working-class widowed father, shoved willy-nilly into the domestic spotlight, crystallized both the fears and the hopes invested in male domesticity.

Part 3 probes the distinction between provider and caregiver by exploring expressions of, and responses to, fatherhood in the context of working-class lives. Did labouring communities have distinctive cultures of fatherhood? How susceptible were they to the hegemonic, middle-class ideals sketched by Sanders, Sabatos and Markwick, and to what extent did they actively resist them? Did working women have the same priorities for fatherhood as middle-class women or working men? Did material circumstances determine or override expectations and ideals? What other factors obtained? Andrew Walker, Helen Rogers and Julie-Marie Strange point to a range of variables conditioning experiences and understandings of working-class paternity: occupation and occupational cultures; local divisions of labour and the corresponding configurations of gender; patterns of migration; the raw practicalities of hardship. All three studies emphasize the importance of specific communities – the embeddedness or otherwise of tradition, political consciousness, networks of solidarity and support, and so on – to the configuration of fatherhood in particular contexts. Again, the figure of the lone father is a test case: as Strange demonstrates, the ordeal of paternal bereavement highlights the reciprocal relationship, and mutual vulnerabilities, between family shape and community solidarity.

Part 4 considers the implications of colonial and post-colonial experiences for constructions of fatherhood, exploring the day-to-day realities of travel, separation, distance and isolation and the consequences of colonial encounters for notions of legitimacy, patrilineage and paternal authority. If, as we have argued, fatherhood was a more nebulous and variable construction than has often been supposed, what happened in the meetings of different cultures of paternity, patriarchy and paternalism? What aspects of paternal ideology were transportable; what accommodations had to be made? As Alison Twells shows, the missionary enterprise in the South Seas was conceived as a paternalist venture in which missionaries, as representatives of God the Father, would guide the heathen male subject, as a father would a son, towards Christian adulthood that would be signified, above all, by his fulfilment of the role of domestic father. This paternalist project undercut, however, the ideal of Christian brotherhood and equality to which missions were also committed, putting strain on relationships not only with indigenous men but also with missionaries in the field. The latter were predominantly men of lower-class origins, some of whom proved dangerously attracted to the patriarchal cultures of indigenous societies.

In this colonial venture, the internal contradictions of domestic, Christian manhood were acutely felt.

Migration, and the separation and reconstitution of families in settler societies, put intense pressure on the framework of family law inherited from the English legal system. As Claudia Nelson notes, every state in America enacted public adoption laws between 1851 and 1929, whereas statutory provision for adoption was not introduced in Britain until 1926. In her examination of American fictions of adoptive and biological fatherhood, Nelson discovers a range of father figures from the involved to the tyrannical. In so far as this spectrum is comparable to that found by Markwick in the work of Trollope, we might postulate cross-currents in gender ideology linking the 'old' and 'new' worlds. There are limits to this model, however. Just as American lawyers and legislators interrogated and adjusted Blackstone's concept of the 'empire of the father' in their development of a specifically American body of family law, so some of the fictions studied by Nelson – and written for a transatlantic readership – set the supposedly obsolescent, 'traditional' British standard of fatherhood against a new, American variant.

Geographical and emotional estrangement from children was a reality for many British men serving overseas, and was deeply regretted by some. However, a colonial career enabled others to escape from the confines of domesticity, a prospect that seems to have appealed to growing numbers of men towards the end of the century. At an individual and an institutional level, furthermore, the British in India were more and more free to deny their paternity of and responsibility towards Eurasians, whether they were those they had fathered themselves or the progeny of earlier colonists. As Elizabeth Buettner points out, in this context paternity and patrilineage were contingent on race above biology. The construction of Indians and Eurasians as children who needed to be managed, trained and disciplined, very similar to the discourse identified by Twells early in the century, points to continuities in the ideology of colonial paternalism. Both the insistence of some Eurasians that their paternity be acknowledged and the refusal of Indians to accept their place as 'children' contributed to the dismantling of colonial ideology in the twentieth century.

If the domestic, companionate component of fatherly identity flowed toward the mid-century only to ebb thereafter, as the existing historiography tends to imply, our contributors suggest that it did so unevenly. Domestic fatherliness was never the exclusive property of a single class or generation or even of biological progenitors; rather it was to be found in complex and unpredictable relation to other historical variables, notably institutionally sanctioned prerogatives and economic imperatives. This made fatherly respectability a versatile but also a volatile compound. In its positive articulation it could seem robust and unassailable, yet the ways in which fathers could fail – in the eyes of their children and the world – were legion: too profligate, too parsimonious; too home-centred; too absent; too domineering; too passive. While it is important not to exaggerate the instabilities within what was clearly a resilient construction, it is worth noting that, like Hardy's soldier, even Santa Claus – most revered, most generous, most welcome of father figures – was never quite at home in the Victorian household.

Notes

1. W. Blackstone, *Commentaries on the Laws of England in Four Books* (London: Strahan and Woodfall, 1973), Vol. 1, ch. 16, 'The Rights of Parent and Child', p. 453 and pp. 446–59 *passim*. The 'empire of the father' applied until the child reached the age of 21 – 'the empire of reason' – even if the father died, since his empire could be continued through the appointment of a guardian, whose authority superseded that of the mother.
2. J. Tosh, *A Man's Place: Masculinity and the Middle-Class Home in Victorian England* (New Haven, CT: Yale University Press, 1999), p. 79.
3. His uniform appears to be a composite: the insignia on the bayonet belt and luggage belong to the Grenadier Guards; the spacing of the buttons on his tunic suggests the Coldstream Guards.
4. M. Trustram, *Women of the Regiment: Marriage and the Victorian Army* (Cambridge: Cambridge University Press, 1984).
5. See A. Skelley, *The Victorian Army at Home* (Toronto: McGill-Queen's University Press, 1977), p. 262.
6. K. McClelland, 'England's Greatness, the Working Man', in C. Hall, K. McClelland and J. Rendall, *Defining the Victorian Nation: Class, Race, Gender and the Reform Act of 1867* (Cambridge: Cambridge University Press, 2000), pp. 71–118.
7. Trustram points out that the immediate post-Crimea years were a time of increased concern over the provision for military families (*Women of the Regiment*, pp. 59, 75 and *passim*.)
8. As Trustram notes, and as we discuss below, soldiers were exempted at this time from the legal obligation to support dependants.
9. Hardy's soldier evokes the well-established image of 'the returning artisan': see B. Maidment, 'Domestic Ideology and its Industrial Enemies: The Title Page of *The Family Economist* 1848–1850', in C. Parker (ed.), *Gender Roles and Sexuality in Victorian Literature* (Aldershot: Scolar, 1995), pp. 25–56.
10. S. Butler, *The Way of All Flesh* (1903), E. Gosse, *Father and Son. A Study of Two Temperaments* (1907); J. Galsworthy, *The Man of Property* (1906), the first in a trilogy published as *The Forsyte Saga* (1921); V. Woolf, *To the Lighthouse* (1927).
11. D. Sadoff, *Monsters of Affection: Dickens, Eliot and Brontë on Fatherhood* (Baltimore, MD: Johns Hopkins University Press, 1982), p. 3.
12. H. Schor, *Dickens and the Daughter of the House* (Cambridge: Cambridge University Press, 1999), p. 50; L. Zwinger, *Daughters, Fathers, and the Novel* (Madison, WI: University of Wisconsin Press, 1991), p. 7.
13. The growing body of literary–historical work addressing nineteenth-century masculinities has had remarkably little to say about fatherhood or paternity: no mention, for instance, in the index or bibliography of C. Lane's *The Burdens of Intimacy: Psychoanalysis and Victorian Masculinity* (Chicago: University of Chicago Press, 1999). This is because the 'burden of intimacy' is defined largely as the medical, legal and cultural rescripting of Victorian men's relationships to their bodies, desires and identities that took place along the homosocial–homosexual axis during the nineteenth century. Such studies tend to steer clear of the implications of this tendency for men as fathers (or indeed as sons), or for the reproduction of family relations and domestic scenarios over time.
14. M. Anderson, *Family Structure in Nineteenth Century Lancashire* (Cambridge: Cambridge University Press, 1971); P. Laslett, *Household and Family in Past Time* (Cambridge: Cambridge University Press, 1972); L. Stone, *The Family, Sex and Marriage in England 1500–1800* (London: Weidenfeld and Nicolson, 1977);

T. Hareven, *Family Time and Industrial Time* (Cambridge: Cambridge University Press, 1982). A. Macfarlane, *Marriage and Love in England, 1300–1840* (Oxford: Blackwell, 1987); K. Ittman, *Work, Gender and Family in Victorian England* (Basingstoke: Macmillan, 1995); L. Davidoff, M. Doolittle, J. Fink, and K. Holden, *The Family Story: Blood, Contract and Intimacy, 1830–1960* (London: Longman, 1998).

15. J. A. Mangan and J. Walvin (eds), *Manliness and Morality: Middle-Class Masculinity in Britain and America, 1800–1940* (New York: St Martin's Press, 1987); M. Roper and J. Tosh (eds), *Manful Assertions: Masculinities in Britain since 1800* (London: Routledge, 1991); M. A. Danahay, *A Community of One: Masculine Autobiography and Autonomy in Nineteenth-Century Britain* (Albany, NY: State University of New York Press, 1993); J. E. Adams, *Dandies and Desert Saints: Styles of Victorian Masculinity* (Ithaca, NY: Cornell University Press, 1995); H. Sussman, *Victorian Masculinities: Manhood and Masculine Poetics in Early Victorian Literature and Art* (Cambridge: Cambridge University Press, 1995).

16. The last decade, however, has seen the publication of illuminating cultural histories of fatherhood in America. See, for instance, R. Griswold, *Fatherhood in America: A History* (New York: Basic Books, 1993); R. LaRossa, *The Modernization of Fatherhood: A Social and Political History* (Chicago: University of Chicago Press, 1997); S. Frank, *Life with Father: Parenthood and Masculinity in the Nineteenth-Century American North* (Baltimore, MD: Johns Hopkins University Press, 1998); Shawn Johansen, *Family Men: Middle-Class Fatherhood in Early Industrializing America* (London: Routledge, 2001).

17. D. Gittins, *The Family in Question: Changing Households and Familiar Ideologies* (London: Macmillan, 1985); J. Lewis (ed.), *Labour and Love: Women's Experience of Home and Family, 1850–1940* (Oxford: Blackwell, 1986); C. Smart (ed.), *Regulating Womanhood: Historical Essays on Marriage, Motherhood and Sexuality* (London: Routledge, 1992); E. Ross, *Love and Toil: Motherhood in Outcast London, 1870–1918* (Oxford: Oxford University Press, 1993).

18. L. Davidoff and C. Hall, *Family Fortunes: Men and Women of the English Middle Class 1780–1850* (London: Hutchinson, 1987), pp. 33–4; Amanda Vickery, 'Golden Age to Separate Spheres: A Review of the Categories and Chronology of English Women's History', *The Historical Journal*, 36.2 (1993), pp. 383–414; Tosh, *A Man's Place*.

19. For important exceptions, see: J. Nash, 'Historical and Social Changes in the Perception of the Role of the Father', in M. Lamb (ed.), *The Role of the Father in Child Development* (New York: Wiley, 1976), pp. 62–88; D. Roberts, 'The Paterfamilias of the Victorian Governing Classes', in A. Wohl (ed.), *The Victorian Family: Structures and Stresses* (London: Croom Helm, 1978), pp. 59–81; N. Lowe, 'The Legal Status of Fathers Past and Present' and T. Lummis, 'The Historical Dimension of Fatherhood: A Case Study 1890–1914', in L. McKee and M. O'Brien, *The Father Figure* (London: Tavistock, 1982), pp. 26–42 and 43–56.

20. C. Nelson, *Invisible Men: Fatherhood and Victorian Periodicals, 1850–1910* (Athens, GA and London: University of Georgia Press), and M. Doolittle, 'Missing Fathers: Assembling a History of Fatherhood in Mid-Nineteenth Century England', Ph.D. thesis, University of Essex, 1996.

21. R. Trumbach, *The Rise of the Egalitarian Family: Aristocratic Kinship and Domestic Relations in Eighteenth-Century England* (New York: Academic Press, 1978); A. Fletcher, *Gender, Sex and Subordination in England, 1500–1800* (New Haven, CT: Yale University Press, 1995).

22. J. R. Gillis, *A World of Their Own Making: Myth, Ritual, and the Quest for Family Values* (Cambridge, MA: Harvard University Press, 1997), p. 181.
23. Tosh, *A Man's Place*, p. 7.
24. Gillis, *A World of their Own Making*, pp. 179–81.
25. *Ibid.*, pp. 145–94.
26. W. Seccombe, *Weathering the Storm: Working-Class Families From the Industrial Revolution to the Fertility Decline* (London: Verso, 1993), pp. 55–60.
27. *Ibid.*, pp. 133–42, 204–7.
28. Throughout the century, suggests Martin Francis, men's responses to domesticity may have 'remained complex and ambivalent', while 'domestic manliness' was 'simultaneously [...] embrace[d] and reject[ed]'. See his insightful overview, 'The Domestication of the Male? Recent Research on Nineteenth- and Twentieth-Century British Masculinity' in *The Historical Journal*, 45:3 (2002), pp. 637–52; p. 643.
29. Gillis, *A World of their Own Making*, pp. 181–3.
30. The most famous was that of the writer Caroline Norton, whose lawyer, Sergeant Talfourd, moved the Custody Bill through Parliament; see M. Poovey, *Uneven Developments: The Ideological Work of Gender in Mid-Victorian England* (Chicago: Chicago University Press, 1988), pp. 51–88.
31. Introduction of Access of Parents to Children Bill, 14 December 1837, cited in *Hansard*, XXXIX, 1085–7.
32. Edward Sugden, cited in *Hansard*, XXXIX, 1091.
33. *Ibid.*, 1115.
34. L. Holcombe, *Wives and Property: Reform of the Married Women's Property Law in Nineteenth-Century England* (Toronto: University of Toronto Press, 1983).
35. For the development of child custody law, see S. Maidment, *Child Custody and Divorce* (Beckenham: Croom Helm, 1984) and M. Shanley, *Feminism, Marriage and the Law in Victorian England, 1850–1895* (London: I. B. Tauris, 1989).
36. B. Griffin, 'Class, Gender, and Liberalism in Parliament, 1868–1882: The Case of the Married Women's Property Acts', *The Historical Journal*, 41:1 (2003), pp. 59–87; pp. 83–6.
37. A. J. Hammerton, *Cruelty and Companionship: Conflict in Ninteenth-Century Married Life* (London: Routledge, 1995).
38. M. J. Wiener, *Men of Blood: Violence, Manliness and Criminal Justice in Victorian England* (Cambridge: Cambridge University Press, 2004).
39. Hammerton, *Cruelty and Companionship*.
40. Wiener, *Men of Blood*, pp. 158–9. See also S. D'Cruze, *Crimes of Outrage: Sex, Violence and Victorian Working Women* (London: UCL Press, 1998).
41. Cooter, R. (ed.), *In the Name of the Child: Health and Welfare, 1880–1940* (London: Routledge, 1992); H. Hendrick, *Child Welfare: England, 1872–1989* (London: Routledge, 1994).
42. J. Zainaldin, 'The Emergence of a Modern American Family Law: Child Custody, Adoption, and the Courts, 1796–1851', *Northwestern University Law Review*, 73 (1979), pp. 1038–89.
43. S. Rose, *Limited Livelihoods: Gender and Class in Nineteenth-Century England* (Berkeley, CA: University of California Press, 1992); A. Clark, *The Struggle for the Breeches* (Berkeley, CA: University of California Press, 1995).
44. Blackstone, *Commentaries*, Vol. 1, ch. 16, pp. 458–9.
45. Poor Law Commission Report, 1832, p. 197, cited by U. Henriques, 'Bastardy and the New Poor Law', *Past and Present*, 37 (1967), pp. 103–29, p. 109; A. Levene, S. Williams, T. Nutt (eds), *Illegitimacy in Britain, 1700–1920* (Basingstoke: Palgrave, 2005).

46. Trustram, *Women of the Regiment*; J. Walkowitz, *Prostitution and Victorian Society: Women, Class, and the State* (Cambridge: Cambridge University Press, 1980).
47. Couples either went out of the country to marry legally if they could afford to do so, or – what was more risky – lied about their 'degree of affinity', or simply found a minister willing to marry them despite the law. On the pressures on poorer widowers, see C. F. Behrman, 'The Annual Blister: A Sidelight on Victorian Social and Parliamentary History', *Victorian Studies* 11: 4 (June 1968), p. 491.
48. For an alternative reading of the controversy, see M. M. Gullette, 'The Puzzling Case of the Deceased Wife's Sister: Nineteenth-Century England deals with the Second-chance Plot', *Representations*, 31 (Summer 1990), pp. 142–66.
49. Nelson, *Invisible Men*, p. 5.
50. S. S. Ellis, *The Women of England, Their Social Duties, and Domestic Habits* (London: Fisher, 1839, 2nd edn), p. 56 and pp. 55–8, 106–7, 211–12, 250–63, 344–6 and *passim*.
51. *Ibid.*, pp. 55–6.
52. P. Stoneman, *Elizabeth Gaskell* (Brighton: Harvester, 1987).
53. C. Gallagher, *The Industrial Reformation of English Fiction: Social Discourse and Narrative Form, 1832–1867* (Chicago: Chicago University Press, 1985).
54. E. Gaskell, *North and South* (Oxford: Oxford University Press, 1998), pp. 118–23.
55. D. Reid, 'In the Name of the Father: A Language of Labour Relations in Nineteenth-century France', *History Workshop Journal*, 33 (1994), pp. 1–22.
56. R. Gray, *The Factory Question and Industrial England, 1830–1860* (Cambridge: Cambridge University Press, 1996), pp. 46–58; D. Roberts, *Paternalism in Early Victorian England* (London: Croom Helm, 1979).
57. Cited by Gray, *The Factory Question*, p. 123. For mid-late Victorian paternalism, see Gray, *The Factory Question*, pp. 121–30, 213–34 and P. Joyce, *Work, Society and Politics: The Culture of the Factory in Later Victorian England* (Brighton: Harvester, 1980).
58. Rose, *Limited Livelihoods*, pp. 39, 34, 40 and 33–49. For gendered paternalist practices, see J. Lown, *Women and Industrialization* (Cambridge: Polity, 1990).
59. Rose, *Limited Livelihoods*, pp. 39–41 and Gray, *The Factory Question*, pp. 48–50.
60. Reid, 'In the Name of the Father', pp. 15–16; Joan Scott, *Gender and the Politics of History* (New York: Columbia University Press, 1988).
61. Gaskell, *North and South*, pp. 431–2.
62. Davidoff and Hall, *Family Fortunes*, p. 76.
63. G. Gilfillan, *The Grand Discovery; or, The Fatherhood of God* (London: Blackader, 1854), pp. 6, 13.
64. J. A. James, 'The Young Man from Home,' quoted in Davidoff and Hall, *Family Fortunes*, p. 113.
65. See R. Mitchell, *The Fatherhood of God* (London: Hamilton Adams; Glasgow: Thomas Morison, 1879), p. 16; also *Proceedings of a General Meeting held at the Freemason's Hall, London, on Wednesday July 20th 1870, Having for its object the formation of a society to be founded on a belief in the Fatherhood of God and the Brotherhood of Man* (London: Longmans, Green, 1870).
66. Gilfillan, *The Grand Discovery*, p. 13.
67. Mitchell, *The Fatherhood of God*, pp. 150, 152.
68. Gilfillan, *The Grand Discovery*, p. 84.
69. J. Smith, *Our Heavenly Father, or, God a Refuge and Strength* (London: Nelson, 1856), pp. 5–6.
70. Smith, *Our Heavenly Father*, p. 5; T. Griffith, *The Fatherhood of God* (London: Hatchard, 1862), p. 214.

71. Mitchell, *The Fatherhood of God*, p. 183.
72. Smith, *Our Heavenly Father*, p. 24; see also Gilfillan, *The Grand Discovery*, p. 6.
73. W. Forster, *The Fatherhood of God: The Subject-Matter of Christ's Mission, Clouded by the Creeds of Christendom* (London: Whitfield, 1857).
74. Gilfillan, *The Grand Discovery*, p. 18.
75. C. Hall, *Civilising Subjects: Metropole and Colony in the English Imagination, 1830–1867* (Cambridge: Polity, 2002), pp. 84–161.
76. Nelson, *Invisible Men*; Doolittle, 'Missing Fathers'.
77. Zwinger, *Daughters, Fathers and the Novel*; P. Stallybrass and A.White, *The Politics and Poetics of Transgression* (Ithaca, NY: Cornell University Press, 1986).
78. Note, however, that, in any one year, a child was slightly more likely to lose a father through an accident than a mother through childbirth, when the loss of the chief male wage-earner could have calamitous consequences for the income of a working-class family. See R. Woods and N. Shelton (eds), *An Atlas of Victorian Mortality* (Liverpool: Liverpool University Press, 1997).
79. B. Caine, *Bombay to Bloomsbury: A Biography of the Strachey Family* (Oxford: Oxford University Press, 2005), p. 83 and *passim*.
80. S. Szreter, *Fertility, Class and Gender in Britain, 1860–1940* (Cambridge: Cambridge University Press, 1996), pp. 530–1.
81. A. McLaren, 'The Sexual Politics of Reproduction in Britain', in J. R. Gillis, L. A. Tilly and D. Levine (eds), *The European Experience of Declining Fertility, 1850–1970: The Quiet Revolution* (Oxford: Blackwell, 1992), p. 85.
82. A. McLaren, *Birth Control in Nineteenth-Century England* (London: Croom Helm, 1978); J. A. Banks, *Victorian Values: Secularism and the Size of Families* (London: Routledge and Kegan Paul, 1981); M. Doolittle, 'Sexuality, Parenthood and Population: Explaining Fertility Decline in Britain from the 1860s to the 1920s', in J. Carabine (ed.), *Sexualities: Personal Lives and Social Policy* (Bristol: Policy Press, 2004), pp. 49–84; H. Cook, *The Long Sexual Revolution: English Women, Sex, and Contraception 1800–1975* (Oxford: Oxford University Press, 2005).
83. Tosh, *A Man's Place*, pp. 93–101.

Part 1
Rights and Responsibilities

Fatherhood, Religious Belief and the Protection of Children in Nineteenth-Century English Families[1]

Megan Doolittle

Throughout the nineteenth century in England, fathers stood at the symbolic centre of family, home and household, and of relationships between families and other social and political worlds. This position was not just symbolic, as fathers were invested with considerable power and authority, invisibly built into many social institutions. As this chapter will show, an implicit and often taken-for-granted aspect of fatherhood was providing protection for dependants, a complex role which shaped inequalities of power between genders and generations. Both formal and informal sanctions against fathers who were unable or unwilling to fulfil this role were at a historically low ebb as community governance of aberrant fatherhood was in decline, and legal remedies were limited.[2] Nevertheless, the rights of fathers were challenged at many levels, from everyday family dynamics to the political movements for women's rights and child protection which gathered momentum over the century. The transmission of religious and moral orthodoxies between generations thus emerged as a key index of fatherly competence and a significant arena for the reshaping of familial relationships.

Protection is a significant marker of parenthood in many cultures and historical periods, and is a feature of kinship and other dependency relations. At its most basic level, it reflects the differences in the capacities of young and adult humans, and the shielding of children from life's dangers forms a core element of parents' relationships with their children. Over the nineteenth century, the long and uneven transition towards the prolonged, sheltered childhood familiar to us today transformed these relationships,[3] reshaping the roles of fathers and father figures, especially in the responsibilities and expectations of being a protector. The social arrangements of protection are constructed through relations of power, as Pathak and Rajan argued: 'the will to power contaminates even the most sincere claims of protection. There are multifarious relations of dominance and subordination that circulate within the term "protection".'[4] In the nineteenth century, within unequal relationships between generations, abuse and neglect were only the most extreme forms of domination available to parents. While children were seen as offering comfort and pleasure to their parents, obedience to adults in general and parents in particular was constantly evoked as a requirement of the protected child.

The protection of children was deeply embedded in constructions of masculinity and adulthood, partly because of its close association with being a provider. For the vast majority of families, income and property were acquired from a variety of earners and sources, but it was husbands and fathers who were understood to have responsibility for providing for those under their authority.[5] In early modern societies an important characteristic of full manhood was independence, partly defined as not living under the protection of another, and best demonstrated through the ability to support a range of dependants.[6] These ideas underpinned the economic and social changes from which the breadwinner model emerged during the nineteenth century.[7]

On the other hand, protection increasingly came to be associated with care in this period, and mothers were most often charged with the day-to-day care of children. Care might be understood in this context as having two meanings – caring *about* and caring *for*.[8] Thus fathering included a protective caring *about* children while they were growing up, while the day-to-day caring *for* children was very often delegated to others.[9] As family life was increasingly associated with the home as a protected domestic space, the enjoyment of children's company became interwoven with care, comfort and pleasure for fathers.[10]

Alongside providing and caring, parents were expected to protect their children from exploitation and abuse within the norms of their class and culture. By the end of the century there was a widespread belief that this could not be left to families on their own, particularly those defined as deviant and/or poor, reflected in the growing body of legislation to limit the employment of children and the rise of the child protection movement.[11] Campaigners for a greater role for the state and philanthropists in child welfare focused on the role of wives and mothers, rarely directly challenging the authority of fathers.[12] When women contested the extensive formal powers of fathers, they argued that they required more authority in the family to protect their children, particularly where husbands and fathers abused their position.[13]

However, there was another important dimension to protective parenting relating to the spiritual and moral dangers faced by the young, and this forms the focus of the case studies below. At a time when control over environment and health were difficult, if not impossible, for most families to sustain, questions of mortality were often very much at the surface of everyday life. Across all denominations, the comforts of religion and in particular the Christian promise of reunion with loved ones in the afterlife were constantly invoked to inculcate in children the perils of unbelief.[14]

Religious orthodoxy also offered demonstrable conformity with a widely understood set of moral precepts, without which a child could face social ostracism. A significant element of conventional morality was the growing Romanticist association of childhood with innocence[15] achieved by the concealment of adult knowledge of sexuality, money, violence and death,[16] and reflected in the pervasive Victorian image of the redemptive innocence of children.[17] The role of parents in inculcating an appropriate religious orthodoxy and concealing adult knowledge became a focus of contestation as the three case studies below demonstrate.

These case studies have been selected to show fathers who faced particularly acute difficulties in managing their role in the moral education of their children, each one resulting in conflict which emerged into public discourse. The first two involve well-known figures, Percy Bysshe Shelley and Annie Besant, whose disputes ended up in court cases; the third is Chester Armstrong, who expressed this aspect of his life in his autobiography. All of these parents were married and had at least one son and daughter. Though the families came from very different social circumstances, their association with radical politics and unconventional religious beliefs formed the crux of their familial difficulties. While these cases cannot represent the highly diverse practices and contexts for family life in this period, they provide a framework for exploring the tensions between conventional fatherhood and those who contested it.

I

The poet Percy Bysshe Shelley was one of the very few fathers to be legally deprived of his children during the first half of the nineteenth century in an 1817 court case which was drawn upon and reiterated for more than a hundred years. Shelley was the heir of a landed family, whom he defied at the age of 19 by eloping and marrying Harriet Westbrook, the 16-year-old daughter of a well-to-do coffee shop proprietor.[18] When they separated three years later, Harriet had a daughter and was pregnant with his son, and Shelley had fallen in love with Mary Wollstonecraft Godwin, then only 17 years old. Harriet and her children went to live with her father. She drowned herself in the Serpentine in 1816, begging her sister to look after the children. Her suicide was hushed up, but her father then went to the Court of Chancery to make the children wards of court to prevent Shelley from bringing them up. Within a few days of hearing of Harriet's death, Shelley and Mary married, partly to strengthen his custody case, to heal their rift with Mary's father William Godwin, and to legitimate the baby Mary was about to give birth to – her third pregnancy.

Under most circumstances, Shelley would have won this case. Fathers' common-law rights over legitimate children were virtually limitless, and desertion, adultery or impoverishment were rarely significant barriers to retaining custody.[19] Shelley had access to a limited income from his family's estate, and his legitimate heir (Harriet's son) had considerable 'prospects' of inheriting land and title.

However, Shelley was an avowed and published atheist[20] who publicly stated that he would bring his children up as atheists, the most significant factor in the ensuing case. While a Catholic, Jewish or Muslim father could not be prevented from bringing up his children in his own faith, an atheist was seen as depriving his children of eternal life, a pressing concern in an age of high infant and child mortality. Only two children from the seven pregnancies of Harriet and Mary survived into adulthood. Shelley's lack of faith thus seriously offended deeply entrenched religious orthodoxies because he was refusing his children the protections of religion. Moreover, Shelley flagrantly transgressed moral codes about the sanctity of marriage in his class, and in the middle class to which Mary Shelley, the Westbrooks and Lord Eldon, the judge, belonged.[21] It was only through marriage that children were legally bound to their fathers, who had no rights or duties over illegitimate offspring, except for the provisions of the Poor Law.[22] Shelley argued in court that marriage should be terminable whenever spouses wished, a deeply radical stance when divorce was only available through an Act of Parliament.

When giving judgement in the case, Lord Eldon, the Lord Chancellor, is reported as saying:

> This is a case in which, as the matter appears to me, the father's principles cannot be misunderstood, in which his conduct, which I cannot but consider as highly immoral, has been established in proof . . . which he represents to himself and others, not as conduct to be considered as immoral, but to be recommended and observed in practice, and as worthy of approbation.[23]

Shelley deemed it his duty to raise his children according to his principles, but Eldon stated, 'the law calls upon me to consider [his principles] as immoral and vicious . . . I cannot, therefore think that I should be justified in delivering over these children for their education exclusively, to what is called the care to which Mr S. wishes it to be intrusted'.[24] In Eldon's view, fathers should form the 'opinions and habits' of their children, but he thought that, in this case, Shelley's views would injuriously affect both the children and society more generally.

An argument was made that removing the children to the guardianship of the Westbrooks would threaten their prospects of inheritance from the Shelley estate. But Eldon decided that protecting their moral and spiritual well-being was more important than the social and material advantages of landed wealth: 'I should deeply regret it if any act of mine materially affects those interests. But to such interests I cannot sacrifice what I deem to be interests of greater value and higher importance.'[25]

Thus Shelley lost possession of the children. The Master of the Court investigated their circumstances and, five months later, a guardian was appointed (Mr Westbrook having died) and they were sent to Church of England schools in the country. Shelley was given limited rights of supervised access and attempted to see them before leaving England to live in Italy, but he never saw them again.[26] They outlived Shelley, but Charles died aged 11 while in the care of Shelley's father. Iolanthe lived to become a respectable married woman, having been cared for by Harriet's sister.

The point at issue in the case was the protection of the children from godlessness, immorality and political radicalism, a powerful mix during this turbulent period. Their father was refusing to protect them from damnation in the next life, and from social ostracism within both Shelley's and Harriet's class. It was one thing for an adult to renounce religion in all its forms, but to withhold it from children was seen as putting them in extreme spiritual, moral and social danger, risking their future opportunities to find a respectable living or to marry, leaving them open to exploitation and hardship.

Wardship through the Court of Chancery was constructed as a relationship of protection, and thus seen as highly appropriate in this case. Acting through the Lord Chancellor, the monarch was seen as the symbolic parent of a ward, as *parens patriae*. Wardship originated in early modern England as a way of protecting the landed property of young orphans, but by this time wardship arrangements included other provisions for the care of wealthy children, particularly in respect of education and, most importantly, their religious upbringing.[27] In earlier times, the Lord Chancellor would bring together all wards of court each year for a tea party, a ritual occasion which confirmed their position as children of the Crown.[28] With the exception of the Poor Law, wardship provided the only alternative to informal kinship or neighbourhood sources of protection for children, and its use delineates for us some of the boundaries and inflections of the role of protector which fathers were expected to perform.

However, as Shelley's case demonstrates, it was not unusual for some protection to be delegated to mothers, kin, servants and schools. Mothers in particular were seen as important in providing moral protection, especially for daughters and 'infants', legally defined as under the age of seven. This was reflected in separation agreements, which were private legal contracts between spouses drawn up to avoid divorce proceedings, which set out maintenance and custody arrangements.[29] It was common for wives to take custody of girls, and husbands of boys, with access arrangements for children to see each other and the other parent.[30] This reflected the different roles of mothers and fathers in protecting children, whereby girls were seen to require female company and chaperoning, whereas boys needed to be introduced to the increasingly homosocial worlds of business, profession, or landed responsibilities. John Tosh points to the crucial role of fathers in the transition from boyhood to manhood in middle-class families, part of which involved easing sons into a profession or position in business.[31] Daughters without a mother were undoubtedly vulnerable, and substitutes were seen as vital to girls if their own mother was not present.[32] Thus men relied on female figures, whether relatives, adult daughters, paid companions or schools, to provide suitable company for their daughters, to protect their reputations and to prepare them for a dependent womanhood.

II

By mid-century, mothers had gained limited rights to custody of their children if separated or divorced.[33] However, the underlying principle of fathers as moral and religious protectors was still very much present, as shown in the complex court dispute between Annie Besant and her husband in 1879.[34] Born in 1847, she married Frank Besant, a Church of England minister in 1867, and had a son and a daughter, living as a vicar's wife in a remote Norfolk parish. After her young daughter survived a life-threatening illness, she lost her faith. She separated from her husband and became an activist in the secularist movement before becoming a prominent socialist, a leading theosophist and an Indian nationalist.[35] The separation agreement provided that her son should stay with his father and she should have custody of her daughter. After Besant was prosecuted with Charles Bradlaugh, and acquitted on a technicality, for publishing the *Fruits of Philosophy*, an American birth control pamphlet[36], her husband applied to Chancery that his daughter be made a ward of court and that he be appointed guardian and have custody.[37]

The Custody of Infants Act of 1873 allowed separated wives to have custody of their children, overriding the common-law rights of fathers, by giving legal recognition to private separation agreements. But there was an important caveat: the agreement would not stand if it were not for the benefit of the child.[38] Frank Besant argued that raising a daughter as a Christian and protecting her from unsuitable company overrode any legal rights which mothers had acquired under the Act. As in Shelley's case, he supplemented the argument that the girl should be raised as a Christian by successfully claiming that her mother was guilty of immoral behaviour in publishing an obscene pamphlet. Annie Besant lost custody of her nine-year-old daughter.

The father's right to determine his children's religious education was established by legislation under Charles II,[39] and was deeply connected to the regulation of religious orthodoxy and the reassertion of order based on patriarchal relations in the early modern sense of rule over households. In addition to arguing that his estranged wife could not protect her daughter from religious and moral dangers and was thus an unfit guardian, Besant also drew upon this paternal right to determine religious teaching, which persisted well into the twentieth century.[40] Like Westbrook, Besant thought that radical ideas about class and religion, equality and morality exposed children to social, spiritual and moral danger and exclusion.

Although as a married woman she was unable to act on her own behalf, Annie Besant mounted an appeal, but this also failed. Lord Justice James commented,

> the conduct of the Appellant in writing and publishing such works is so repugnant, so abhorrent to the feelings of the great majority of Englishmen and Englishwomen, and would be regarded by them with such disgust, not as matters of opinion, but as violations of morality, decency, and womanly propriety, that the future of a girl brought up in association with such a propaganda would be incalculably prejudiced.[41]

He stated,

> the Court cannot allow its ward [the daughter] to run the risk of being brought up, or growing up, in opposition to the views of mankind generally as to what is moral, what is decent, what is womanly or proper, merely because her mother differs from those views and hopes that by the efforts of herself and her fellow-propagandists the world will be some day converted. If the ward were allowed to remain with the mother, it is . . . not improbable, that she would grow up to be

the writer and publisher of such works . . . From such a possible future the Master of the Rolls thought it his duty to protect her, and we have no hesitation in saying that we entirely concur with him.[42]

Annie Besant was never accused of adultery in court, but a woman separated from her husband was highly vulnerable to losing rights of custody because such rights were always, automatically, refused to adulterous wives[43] who were considered incapable of protecting children from sexual knowledge. Adulterous fathers, by contrast, were not seen as subjecting their children to moral risks as long as the children were not brought into direct contact with their lovers.[44] The sexual double standard thus ensured that adultery had radically different implications for mothers and fathers, a point which formed a crucial argument in the passing of the 1857 Divorce Act. The consequent changes in custody whereby children were cared for by the 'innocent' party emphasized the growing importance of their protection from the taint of sexuality outside marriage.

Underpinning these debates was the fear that a divorced or widowed wife's second husband would be able to influence her with respect to her children, supplanting the role of their 'natural' father, potentially exposing children to forms of education and upbringing which he would not have condoned, especially relating to religious denomination.[45] A wife could not protect her children from a stepfather's 'fathering', because wives were expected to submit to the wishes of their husband just as children were constantly reminded to obey their fathers. Thus a man's inability to bring up his children according to his own beliefs was a sign of a lack of authority and control over his wife as well as a failure to protect his children's spiritual well-being. Frank Besant successfully asserted himself on all fronts, as a minister of religion, a father and a husband, in the face of an exceptionally strong-willed and determined adversary. Despite several subsequent attempts, Annie Besant never obtained a judicial separation or divorce from her husband, nor did she regain custody of her daughter. Both of the Besant children were subsequently raised by their father as orthodox Christians, and when both returned to support and befriend their mother once they were adults, he disowned them.[46]

III

The third case study is drawn from the autobiography of a mine-worker, Chester Armstrong, (born 1868), who lived in Ashington, a coal-mining town near Newcastle upon Tyne, who married in 1893 and had eight children, six of whom lived into adulthood.[47] His autobiography relates his intellectual and political journey through a crisis of faith: a turning against institutional Christianity towards free thought, radical socialism and the Independent Labour Party. This was inspired by reading Shelley and other Romantic poets before moving on to secularists such as Charles Bradlaugh, all of whom deeply influenced his religious and moral development. He also studied the works of sexual radicals, including Edward Carpenter. His active membership in local literary and political groups entailed much discussion of these ideas and how they should be applied in the working-class political movement.

Armstrong's journey was not just an intellectual one. He sought to change his personal and domestic life to reflect his increasingly unconventional views, describing this process as 'a great experiment'.[48] He was determined 'to correct what [he] regarded as errors of [his] own upbringing as a child, especially those that spelt repressive discipline, and particularly that of imposing the religious beliefs of the parent on the plastic mind of the child before such beliefs can be understood' (p. 280). He felt it was essential to win the agreement of his wife, who did not share his interest in radical ideas, because '[he] had already dispensed with that idea of overlordship involved in the marriage vows; which implies obedience on the part of the wife' (p. 197). Putting his ideas into practice profoundly affected their parenting:

> I had dispensed with theological sanctions. So we bent ourselves to the task of providing that spiritual nurturing, of a moral and ethical kind, which, as I assumed, would be of basic value to our children when they came to confront the problems of life on their own accord. I was fully conscious of the responsibility involved in such an experiment, since it was a departure from commonly accepted standards (p. 130).

However, he recognized that this task would involve imposing his views upon his family, and this provoked anxieties not only because it carried social risks for his dependants, but also because it exposed his position of authority and the inequalities of power in the family. 'How were my [domestic] obligations to be adjusted in accordance with this new attitude of mind? Was it right that I should impose this attitude of mind on my wife and family?' (p. 196).

Armstrong knew that his children were in no position to make a real choice about spiritual and moral concerns until they were old enough to trace his steps through doubt and understanding, but felt that in the end 'a very real form of freedom became the normal standard of [their] home life' (p. 197). The act of removing his children from Sunday school publicly marked his determination to challenge and reshape social norms:

> Imbued with a due sense of parental responsibility, ultimately I withdrew our children from the Sunday school, with the determination to attend to their moral well-being within the limits of my powers. There seemed no other course that was consistent with my new convictions. Emboldened by the adventurous sense of entering upon a new experiment, I thus came to reverse a traditional family order. In doing this I also felt that the moral rectitude of my children would be more assured ultimately by saving them from being befogged by theological impossibilities (p. 196).

We know much less about Chester Armstrong's family life than that of Shelley and Besant not least because its tensions were not aired in the courts. His marriage did not come to an early end, and questions of sexual morality did not appear in his rejection of convention in his own life story.[49] As a working-class family, the Armstrongs faced challenges of insecurity and poverty, as well as being deeply embedded in local and community life in ways which were not experienced by the more cosmopolitan Shelleys and Besants.

Armstrong shows how one individual took to heart the radical ideas of Shelley and Besant, and how difficult it was to put them into practice in everyday life. He thought he had succeeded, but at the beginning of the twentieth century it still felt like a dangerous experiment. Many decades after Shelley's moral precepts were publicly rejected, deep anxieties about shaping family life around notions of equality and freedom can still be traced, indicating that social norms about the protection of children were very deeply embedded in family life as well as legal and state institutions.

Throughout this period, these anxieties were expressed through debates about conventional religious teaching and its associated moral codes about sexual and family relationships. While mothers were seen as playing an essential role in inculcating these ideas, protection was framed around the presence of a father who was both responsible and in control of the moral protection of his children. When protection was defined in this way, only the most 'unnatural' or unsuccessful father could fail. However, among the fathers in these case studies, there were few who completely conformed to the norms of protective fatherhood: Frank Besant, who sought to keep his daughter safe from the freethinking company of his estranged wife, and Harriet Westbrook's father who, unable to protect his daughter from a fatal marriage, removed his grandchildren from further involvement with Shelley. Other fathers struggled to do what they thought was right, overriding conventions of morality and religion to pass on their values and ideals to their children.

The ways of carrying out protective fathering were thus very diverse, but always highly gendered processes. Through these conflicts and interactions, family life and the position of fathers within it were subject to examination and transformation. On the one hand, mothers claimed a stronger voice in bringing up children through linking their more accepted concern with caring for children with a desire to be effectively protective. On the other, there was a growing view that fathers should offer a protectiveness which would allow their children to grow and develop as individuals, rather than imposing rigid conventions and discipline upon them.

When we turn to fatherhood as a role, a status and a position in families and in the social world, we can see from these cases that being responsible for protecting children was constructed as an attribute of masculinity, as a marker of adult manhood. This was contingent, not just on being a father or the activities of fathering, but on marriage, the basis for social recognition of men's relationships with their children and also the institution within which their duties and rights were delineated. Protection was sited at the centre of fatherhood, where the duties, rights and pleasures of being a parent were deeply embedded in daily life as well as social and economic structures and processes. Historical constructions of fatherhood in these cases show the anxieties and challenges of negotiating power relations not only within families but also between families and those wider social forces which were both shaped by and shaped family life.

Notes

1. I should like to thank the many people who have discussed this paper with me, especially Katherine Holden, Janet Fink, Leonore Davidoff, the Social Policy Department at the Open University and the editors.
2. Community sanctions had included 'rough music' which publicly shamed those deemed inadequate. For discussion from this period in the context of domestic violence, see Hammerton, *Cruelty and Companionship*, pp. 15–33. For changes in formal rights and duties, see M. Finer and O. R. McGregor, *The History of the Obligation to Maintain. Report of the Committee on One Parent Families*, PP 1974 [Cmnd. 5629] XVI, App. 5 (London: HMSO, 1974), pp. 100–1.
3. A. Davin, *Growing Up Poor: Home, School and Street in London 1870–1914* (London: Rivers Oram Press, 1996), p. 3.
4. Z. Pathak and R. Rajan, 'Shahbano', in J. Butler and J. W. Scott (eds), *Feminists Theorize the Political* (New York and London: Routledge, 1992), p. 265.
5. See L. Davidoff and C. Hall, *Family Fortunes* for the middle classes and Seccombe, *Weathering the Storm* for the working class.
6. Rose, *Limited Livelihoods*, pp. 138–41.
7. For a discussion about explanations for the emergence of the male breadwinner, see C. Creighton, 'The Rise of the Male Breadwinner Family: A Reappraisal', *Comparative Studies in Society and History*, 38, No. 2 (1996), pp. 310–37.
8. J. Fink, 'Questions of Care,' in Fink (ed.), *Care: Personal Lives and Social Policy* (Bristol: Policy Press, 2004), pp. 6–8.
9. Nelson discusses the differences between motherhood and fatherhood which included discussions about whether caring about children implied a feminization of men, C. Nelson, *Invisible Men: Fatherhood in Victorian Periodicals, 1850–1910* (Athens GA and London: University of Georgia Press, 1995), ch. 2.
10. Gillis, *A World of Their Own Making*, pp. 109–29. Tosh, *A Man's Place*, pp. 27–50.
11. There is an extensive literature on child labour. See, for example, E. Hopkins, *Childhood Transformed: Working Class Children in 19th Century England* (Manchester: Manchester University Press, 1994). On child abuse, see L. Jackson, *Child Sexual Abuse in Victorian England*, (London and New York: Routledge, 2000). especially pp. 120–2 and G. K. Behlmer, *Child Abuse and Moral Reform in England, 1870–1908* (Standford, CA, Stanford University Press, 1982).
12. This arose most sharply in the anti-vaccination campaigns and the introduction of compulsory schooling: N. Durbach, 'Class, Gender and the Conscientious Objector to Vaccination, 1898-1907,' *Journal of British Studies*, 41 (January 2002), pp. 58–83; G. Behlmer, *Friends of the Family: The English Home and its Guardians, 1850–1940* (Stanford, CA, Stanford University Press, 1998), pp 92–103, For a discussion of the shift towards identifying mothers as the source of parental failure, see M. Arnot, 'Infant Death, Child Care and the State: The Baby Farming Scandal and the First Infant Life Protection Legislation of 1872', *Continuity and Change*, 9 (1994), pp. 271–311.
13. Griffin, 'Class, Gender and Liberalism in Parliament, 1868–1882', pp. 59–87; K. Gleadle, *The Early Feminists: Radical Unitarians and the Emergence of the Women's Rights Movement* (Basingstoke: Macmillan, 1995), pp. 97–196; Poovey, *Uneven Developments*, Ch. 3.
14. Tosh, *A Man's Place*, p. 38 discusses the importance of evangelical constructions of the family united after death.
15. H. Cunningham, *Children and Childhood in Western Society since 1500* (London: Longman, 1995), pp. 74–8.

16. R. Mills, 'Perspectives on Childhood,' in J. Mills and. R. Mills (eds), *Childhood Studies: A Reader in Perspectives of Childhood* (London: Routledge, 2000), pp. 12–16.
17. Nelson, *Invisible Men*, p. 72.
18. Biographical details are from W. St Claire, *The Godwins and Shelleys: The Biography of a Family* (London: Faber and Faber, 1989); C. Tomalin, *Shelley and his World* (London: Thames and Hudson, 1980), F. L. Jones (ed.), *Letters of Percy Bysshe Shelley*, Vol. 1 (Oxford: Clarendon, 1964).
19. M. L. Shanley, *Feminism, Marriage and the Law in Victorian England, 1850–1895* (Princeton, NJ: Princeton University Press, 1989); Lowe, 'The Legal Status of Fathers: Past and Present'.
20. P. B. Shelley, *The Necessity of Atheism* (1811).
21. Eldon's father was a coal factor in Newcastle upon Tyne. Eldon had eloped with his wife at the age of 21, but was an arch-conservative on questions of marriage and sexuality, arguing for the criminalisation of adultery in 1800, and was an opponent of divorce. R. A. Melikan, *John Scott, Lord Eldon, 1751–1838: The Duty of Loyalty* (Cambridge University Press, 1999), p. 157.
22. I. Pinchbeck and M. Hewitt, *Children in English Society*, Vol. II (London: Routledge and Kegan Paul, 1973), pp. 582–600.
23. Shelley v. Westbrook, *English Reports* (Chancery, 1817), p. 850, p. 851.
24. Ibid.
25. Ibid., pp. 851–2.
26. Jones, *Letters of Percy Bysshe Shelley*, pp. 553–5 shows a draft letter to the Lord Chancellor in September 1817 requesting that he be allowed to see his children after the Westbrooks had refused him access.
27. J. Seymour, '*Parens Patriae* and Wardship Powers: Their Nature and Origins,' *Oxford Journal of Legal Studies*, 14, No. 2 (1994), pp. 159–88.
28. N. V. Lowe and R. A. H.White, *Wards of Court* (London: Butterworths, 1979), pp. v.
29. L. Stone, *Road to Divorce: England 1530–1987* (Oxford University Press, 1990), p. 174–80.
30. See, for instance, the case of 'Vansittart v. Vansittart,' in *English Reports* (Chancery, 1858), p. 26, and Annie Besant's case, discussed below.
31. Tosh, *A Man's* Place, pp. 115–16.
32. Davidoff, Doolittle, Fink and Holden, *The Family Story*, pp. 115–6.
33. Shanley, *Feminism, Marriage and the Law*, pp. 136–40.
34. There is an extensive discussion of this case in N. F. Anderson, '"Not a Fit or Proper Person", Annie Besant's Struggle for Child Custody, 1878–9', in C. Nelson and A. S. Holmes (eds), *Maternal Instincts: Visions of Motherhood and Sexuality in Britain, 1875–1925* (Basingstoke: Macmillan, 1997), pp. 13–36.
35. Biographical details are from Taylor, *Annie Besant*.
36. Taylor, *Annie Besant*, pp. 127–37.
37. *In re* Besant, in *Law Reports* XI (Chancery, 1878) p. 508.
38. Shanley, *Feminism, Marriage and the Law*, pp. 139–41.
39. Pinchbeck and Hewitt, *Children in English Society*, p. 362.
40. See, for example, In re Agar Ellis, in Law Reports X (Chancery, 1878), p. 49.
41. In re Besant (Appeal), in *Law Reports* XI (Chancery, 1879), p. 515, p. 521.
42. Ibid., p. 521.
43. See, for example, early cases in the new Divorce Court: Bent v. Bent, in *English Reports* (Divorce, 1861), p. 1047 and Clout v. Clout and Hollebone, in *English Reports* (Divorce, 1861), p. 1047. However, after the passing of the *Guardianship*

of Infants Act 1886, the courts were slightly more flexible: for example, *In re* A and B (Infants), *Law Reports* (Court of Appeal, 1896), p. 786.
44. R v. Greenhill, in *English Reports* (Kings Bench, 1836), p. 922.
45. See, for example, Austin v. Austin, in *English Reports* (Chancery, 1865), p. 1098.
46. Taylor, *Annie Besant*, p. 252.
47. C. Armstrong, *Pilgrimage from Nenthead: An Autobiography* (London: Methuen & Co., 1938).
48. Armstrong, *Pilgrimage*, p. 130.
49. However, for many autobiographers at this time, constructing their stories involved the repression of family conflict and shame, so it is difficult to make any assumptions about how Armstrong's wife and children experienced and understood his intellectual and moral positions. See J. Peneff, 'Myths in Life Stories,' in R. Samuel and P. Thompson (eds), *The Myths We Live By* (London: Routledge, 1990), p. 39.

'Married Men and the Fathers of Families': Fatherhood and Franchise Reform in Britain

Matthew McCormack

Fatherhood is generally regarded as being a private matter, since it concerns personal relationships within the familial and domestic spheres. The public implications of fatherhood are rather more difficult to establish, not least because we are accustomed to conceptualizing formal politics as a sphere that is separate from 'the private', and because historians tend to assume that men have dominated the political world without critiquing these roles. The pioneers of the history of masculinity, however, always asserted that familial and public masculinities were inseparable. Michael Roper and John Tosh argued in 1991 that men's power in the political domain has historically been justified along patriarchal lines, in terms of the relationships 'between father figures and their dependants'.[1] This chapter will therefore focus upon the debates surrounding the parliamentary franchise in Britain in the late eighteenth and nineteenth centuries, but will place the issue of fatherhood at the centre of the question. In this way, it will explore both the implications of gender for this key constitutional debate and the place of politics in nineteenth-century ideologies and practices of the family.

The story of parliamentary reform in Britain is well-trodden historical ground, and its usual Whiggish outlines are very familiar. Electoral reform, we have always been told, is a tale of gradual democratization, of timely Reform Acts granted by enlightened public men, which peacefully delivered Britain into an era of mass representative politics. In recent years, however, this narrative of progress has been superseded by a new interpretation, one informed to a large degree by the 'postmodern' current in cultural history. Rather than emancipation, it is instead a story of control, attentive to the twin concerns of knowledge (how human society is classified) and power (how it is governed). In particular, the language of the reform legislation and the debates surrounding it have been scrutinized in an attempt to understand how contemporaries ordered their world. Focusing in particular upon the Second Reform Act of 1867, historians have reconstructed the debate concerning what sorts of people should be admitted to official politics and – equally importantly – who should not.[2] This body of work constitutes a new cultural history of citizenship, concerned with how the legitimate political subject is defined, both as an individual and as a member of a social, national and political community. Given that this new history is preoccupied with the cultural construction of the political self, it has been a particularly productive 'way in' to politics for historians of gender.

The key work in this revisionist mould is *Defining the Victorian Nation: Class, Race, Gender and the Reform Act of 1867*, jointly authored by Catherine Hall, Keith McClelland and Jane Rendall. Tellingly, none of these authors would claim to be mainstream political historians – arriving at the subject via the histories of empire, labour and women – and they therefore make the case that there was a lot more at stake in 1867 than the quantitative shape of the new electorate. As the title suggests, they place the debate about parliamentary reform in the context of discourses on class, race and gender, in order to assess how mid-Victorians defined access to the national political community. The citizen of 1867, they argue, was the respectable British working man. These characteristics were very much bound up together, and were respectively defined against the perceived absence of the same attributes in the 'rough', the foreigner, the pauper and the female (or the effeminate). Fundamentally, the citizen should be an independent householder: he should possess a free political will because he should be able to support himself and his dependants by his own labours, with all the moral character and respectability that that implied. Archetypically, he should be a father. As the radical J. A. Roebuck put it during the debates in the Commons, 'if a man has a settled house, in which he has lived with his family for a number of years, you have a man who has given hostages to the state, and you have in these circumstances a guarantee for that man's virtue'.[3]

To date, historians in this area have been satisfied that this preoccupation with the moral and domestic qualities of the male citizen was a specifically Victorian phenomenon. Whereas parliamentarians of the 1860s reiterated the moral character, religious virtue and respectability of the father-citizen, this apparently played little role in the debates leading up to the First Reform Act of 1832.[4] This chronology is consistent with the dominant account of middle-class Victorian masculinity, which asserts that the mid-nineteenth century saw the high-water mark of the domestic father ideal.[5] This essay, however, will revisit the debate on electoral citizenship prior to the Victorian period, in order to extend our understanding of the place of fatherhood in British political culture. 'Citizenship', of course, involves many activities, memberships and commitments beyond electoral participation, but it is useful to focus here upon the parliamentary franchise: in this period it was regarded as a badge of human dignity and the marker of full political inclusion, and contemporaries had tremendous faith in its capacity to achieve real change.[6] By focusing specifically upon the issue of fatherhood in relation to the vote, it is possible to reconstruct the elements of a pro-reform argument that was both remarkably consistent and difficult to contest. Indeed, their opponents generally avoided engaging them on these grounds: before the principle was conceded in 1832, anti-reformers insisted that the moral worthiness of the individual citizen was not up for debate because, in practice, you either had the vote or you did not. As such, this chapter will focus upon reformist discourse. It will demonstrate that a model of heterosexual masculinity based upon the related stations of father, husband and householder was central to the British parliamentary reform project from its inception in the last third of the eighteenth century. This is an important example of the ways in which domestic masculinities could have crucial public ramifications.

I

The story of franchise reform during Britain's long nineteenth century – from the Georgian radicals to the suffragettes – fundamentally revolved around questions of gender. As historians such as Anna Clark have demonstrated, Georgians and Victorians had a highly gendered notion of political entitlement.[7] Most commentators agreed that political power should only be wielded by responsible and free persons, virtues that were explicitly conceptualized in terms of masculinity. To a large extent, the debate on who should be admitted to official politics revolved around negotiating what sorts of people met this standard: it is possible to view the first three Reform Acts as successively modifying this definition in order to extend the franchise to men further down the social scale – whilst carefully excluding women and other sorts of men. Since fatherhood was a male station that was relatively accessible, and was associated with authority and responsibility, it was commonly invoked as grounds for widening the male suffrage.

Being the master of a family was politically important, since the household was central to the theory and practice of citizenship. Although the variety of local electoral qualifications before the Reform Act made the distribution of the franchise uneven, in theory the vote was exercised by heads of household. Most of the proposals aired in the Commons to reform the franchise in the early nineteenth century involved making this electorate of 'independent' householders more systematic in practice.[8] As well as being an important measure of masculinity, 'independence' was a key political value in a system where voting was open, patronage was commonplace and constitutional theory emphasized the need for checks and balances.[9] The 'independence' of the householder was partly founded upon his ownership of property: it connoted a stake in the country, a basic guarantee of status and – crucially – enabled the voter to avoid compromising dependencies upon forms of political influence. To a large extent, though, the 'independent' political personality of the householder was predicated upon his relationships with others in the household. According to classical theory, only the head of the patriarchal household was capable of acting for the public good, since those who depended upon him – wife, children and servants – could have no free political will. The implications of this were not just exclusionary, however, and were concerned with a man's domestic attachments as well as his freedom from obligation. Access to the political world was fundamentally concerned with the stations the householder occupied within the home as father, husband and master.

First, when a householder participated in public life, he did so on behalf of those he governed in the household. Georgian constitutional theory had it that even those who did not have direct access to political power – such as people who lacked the vote, or parts of the country or empire that lacked representatives – were 'virtually represented' by a parliament that spoke for the whole nation.[10] Increasingly, this argument was employed in relation to the household by reformers who supported the enfranchisement of more men. As the radical paper *The Gorgon* argued in 1818, children were 'under the controul of their parents' and were therefore 'represented by those to whom they were indebted for support and existence. Hence it follows, that *virtually*, both *females* and *minors*, would be represented, by extending the elective suffrage to males, 21 years of age.'[11] More pervasively, there was a sense in which the political personalities of women and children were merged with that of the male household head: they therefore did not require political rights, but he did in order to act on their behalf.[12] The father's supposedly natural role of speaking for his children was mobilized in order to make a case for his access to political power.

Secondly, by exercising authority within the household, the master had demonstrated some capacity for government. As James Harrington had put it in the 1660s, when 'a man has some estate, he may have some servants and a family, and consequently some government, or something to govern; if he has no estate, he can have no government'.[13] Conversely, a man who failed to govern his wife and children was unfit for public life. William Cobbett, writing a century and a half later, made a similar elision between property, domestic authority and political power when he discussed the dangers of a man being overawed by his wife:

> A husband thus under command is the most contemptible of God's creatures. Nobody can place reliance on him for anything . . . No bargain is firm, no engagement sacred, with such a man . . . Such a man has, in fact, no property; he has nothing that he can rightly call his own; he is a beggarly dependant under his own roof . . . 'A house divided against itself,' or, rather, in itself, 'cannot stand;' and it is divided against itself if there be a divided authority.

For Cobbett, the will of the household had to be unanimous, and it was the master who should express it. The opinions of the wife should be 'patiently heard', but when it comes to 'the principles that he is to adopt as to public matters . . . these must be left solely to the husband; in all these he must have his will; or there can never be any harmony in the family'.[14] Whether this happened in practice is more difficult to establish. It was recognized that husbands commonly consulted their wives about how the household vote was to be cast, and women were therefore canvassed at elections and were directly addressed in election propaganda.[15] Given the inclusive, communal nature of Georgian election rituals, women and children could participate in the festive public events. In a sense, they were as much members of the political community as the many men who could not vote, since all were 'virtually' represented by those who could.

It was in the interest of male radicals, however, to depict the political structure of the family in more black-and-white terms. The independence required for citizenship had formerly been associated with landed property and rank, so radicals attempted to realign the debate along the lines of gender in order to make a case for *male* political inclusion. A common rhetorical device among radicals was to emphasize the political unfitness of 'dependent' groups – lumping together women, children, criminals and the insane – in order to demonstrate the inherent political fitness of men.[16] Fatherhood therefore suited radical argument: it was accessible to men, involved the representation of others, demonstrated capacity for government, and underlined the contrast between the citizen and his dependants.

II

Fatherhood also had more empathetic connotations, and these too were reiterated by radicals and reformers. There is commonly a sense in reformist writing that fatherhood is an admirable institution. William Cobbett addressed this explicitly in his prescriptive text of 1829, *Advice to Young Men*. The work is structured around a series of letters dealing with the various stages and stations of a man's life, but the last two – 'Advice to a Father' and 'Advice to a Citizen' – are of particular interest here. Cobbett clearly valorises fatherhood and regards it as the touchstone of manly character:

> Being fond of little children argues no effeminacy in a man, but, as far as my observation has gone, the contrary . . . This fondness manifestly arises from a compassionate feeling towards creatures that are helpless, and that must be innocent. For my own part, how many days, how many months, all put together, have I spent with babies in my arms![17]

Cobbett discusses his own experiences of parenting in detail and espouses an active and involved model of fatherhood, both with infants and with older children. This is especially true of his sons, whom he carefully prepares for manhood and citizenship. For Cobbett, there is apparently no contradiction between the strikingly sentimental accounts of his relationships with his children and the firm authority that he expects to exercise as master of the household.

Fatherhood, however, also has implications beyond the household. A recurring theme in *Advice to Young Men* is the way that the author always claims to have combined domestic involvement with his public business.[18] For Cobbett, fatherhood and citizenship are not separate duties, but are very much bound up together:

> To say of a man that he is fond of his family is, of itself, to say that, in private life at least, he is a good and trustworthy man; aye, and in public life, too, pretty much; for it is no easy matter to separate the two characters; and it is naturally concluded that he who has been flagrantly wanting in feeling for his own flesh and blood will not be very sensitive towards the rest of mankind.[19]

Reformers such as Cobbett therefore argued that public and private masculinities were inextricably linked. Although the father–child attachment is necessarily a private one, it also demonstrates the man's sympathy with others, the basis of public spirit. In a culture where political subjects had to be manly, and where women and children were their cherished objects, the citizen's claim was underlined by being a good father.[20] As a radical, Cobbett was quick to emphasize the democratic implications of all this. He frequently insists that humble folk make better parents than the upper classes: the former do not delegate childcare to nurses and therefore have a closer relationship with their children.[21] Implicitly, they are morally superior and more deserving of political entitlements as a result.

In a symbolic sense, too, the father was a key figure in radical culture. British constitutionalism placed a great deal of emphasis upon historical rather than abstract or natural rights. The radical interpretation of the ancient constitution posited that freedoms had been won in the past by their ancestors and that it was their duty to maintain these rights or, where they had become corrupted or usurped, to restore them to the present generation. The language of 'fathers' and 'forefathers' therefore recurred in popular political culture, urging (or often shaming) citizens in the present to live up to their example and to protect their political inheritance.[22] In 1832, for example, the radical Thomas Hardy published a history of the London Corresponding Society, which described the hardships that activists such as himself had endured in the age of the French Revolution. As he explained, he did so in order 'that the present generation may see the severity with which liberal principles were dealt with in the days of their fathers, and if these fathers did not recover the liberty that had been wrested from their ancestors, it was not for want of struggling, and braving every danger in the cause'.[23] Radicals' connection with the past and also with the future was therefore expressed in familial terms, in the language of fatherhood and generations. Cobbett urged his readers to strive to maintain their political rights, and not only for their own sake: 'For, besides the baseness of the thought of quietly submitting to be a slave oneself, we have here, besides our duty to the community, a duty to perform towards our children and our children's children.'[24] Citizens were aware that political rights were a national inheritance which they passed from their ancestors to their descendants, and which deserved all the vigilance that would be due to a family possession. This inheritance was patrilineal, however, since it was to be enjoyed only by successive generations of men.

III

Fatherhood therefore played an important role in radical culture and in Georgian understandings of the political system. I now want to turn to the franchise debates themselves in order to explore the ways in which the proponents of reform drew on the idea of fatherhood. Reformers argued that the father and master require the vote so that he could protect his dependants. This went beyond a bland restatement of 'virtual representation', and suggests that political action on behalf of one's family was regarded in the most chivalric terms. Let us start by considering John Wilkes, who is credited with presenting the first ever parliamentary reform motion in Westminster, and who is often regarded today as being the epitome of radical hypermasculinity. In the 1760s, Wilkes had been a famous libertine: he abandoned his wife, and sexual hedonism became an important aspect of his libertarian persona.[25] However, his opponents increasingly cited his private vices in order to cast doubt on his public virtue, so in the very different moral climate of the 1770s he reinvented himself as a family man. He had always doted upon his daughter Polly, but he consciously presented himself as an adoring father during his period as Mayor of London. It was as father and daughter that the Wilkeses won the hearts of Londoners in the 1770s: as a contemporary noted, Polly filled the situation of lady-mayoress 'with great honour to herself, and infinite satisfaction to all the visitors at the mansion-house'.[26] Wilkes's correspondence with his daughter was printed in a lavish multivolume set, as a sentimental complement to his published political correspondence with leading public men.[27] And a portrait by J. Zoffany of 1779 depicted the Wilkeses with father seated and daughter standing. His disfiguring squint – famously rendered as a threatening leer by Hogarth – was therefore transformed, with his head tilted on one side as he gazed up at her with paternal affection.[28] His transition from libertine to father figure was complete.

When Wilkes presented his reform motion in 1776, his arguments were consistent with his reformed masculine image. He argued that a man required the vote in order to protect the 'personal liberty . . . of his wife and children'. He also indulged in melodrama, invoking the figure of the pure woman oppressed (rather ironically in his case) by a tyrannical libertine: 'Each law relative to marriage, to the protection of a wife, sister, or daughter, against violence and brutal lust, to every contract with a rapacious or unjust master, is of importance to the manufacturer, the cottager, the servant, as well as to the rich subjects of the state.'[29] This melodramatic scenario pervaded English political aesthetics, spurring men to acts of heroism by portraying political villainy in terms of sexual danger: at election time in particular, handbills warned men of the horrors that would befall their wife and children if they did not perform as required.[30] From the point of view of parliamentary reform, this was a democratic argument: as Wilkes does here, reformers cited the example of the father's desire to protect his children as an argument for enfranchising humble men. Forty years after Wilkes's speech, the reformer Thomas Oldfield similarly argued that many men with no property 'have yet wives and children, in whom they have a right', and even paupers need the franchise in order to defend 'the virtue of their wives and daughters'.[31]

It may be surprising to us that reformers placed so much emphasis upon the capacity of the vote to protect the family, but this serves to underline the importance of the parliamentary franchise in this period. Georgians and Victorians had considerable faith in the efficacy of representative politics, and believed that political action was necessary in order to safeguard their everyday lives. The unreformed Parliament was perceived to legislate in the interests of the monopoly, so change in the social, economic and legal realms would only come about if the Commons was rendered representative of the people. As such, reformers emphasized that male householders needed political rights because the state had the capacity to penetrate and disrupt the domestic sphere. First, the state took money from households in the form of taxation. It was a long-held maxim in Anglophone political thought that taxation should be linked to representation but, in the wake of the heavy taxes levied to fund the French Wars, radicals emphasized its effect on already poor working people. As Sir Francis Burdett argued when he outlined his proposal for parliamentary reform in the Commons in 1818, the people 'asked no bread but that which was earned by the sweat of their brows; and when they had earned it, they asked nothing but that it should not be wrenched from them and their children by the hand of fiscal rapacity, to feed the profligate and unprincipled sons and daughters of corruption'.[32]

Secondly, householders could be called upon to serve in the military. Again, it was a common argument that citizens who defended the state were entitled to a say in how it was run,[33] but reformers dramatized the issue by emphasizing that a man could be enlisted against his will. Burdett noted that the government 'exercised a power of taking men by force from their homes and families' in order to serve in the militia or be pressed into the fleet.[34] Thirdly, radicals emphasized the capacity of the state to incarcerate its critics. Radicals who were arrested under the repressive legislation of the 1790s and the 1810s emphasized the effect that this had upon their families in their memoirs. When Thomas Hardy was seized in May 1794, he described the distress that this caused to his heavily pregnant wife (who had already borne him five children who had died in infancy). While he was in prison, a loyalist mob surrounded the house and Mrs Hardy was forced to escape through a small back window, which caused her substantial injury. She died soon afterwards delivering a stillborn child, a tragedy that Hardy blamed squarely on the government. Upon his release he petitioned the King with his complaints:

> SIRE
> Your Ministers have bereaved me of my wife and my child . . . There was, indeed, a time when I could have addressed you as a father – a husband – a man – I could have called on you, on the pledge of these relations, to pity my sufferings; – that time is past: – I now ask only for justice.[35]

Hardy presents his claim to being 'a man' – and therefore a political subject – as being bound up with his stations as father and husband, stations that the authorities had robbed from him. In common with other radicals, then, Hardy emphasized the power of the state to affect the family. Fathers and husbands required political rights in order to protect their dependants from the harm that it could cause.

Reformers argued not only that fathers needed the vote, but that they could be relied upon to exercise it responsibly. This was a recurring theme in a Commons debate in 1797, when reformers within the Whig party moved a motion for parliamentary reform. Given that it was at the height of the French

Revolution, the Whigs presented their measure as a moderate reform that would head off radical protest, and they underlined the responsibility of the householder-citizen by identifying him with the father. A voter with children, they argued, would always act responsibly because of his regard for their welfare. Charles Grey argued that 'a man, arrived at the respectable situation of being a father, and consequently master of a family, having given hostages, as it were, to society, as an assurance of his interest in its welfare, was not unworthy of a share in the legislation of the country'.[36]

Thomas Erskine followed Grey in the debate and evoked a romantic family scene – 'a little circle round his fireside' – challenging anybody to deny that the humble father had a 'stake in the public fate'.[37] Grey and Erskine presented paternal affection as the norm within the late-Georgian sentimental family – but they did so to political effect, in order to claim wider enfranchisement for men. In his survey of the electoral system, Oldfield also used the language of 'hostages to society', and argued that the position of the father as the 'guardian and virtual representative' of his family was founded in nature: 'The relations and duties that belong to it are antecedent to all positive institutions, and constitute at once the basis and the security of civil society.'[38]

Finally, these reformers all agreed that fatherhood represented a position of respectability and responsibility and, as such, was a guarantee of the voter's moral character. As I have shown, the reformist left celebrated fatherhood as being an admirable institution. Fatherhood was a 'respectable situation', a 'character' in which a man had 'personal credit and respect to maintain'.[39] There is a sense throughout these writings that fatherhood and electoral citizenship should be held up as stations to which all men should aspire. Throughout the nineteenth century, the radical and liberal left argued that men should demonstrate their capacity for political rights through effort and self-improvement, and that citizenship – like fatherhood – should not be beyond the reach of any worthy man. The ten-pound electoral qualification in 1832 was explicitly presented in such terms: although it was exclusive in the short term, it was presented as being a reachable goal for the industrious. As Grey argued, however, meeting the householder qualification involved a lot more than just owning property:

> [the new citizenry] from the very circumstance of their occupying a 10*l*. house . . . have given a sort of guarantee of their holding a certain station in life – who thereby exhibit an open sign of their possessing some property – who have given a pledge to the community for their good conduct – and who for the most part are married men and the fathers of families.[40]

IV

What, then, is the significance of these links between fatherhood and political reform? It suggests that the type of analysis that has been carried out of the Victorian period needs to be extended right back to the inception of British reformism in the previous century. As this study of fatherhood shows, the project of redefining political citizenship in Britain had always been centrally concerned with issues of gender. In this broader chronological perspective, it is the First Reform Act of 1832 – not the Second of 1867 – that becomes the crucial turning point: the moment at which the reformers' gendered critique of the political system becomes the official criterion for citizenship.

From the point of view of political studies, it is clear that there needs to be a more thoroughgoing engagement with the history of gender. In particular, the aspects of an individual's social being that are relevant to electoral citizenship need to be defined more broadly. Too often, political historians focus merely upon property, work and class as the qualifying criteria for the franchise in this period, whereas this focus on fatherhood suggests that political entitlement was viewed in far more qualitative terms. Placing the family at the centre of political culture enables us both to broaden our conception of what constitutes 'the political', and to deepen our understanding of the central institutions such as the electoral system that necessarily dominate our accounts. It is well established that patriarchy was a dominant concept in early modern political theory, when the good ordering of the state was commonly held to be dependent upon that of the household.[41] The history of parliamentary reform, however, suggests that 'the rule of the father' was also taken literally in nineteenth-century politics.

Gender studies, too, has much to gain from an engagement with political culture. In particular, historians of masculinity need to pay more attention to the public aspects of masculine being – especially where, as in the case of citizenship, they are inseparable from the private. This was an agenda suggested by Davidoff and Hall's *Family Fortunes* in 1987, but it is one that has not really been followed through since.[42] In the subsequent rush to deconstruct 'separate spheres', we have lost sight of the need to have some meaningful way of understanding how these aspects of human life relate to one another. There is also a clear need to put politics back into our understanding of gender change in this period. The fact that this model of fatherhood was being trumpeted by a particular section of the political spectrum reminds us that domestic ideology was fundamentally political in nature: a way for working and middling men to assert their moral superiority in relation to those socially above and below them, and of claiming their right to political inclusion. By identifying citizenship with the stations of father, husband and master, they sought to render political life more accessible to men – even if this made it less accessible for women. From a gender perspective, then, the story of parliamentary reform is not one of progress and empowerment; rather, it represents a reiterated commitment to a patriarchal notion of political entitlement.

Notes

I should like to thank Julia Bush, Francis Dodsworth, Catriona Kennedy, participants at the 'Father Figures' conference and the editors for their useful comments upon this work.

1. Roper and Tosh (eds), *Manful Assertions*, p. 10.
2. J. Vernon, *Politics and the People: A Study in English Political Culture, 1815–67* (Cambridge: Cambridge University Press, 1993); C. Hall, 'Rethinking Imperial

Histories: the Reform Act of 1867', *New Left Review*, CCVIII (1994), pp. 3–29; A. Clark, 'Gender, Class and the Constitution: Franchise Reform in England, 1832–1928', in J. Vernon (ed.), *Re-Reading the Constitution: New Narratives in the Political History of England's Long Nineteenth Century* (Cambridge: Cambridge University Press, 1996), pp. 239–53; Hall, McClelland and Rendall, *Defining the Victorian Nation*.
3. 12 April 1867: quoted in Hall, McClelland and Rendall, *Defining the Victorian Nation*, p. 98.
4. D. Wahrman, *Imagining the Middle Class: The Political Representation of Class in Britain, 1780–1840* (Cambridge: Cambridge University Press, 1993), p. 381; Clark, 'Gender', p. 234.
5. Tosh, *A Man's Place*.
6. For this study, I am excluding the municipal franchise; at the time it was regarded as a separate issue and had a different cultural and political status to its parliamentary equivalent. It is an area that requires more work, however, and is especially interesting in the gender context, as women began to participate in local government elections long before they were given the parliamentary franchise. See P. Hollis, *Ladies Elect: Women in English Local Government, 1867–1914* (Oxford: Clarendon Press, 1987).
7. Clark, 'Gender'.
8. See the motions by Sir Francis Burdett (15 June 1809): *Parliamentary Debates* XIV, pp. 1041–63; Thomas Brand (21 May 1810): XVII, pp. 123–64; Brand (8 May 1812): XXIII, pp. 99–157; Burdett (2 June 1818): XXXVIII, pp. 1118–81; and John Lambton (18 April 1821): New Series V, pp. 360–450.
9. M. McCormack, *The Independent Man: Citizenship and Gender Politics in Georgian England* (Manchester: Manchester University Press, 2005).
10. See the speech by D. Giddy in the Commons (21 May 1810): *Parliamentary Debates* XVII, pp. 133–5; P. Langford, 'Property and Virtual Representation in Eighteenth-Century England', *Historical Journal*, XXXI (1988), pp. 83–115.
11. *The Gorgon* (5 September 1818), p. 123. See also Thomas Erskine (Commons: 26 May 1797): *Parliamentary History of England* XXXIII, p. 665. Julia Bush has pointed out to me that these same arguments were employed by opponents of women's suffrage even into the early twentieth century.
12. J. Mill, 'Essay on Government', in J. Lively and J. Rees (eds), *Utilitarian Logic and Politics* (Oxford: Oxford University Press, 1978), p. 79.
13. J. Harrington, *A System of Politics* (c. 1661) in J. G. A. Pocock (ed.), *The Commonwealth of Oceana* (Cambridge: Cambridge University Press, 1992), p. 269, pp. 267–93.
14. W. Cobbett, *Advice to Young Men* (1829), ed. by George Spater (Oxford: Oxford University Press, 1980), pp. 179–84.
15. *History of the Contested Election in Chester, 1812* (Chester, c. 1812), p. xv; 'To the Electioneering Ladies of Liverpool', in *The Liverpool Squib Book* (Liverpool, 1820), p. 38.
16. *The Black Dwarf* (4 June 1817); *The Gorgon* (22 August 1818); J. Wade, *The Extraordinary Black Book* (Shannon: Irish University Press, 1971), pp. 560–1.
17. Cobbett, *Advice*, p. 175.
18. For example, Cobbett, *Advice*, pp. 157, 162, 165.
19. Cobbett, *Advice*, p. 234.
20. An interesting comparison can be made with French political culture in this period: J. Landes, 'Republican Citizens and Heterosocial Desire: Concepts of Masculinity in Revolutionary France', in S. Dudink, K. Hagamann and J. Tosh (eds),

Masculinities in Politics and War: Gendering Modern History (Manchester: Manchester University Press, 2004), pp. 96–115.
21. Cobbett, *Advice*, pp. 237–8.
22. It was a recurring motif in electoral culture, for example, *History of the Contested Election in Chester, 1818* (Chester, *c.* 1818), p. viii.
23. T. Hardy, *Memoir of Thomas Hardy, Founder of, and Secretary to, the London Corresponding Society* (1832), in D. Vincent (ed.), *Testaments of Radicalism: Memoirs of Working-Class Politicians 1790–1885* (London: Europa, 1977), pp. 31–102 (p. 52).
24. Cobbett, *Advice*, p. 329.
25. J. Sainsbury, 'Wilkes and Libertinism', *Studies in Eighteenth-Century Culture* XXVI (1998), pp. 151–74.
26. *The Correspondence of the Late John Wilkes with his Friends*, ed. by J. Almon, Vol. IV (London, 1805), pp. 172–3.
27. *Letters from the Year 1774 to the Year 1796 of J. Wilkes, Esq., to His Daughter*, ed. by J. Almon, 4 vols (London, 1805).
28. S. West, 'Wilkes's Squint: Synecdochic Physiognomy and Political Identity in Eighteenth-Century Print Culture', *Eighteenth-Century Studies*, XXXIII (1999), pp. 65–84.
29. John Wilkes (Commons: 21 March 1776): *Parliamentary History* XVIII, p. 1295.
30. For example, the handbills 'To the Worthy Freemen of the Borough of Lancaster' (Lancaster, 1 March 1768) and 'Advertisement Extraordinary' (Shrewsbury, 22 June 1819).
31. T. H. B. Oldfield, *The Representative History of Great Britain and Ireland*, Vol. III (London, 1818), p. 4. See also *The Black Dwarf* (30 April 1817); Wade, *The Extraordinary Black Book*, p. 560; Cobbett, *Advice*, p. 318.
32. Sir Francis Burdett (Commons: 2 June 1818): *Parliamentary Debates* XXXVIII, p. 1136. See also *The Black Dwarf* (30 April 1817); Cobbett, *Advice*, p. 328.
33. J. Cartwright, *The Commonwealth in Danger* (London, 1795).
34. Sir Francis Burdett (Commons: 2 June 1818): *Parliamentary Debates* XXXVIII, p. 1136.
35. Hardy, *Memoir*, pp. 60–1, 85. See also William Cobbett's account of his arrest in *Advice*, pp. 284–9.
36. Charles Grey (Commons: 26 May 1797): *Parliamentary History* XXXIII, p. 650.
37. Thomas Erskine (Commons: 26 May 1797): *Parliamentary History* XXXIII, p. 664.
38. Oldfield, *Representative History* III, p. 6. This passage was quoted as an authority during the debate on Francis Burdett's plan of reform: Madocks (Commons: 15 June 1809): *Parliamentary History* XIV, p. 1060.
39. Oldfield, *Representative History* III, p. 6.
40. Charles Grey (Lords: 9 April 1832), *Hansard's Parliamentary Debates* Third Series XII, p. 19.
41. Fletcher, *Gender, Sex and Subordination*, ch. 11.
42. Davidoff and Hall, *Family Fortunes*.

'What Do You Want to Know about Next?' Charles Kingsley's Model of Educational Fatherhood

Valerie Sanders

'Kiss the darling ducks of children for me,' Charles Kingsley told his wife at the end of a letter of 1849, when he was away in Devonshire trying to recoup his health: 'How I long after them and their prattle. I delight in all the little ones in the street for their sake, and continually I start and fancy I hear their voices outside. You do not know how I love them; nor did I hardly till I came here.'[1]

Kingsley was by all accounts a devoted and demonstrative father, whose letters to his wife are full of affectionate remembrances to his children, for whom he often brought home samples of natural history: 'Tell Rose and Maurice I have got a strange sponge for each of them, which I picked up upon the shore of the Firth of Tay,' he wrote from Edinburgh in 1854;[2] while other trips abroad yielded lava-stones from volcanoes, red and blue locusts, birds' eggs and, on one occasion (when his eldest child Rose was eighteen), 'two pairs of bucks' horns – one for each of them, huge old fellows, almost as big as Baby'.[3] Kingsley assumed that his daughters would be just as interested in natural phenomena as his sons, though he was especially anxious that Maurice, the elder son, would thereby be saved from bad influences: 'I am bringing up my children as naturalists,' he told a friend in 1857, 'my boy as both naturalist and sportsman; and then, whether he goes into the army (Engineers), or emigrates, he will have a pursuit to keep him from cards and brandy-pawnee, horse-racing, and the pool of hell.'[4] As it was, all his children became adventurous achievers. Maurice went out to South America, his second son, Grenville to Australia, his younger daughter Mary became the novelist 'Lucas Malet', and his eldest, Rose, a writer on history and gardening. Kingsley dedicated his first children's book, *The Heroes* (1856) (a rewriting of Greek mythological tales) to his first three children, while as a family anecdote famously recounts, *The Water-Babies* (1863) was written for Grenville, so that 'Baby' would have a book of his own.[5]

At a time when the duties of fatherhood were seen as being primarily to provide for and protect dependent offspring, Kingsley was intensely involved in training his children's minds and stimulating their intellectual curiosity. In this respect, he was similar to several other key educator-fathers of his time, most notably James Mill, Thomas Arnold of Rugby, Philip Gosse, and Edward White Benson, later Archbishop of Canterbury, but known to Kingsley as the first headmaster of Wellington College. Each of these men had an idealized notion of how he wanted to raise his children, and in each household the children were unable to escape a father who was usually at home, or close by; in the cases of Benson and Arnold, he was in an adjacent building teaching other boys, and coming home to oversee the intellectual progress of his own offspring. Terence Copley notes that Dr Arnold 'drew up their syllabus personally' and 'tested his children on Sunday evenings', rewarding good results with toys, while Benson, out walking with his children, encouraged them to be close observers of nature, and to make up rhymes. John Stuart Mill also went on educational walks with his father, who, despite his own heavy workload, spent 'a considerable part of almost every day ... employed in the instruction' of his children'.[6] Edmund Gosse, whose father was another of Kingsley's personal friends, recalls 'preparing little monographs on seaside creatures, which were arranged, tabulated and divided as exactly as possible on the pattern of those which my Father was composing for his *Actinologia Britannica*'.[7] Despite attempts to educate his sons at other public schools, Arnold finally installed them at Rugby, where home and school life so completely converged that their father was also their headmaster. Benson's sons, despite attending other schools, remained intensely conscious of his headmasterly expectations of them. Brian Masters, biographer of E. F. Benson, comments, 'They were to be perfect, he must be proud of them, they must never let him down.'[8] As it happened, while Benson was at Wellington, he was, like Philip Gosse, a near neighbour of Kingsley's, and the two men became such warm friends that Kingsley sent his son Maurice to school at Wellington. Benson's wife Mary recalled that the two fathers' 'talks on education were wonderful'.[9]

As a clergyman, Kingsley worked from home, with his children's activities going on around him. His daughter, Lucas Malet, recalled in an interview of 1896 how fond they were of him as children: 'we made it quite a pleasure to keep quiet when we knew he was at work'.[10] Corporal punishment was never allowed because he felt it degraded both parties, and he did his best to hide from them his own emotional instability and tendency to depression. His son Maurice recalled that he was at once 'the most fatherly and the most unfatherly of fathers – fatherly in that he was our intimate friend, and our self-constituted adviser; unfatherly in that our feeling for him lacked that fear and restraint that make boys call their father "the governor"'.[11]

Maurice's distinction between the two terms gives us some idea of how fatherhood was defined at the time. Though historians such as John Tosh and John Gillis have now indicated the range of parenting styles to be found in Victorian (and other) fathers, Maurice's comments suggest that the norm still included an element of awe. Kingsley himself thought deeply about the role he was performing with his own children, and the relative importance of mother and father in their upbringing – issues he never entirely resolved in his turbulent and restless-sounding educational texts for children, despite an underlying current of self-examination and inward debate. Often away from home, either for health reasons or on church business, Kingsley, in sending regular messages to his children, was reminding them of his presence in their lives: a point reinforced by his return, laden with outlandish gifts of nests and stones and horns. He repeatedly asserted his own role as fatherly educator, urging his wife to 'tell' the children things on his behalf, so that, during his absence, Fanny became his mouthpiece or surrogate educator. In his letters he was in effect employing a woman to pass on useful information, while retaining ultimate control, a model he would perfect in his children's fiction.

His travels often inspired him to plan further exercises for his return: for example, on a visit to Lyons in France he sent messages to his daughter Mary and his son Grenville, promising to pass on his new experiences: 'Tell M. that her letter was delightful, and that I will give her lessons in the geography of France. Tell G. that there is a wonderful mechanical clock in the cathedral here, and when I have seen it, I will write to him all about it.'[12] His writing gives the impression that he never tired of disseminating information; indeed, this was something he seemed to crave, as a validation of his fatherly role. Mary recalled that when she was reading at home as a child, she did so in a desultory way, not bothering to verify what she read: '[I] simply asked my father questions instead of going to a dictionary or encyclopaedia.'[13] Even when his children were practically grown up, Kingsley continued to concern himself with defining the exact role of a father as educator in relation to professional teachers. Enjoying the coincidence of his son Maurice being a Cambridge undergraduate when he himself was Professor of History, he reflected: 'It is quite right that the schoolmasters should have the grounding and disciplining, but the father who can *finish* his boy's education, and teach him something of life besides, ought to be very thankful.'[14] This comment shows that Kingsley thought of himself as engaged with more than just facts: in wanting to teach his son 'something of life', in a moral, experiential sense, he was proposing a masculine model which apparently excluded the boy's mother, however well-informed or well-intentioned she might be. Yet when his youngest child Grenville went to school in 1867, Kingsley reassured his wife that the mother was the more important parent, 'and in the case of the *boy* everything; the child *is* the mother, and her rights, opinions, feelings, even fancies about him, ought to be first regarded.'[15]

Fanny Kingsley's own perspective on parenting is difficult to fathom. Her two-volume biography of her husband is too deferential to expose any rifts between them, though she did not always agree with his plans for their children and made occasional bids to keep them at home. Susan Chitty suggests that she was a devoted mother who became 'hysterical' at the prospect of sending Grenville on his own to Harrow. By way of a compromise, they rented a house there so that his mother could keep a watchful eye on her youngest child. But this was perhaps no stranger than Margaret Oliphant moving to Windsor while her boys were at Eton, or Margaret Ruskin joining her son John in Oxford while he was an undergraduate.[16] Fanny otherwise figures little in the narrative of her children's lives, her recurrent ill health making her the parent who stayed at home, rather than the one who took them on adventures. Gradually, Rose replaced her as her father's companion, and made the strenuous trips around America that Fanny could never have contemplated. Whatever role she had in her children's daily upbringing, Kingsley's writing seems to edge her out of it, and her voice remains essentially private and silent. Her one momentous intervention, recorded in the biography (II, p. 137) is where she announces that 'Rose, Maurice, and Mary have got their book [*The Heroes*], and baby must have his.' This allegedly triggered the writing of *The Water-Babies*.

In his assorted writings, both formal and informal, Kingsley sounds as if he is trying to reassure himself of the father's importance as the ideal educator: a dilemma tied up with his lifelong uncertainties about the relative characteristics of masculinity and femininity, and whether it was ever possible for one individual to combine them both without loss of distinctive gender identity. He felt that women had a particular role for which they were qualified by having experienced the pain and suffering of pregnancy and childbirth, while in practical terms they also ran the household 'while the men [were] away'.[17] To Kingsley it was natural for a mother to care about her children and work for them, but in *Madam How and Lady Why* (1870) he suggests that if 'the father should help likewise,' this is '(as you will find out as you grow older) more wonderful far'.[18] In this passage he is actually referring to starlings, but it is tempting to read it as at least partially applicable to human fathers, implying that active fatherhood does not come naturally to a man. Much of his writing for children works as an attempt to put the father back into a teaching role, while recognizing the all-powerful nature of the mother's position. This is made all the more problematic because of the apparent redundancy of the father's sexuality.

Kingsley's gradual formulation of a role for himself as an educating father has not so far been explicitly connected with his developing sense of himself as a strongly sexualized male. Recent critical discussion of his theories of masculinity stresses his clear differentiation of gender roles, with all the vital energies being attributed to the male. David Rosen argues that Kingsley used the volcano as a metaphor for all the unrepressed 'rage' or 'pluck', otherwise known by the Platonic term *thumos*, which he saw as a vital component of masculinity, and a driving force in the purgation of the world.[19] Apocalyptic volcano images feature in his novels *Yeast* (1848) and *Alton Locke* (1850), besides being discussed in very different contexts in his writing for children. While Kingsley's sexual energy has been examined by biographers and critics in relation to his marriage with Fanny Grenfell, the issue of what happened to it when Kingsley became a father is less clear. The fathering of children, in itself proof of virility, is not just a biological act, but a lengthy, nurturing responsibility, in relation to which displays of aggressive male sexuality are inappropriate. Like many fathers before and after him, Kingsley therefore had to cultivate new skills which would divert his energies in a more suitable direction. According to David Rosen, one of these new qualities was 'tenderness': another side of masculinity which Kingsley valued as much as the volcanic energy, because 'all men learned love at their mother's breast'.[20] Laura Fasick, on the other hand, suggests that he found it difficult to reconcile his 'fondness for hyper-masculinity' with the code of Christian, domestic morality he was expected to propound as a clergyman: 'gentleness, humility, patience – were not the values of the type of masculinity that he prized'.[21] Fasick argues elsewhere that while Kingsley accepted 'a doctrine of complementarity' for the two sexes, he tended to associate vulnerability with the feminine. He may have prized 'tenderness', but there was much in femininity from which he wished to distance himself, not least a kind of long-suffering passivity which was in direct contrast with the male energy he so happily vaunted.[22] These contradictions surface especially in relation to his intended readership: the 'dear little man' he addresses in *The Water-Babies*, and Grenville and his schoolfellows in *Madam How and Lady Why*. If his role is to educate the next generation of men, his function as a virile father is presumably to make them confident in their masculinity. But how can this be done using female teachers, as he does throughout *The Water-Babies*, and by constant reference to the wisdom of 'Madam How' and 'Lady Why'? Is it his role as fatherly narrator to reinforce what the women teach his son, or to override it?

One reason for his uncertainties may be that the tradition of educational children's literature, based on the catechism-style, question-and-answer format, which surely underlies Kingsley's style in *Madam How*, had been very much the province of women in the previous generation. 'In fact,' argues Alan Rauch, 'in the early nineteenth century, children – both male and female – learned most of their science from female authors.'[23] The most famous of these texts was Richmal Mangnall's much-republished *Questions* (1800), the full title of which was *Historical and Miscellaneous Questions for the Use of Young People*. The questions themselves were, according to the preface, not only 'intended to awaken a spirit of laudable curiosity in young minds' but also to 'serve as Exercises for the ingenuity both of pupil and instructor'.[24] Having exhausted their ingenuity on history, readers were rewarded after 1806 with a new section on astronomy, which included such questions as 'What is meant by the Heavenly Bodies?' and 'What is the Solar System?', followed by a neat definition designed to be easily committed to memory. As an aid to knowledge it entirely lacks the moral dimension which is such a notable feature of Kingsley's writing, but a more recent example of a question-and-answer book written by a woman, Jane Marcet's *Conversations for Children; On Land and Water* (1838), is much more of a genuine dialogue, allowing the children to discuss the implications of what the mother-educator figure, 'Mrs B,' tells them. This book followed in the vein of her earlier *Conversations on Natural Philosophy* (1819), designed to introduce children to the elements of basic science, while her *Conversations on Chemistry* (1806) was – rather pointedly perhaps – aimed specifically at girls. The later *Conversations for Children; On Land and Water* incorporates a family of boys and girls who, like Kingsley's son Grenville, are shown in the text asking questions about volcanoes, rivers and lava, to which their mother, 'Mrs B,' responds while the children engage in practical experiments with sand and clay. The children's father makes only the briefest of appearances: for most of the text he is shut up in his chemical laboratory, which they invade in the Seventeenth Conversation, only to be shooed away:

'No, my dears, this is chemistry, which you are much too young to understand; and I am not a conjuror to show off a number of wonderful tricks for the amusement of children, so take them away,' continued he, addressing Mrs B., 'and let me return to my work.'[25]

Mrs B. tries to console her disappointed flock with some 'drawing-room chemistry' involving lucifer matches (p. 177), but she and they have had a firm rebuff: real chemistry is men's work, incompatible with fatherhood, and not for sharing with mothers and children.

In *The Water-Babies*, the narrator shows that he is clearly uncomfortable about these bookish female educators, whom he lampoons as 'Aunt Agitate' (p. 34), a term that may refer to Mrs Marcet, or possibly Harriet Martineau. Either way, such women are too unimaginative to believe in fairies or water-babies, but this is not exclusively a female failing. Kingsley's narrator seems haunted by the spectre of 'Cousin Cramchild's Conversations', probably a reference to the American popularizer of knowledge, Samuel Goodrich, otherwise known as 'Peter Parley', whose books instructed children in history, geography and natural science. What angers Kingsley most about such educators is their lack of faith in anything invisible or mysterious, whether construed as religion or the imaginative world of children's make-believe. Much of *The Water-Babies* in particular is an argument with himself, justifying his way of teaching and attacking all those who insist on children being stuffed to excess with information. Yet this is a temptation to which he succumbs himself in all those texts where he plays the part of educating father.

Kingsley's unresolved theories of sexual difference perhaps go some way towards explaining how he distributes teaching roles among the male and female characters in his children's books, and his casting of himself as the overseeing omniscient narrator in texts otherwise lacking a visible father figure: a pattern he had already established in his writing for adults. The eponymous hero of *Alton Locke* (1850), for example, never knew his father, and was brought up by a harsh and dominant mother: 'My mother moved by rule and method; by God's law, as she considered, and that only. She seldom smiled. Her word was absolute.'[26] Alton's famous Darwinian dream, which re-enacts the stages of evolution, seems to be triggered by a vision of his mother standing at the foot of his bed. When he tries to follow her, his bedclothes swell into the shape of a volcano, which violently erupts and, in his subsequent raging fever, the 'fancy of the mountain returned' (p. 335). His mother, meanwhile, is seen bending the pillars of a Hindu temple: a destructive and irrational force at the heart of the storms and tornadoes that threaten to blind and bury him. Alton's subsequent dream presents him with all the fantastic symbols of the natural world that reappear in Kingsley's writing for children.

Essentially, Kingsley's is a gendered, sexually alive universe, composed of male and female presences. This is particularly the case in his educational writing (not necessarily for children), such as his 1869 lecture 'The Air-Mothers', which characterizes the breezes as female, and the 'great sun' as their 'father'.[27] His children's books likewise divide up the natural and spiritual influences in a child's upbringing into father and mother surrogates. Thus the Father in

Heaven (or 'All-Father' as he is called in *Alton Locke*, p. 344) is complemented by Mother Earth, both of them teacher figures who, in *Madam How*, are supported by the two female figures of the title. Even Mr Grimes, Tom's master and substitute father figure, is complemented by his own mother, the old schoolmistress, who gives Tom some milk in his flight from Harthover Place. Grimes clearly proves his inadequacy as a father when he interrupts Tom's educational dialogue with the gamekeeper about bees:

> 'What are bees?' asked Tom
> 'What make honey.'
> 'What is honey?' asked Tom
> 'Thou hold thy noise,' said Grimes.[28]

Kingsley, by contrast, constantly urges his children and his child-readers to use their eyes and notice their surroundings: an idea he propounded when he addressed a hall of Edward Benson's schoolboys at Wellington in 1863. In a lecture designed to stimulate the boys into collecting exhibits for a college museum, he emphasized his wish, not so much to teach them things as to teach them 'how to *learn* . . . And what does the art of learning consist in? First and foremost, in the art of observing.'[29] Recalling his childhood enjoyment of reading *Evenings at Home* (1792–6), a collection of tales by John Aikin and Anna Laetitia Barbauld, which contained a story called 'Eyes and No Eyes', he urges his boy listeners to be 'Mr Eyes', if only to keep themselves out of trouble and to be happy and successful.

Repeatedly, in his comments on educating boys and men, Kingsley emphasized how much he saw education as an antidote to specifically masculine kinds of vice. This is where we can identify a clear connection between his sense of himself as a man aware of having a strong sexual appetite, and his equally powerful drive to cleanse the world. In his Wellington speech he warns his audience that unless they cultivate a taste for something healthy, such as geography, chemistry or natural history, they will lay themselves open to having nothing worthwhile to do after work but:

> the theatre, or billiards, or the gossip at their club, or if they be out in a hot country, everlasting pale ale; and continually tempted to sin, and shame, and ruin, by their own idleness, while they miss opportunities of making valuable discoveries, of distinguishing themselves, and helping themselves forward in life.[30]

In *Madam How*, where his audience is also schoolboys, but younger ones, he frames the choice in simpler language, asking whether it is not 'altogether naughty and wrong to refuse to learn from your Father in Heaven, the great God who made all things, when he offers to teach you all day long by the most beautiful and most wonderful of all picture-books' (p. x). So far as Kingsley was concerned, the universe was God's book, which he also defined as 'Science', and God himself was a kind of father-teacher whose lessons ignorant mankind too often disregarded. In his view they were a source not only of scientific knowledge but also of goodness, truth and wisdom. Madam How, by contrast, is 'the Housekeeper of the whole Universe' (p. 7), active and unpredictable, constantly rearranging things in order to test the mettle of humankind. She and Lady Why are repeat versions of the two female fairies, Mrs Bedonebyasyoudid and Mrs Doasyouwouldbedoneby from *The Water-Babies*, between them distributing punishment and spiritual enlightenment respectively. In turn, Madam How has two grandsons, Analysis and Synthesis (p. 134), while Mother Carey in *The Water-Babies*, 'the grandest old lady he had ever seen' (p. 148), makes millions of new-born creatures out of the seawater, and tells stories which prove that she is 'perfectly right, as it is [her] custom to be' (p. 150). Alongside these images of all-powerful female fecundity, and faith in the rightness of women's teaching, men and fathers in his imaginative writings for children are curiously unimportant in the day-to-day functioning of the universe. If anything, as Claudia Nelson has argued, men, in *The Water-Babies* at least, have caused most of the death and destruction from which the women need to rescue Tom and Ellie – 'The world of grown men is narrow, exploitative, filthy, and dangerous, even at its most well meaning' – though, as Nelson points out, the text simultaneously celebrates the kind of tough rural masculinity it also blames for Tom's apparent death.[31]

The Water-Babies is full of men, but few of them are fathers. This absence of the father has been noted in a recent article by Laura Fasick, who observes that in his novels Kingsley 'never shows a hero fulfilling himself through paternity'.[32] This may be partly to do with the conventions of the novel during the 1840s and 1850s, when the emphasis was still on the implications of the *Bildungsroman* and courtship, rather than the raising of a family, with *Dombey and Son* a notable exception.[33] But it is true that fathers are curiously absent or unimportant in Kingsley's writing for children, and all the more so in that his intended reader is his son, and boys in general, and his underlying aim the promotion of a very physical kind of masculinity. Tom's own father is in 'Botany Bay' (p. 45), and throughout the text he lacks positive male role models, other than the one constantly held up by the narrator of becoming a brave and decent Englishman. Ellie's father, Sir John Harthover, having twice sent Tom to gaol (p. 7), is viewed primarily as a disciplinarian, though fathers are noticeably missing from the list of cruel adults who are punished in Chapter 5 by Mrs Bedonebyasyoudid: doctors, careless nurserymaids, schoolmasters and foolish mothers who tight-lace their children are all systematically given a taste of their own medicine, but not fathers. Whether this is because fathers are seen as being less directly involved in their children's lives, or whether he simply feels less animosity towards fathers is unclear. Possibly the clue lies with Sir John Harthover, by this time so overcome with remorse for Tom's death that he 'did something as like crying as ever he did in his life, and blamed himself more bitterly than he need have done' (p. 45). In his description of the whole household crying for Tom's loss, Kingsley creates a comic opera of noise which either makes Sir John's grief look ridiculous, or else conceals and minimizes it in the crowds. Either way, it implies that Kingsley feels uncomfortable with this image of unmanliness, and tries to caricature it.

As the only significant image of a father in *The Water-Babies*, Sir John is a contradictory figure, alternately admired for his down-to-earth heartiness, and exposed as an unintentionally clumsy buffoon. When he reappears in the text in Chapter 4, he is seen engaged in manly sports and activities typical of a rural squire: 'Four days a week he hunted, and very good sport he had; and the other two he went to the bench and the board of guardians, and very good justice he did' (p. 79). The narrator commends Sir John's sensible dining habits to his 'dear little man', and begins to offer him as a role model to his son, only to undercut his positive image with accounts of his snoring, and hopelessness as a domestic companion, which drives his wife away to the seaside for a few days' holiday with the children. Ellie's death in the rock-pool is thus the indirect result of Sir John's insensitive behaviour as a father and husband.

In this context, the omnipresence of the narrator's voice – fatherly and authoritarian like God's, but humanly tetchy and interventionist – more than makes up for his shortcomings. Perhaps because he saw God as *the* supreme father and teacher, Kingsley has no positive father figures or male teachers in his children's books, other than the paternal voice of the ever-present narrator. *The Water-Babies* is largely a commentary on different types of education, with the fatherly narrator seeing the world as a giant schoolroom, full of children being miseducated, either by poor teachers or through their own inability to improve. Even whole nations he saw as being like wilful children, many of them too stubborn and immature to learn effectively. For example, he finds it difficult to understand why people continue to live in earthquake zones when they run the risk of having their lives destroyed: a point he pursues both in *The Water-Babies* with the tale of the Doasyoulikes, and in *Madam How*, though he introduced the analogy between nations and children in an earlier book, *The Heroes* (1856). There he describes nations as being 'men and women with children's hearts; frank, and affectionate, and full of trust, and teachable, and loving to see and learn all the wonders round them'.[34] He praises the Greeks for being willing to learn from other nations, and indeed from God, brushing aside the objection that because the Greeks were 'heathens' God taught them nothing.

Essentially, Kingsley's children's books are a dialogue between the father figure who narrates, and the 'dear little man' who is obliged to listen. The protagonist is usually a boy – either Tom in *The Water-Babies*, or Perseus, Jason or Theseus in *The Heroes* – while in *Madam How*, Grenville is clearly both protagonist and addressee. The male heroes of his Greek tales are, like Tom, active voyagers in search of spiritual maturity, and even Grenville is on a kind of journey with his father in *Madam How*: a journey through landscapes, times and a process of knowledge gain. Kingsley plays down the notion of monetary advantage in the story of Jason and the Golden Fleece, and in the tale of Theseus stresses that the hero wants to prove himself worthy of his father's love. This is in fact one of the few places in Kingsley's stories for children where a fictitious father–son relationship is important as an incentive to enacting manly deeds and growing up. Theseus feels he wants to find 'strange adventures, robbers, and monsters' (p. 173) as a means of demonstrating his masculinity.

Accommodating girls in the process was another matter. Although he later gave 'Lectures to Ladies' (1855), his early lectures to adults (such as 'How to Study Natural History' (1846)) assumed an audience of young men seeking in shared study 'a ground of brotherhood with men'.[35] A lecture on 'Heroism' proclaims the hidden deeds of women as 'of the essence of the perfect and womanly heroism, in which, as in all spiritual forces, the woman transcends the man', but he has difficulty in finding a role or reading position for his daughters.[36] It seems significant that it is a girl – Ellie – who confounds the scientist in *The Water-Babies* and causes him such profound embarrassment that he denies the evidence of his own eyes. When Ellie insists that she has seen a water-baby, the Professor is too proud to admit in front of a child (and a girl at that) that he could be wrong in denying their existence, telling her, '"My dear little maid, you must have dreamt of water-babies last night, your head is so full of them"' (p. 86). The fact that the Professor cannot speak the truth here stresses the unnerving impact of the little girl's intervention in the text as scientific questioner. Perhaps this is the reason she is 'punished' with a fall and a bang on the head, causing her death – so far as anyone does actually die in *The Water-Babies* – but when she revives, Ellie becomes Tom's teacher.

Ellie is perhaps the supreme amalgam of all perfect female teachers: 'She taught him, first, what you have been taught ever since you said your first prayers at your mother's knees; but she taught him much more simply' (p. 120), in other words, without resorting to the pretentious, incomprehensible, scientific language which Kingsley both relishes and parodies in the story. This is perhaps Kingsley's chief difficulty as a father–teacher: however hard he tries to counteract the effects of femininity in his writing with rousing doses of bull-dog Englishness, girls and women emerge as the ideal teachers. Essentially, Kingsley defines female characters in his tales as mothers with an educational mission, both punitive and loving in relation to erring children, while the father figure is more self-centred in his godlike authority, constantly goading his son into asking questions so that he can demonstrate how much he knows. The male 'Cousin Cramchild' is someone to be resisted, by both the child and the educating father: 'Don't be put down by any of Cousin Cramchild's arguments,' the narrator insists, 'but stand up to him like a man.' (p. 42).

Kingsley presents himself in his narratives as a father who urgently wants to be asked questions by his son, in a form of 'reverse interrogation' which forces Grenville into acts of spontaneous curiosity.[37] This even happens in the occasional lecture, such as 'The Air-Mothers,' where in the style of *Madam How*, a dialogue with 'my little man' about ensuring clean water supplies suddenly invades the address. This is manly talk, with no sisters or mothers present, no 'little maids' to add a distracting layer of romance and stubbornness. It was his view that God had made children naturally inquisitive so that they would constantly seek for knowledge and come to understand the wonders of the God-created universe, but the questions needed to be asked. If necessary, Kingsley was prepared to ask them himself, in Grenville's voice. 'I would sooner answer one question of yours than tell you ten things without your asking,' Kingsley urges at a point in *Madam How* when he has been carried away by his own eloquence (p. 76).

Within his portrayal of the questioning child, however, Kingsley includes a subtext of rebellion. If Ellie refutes the Professor's logic, Grenville is not always willing or able to ask a question, and sometimes he feels tired of listening to the answers. In *The Water-Babies*, the narrator offers less hectoring prompts, such as on the occasion when Tom first meets another water-baby: 'you will, no doubt, want to know how it happened, and why Tom could never find a water-baby till after he had got the lobster out of the pot' (p. 100). He also assumes that his child reader will be unfamiliar with difficult words, such as 'amphibious', but gives a comic answer, referring him to 'the nearest Government pupil–teacher', who will provide a suitably dry definition (p. 47). In *Madam How*, which is more directly didactic, the narrator repeatedly prompts Grenville with phrases such as 'What do you want to know about next?' (p. 105) or 'You want to know then, what chalk is?' (p. 134) Finally, the child has had enough, and the narrator imagines him asking, 'This is all very funny: but what is the use of knowing so much about things' teeth and hair?' (p. 245) or commenting, 'I wanted to ask you a question, but you wouldn't listen to me' (p. 258). By inscribing the son's frustrations within the text, Kingsley seems to be acknowledging, however fleetingly, that his paternal urge to educate has reached a dangerous point. Indeed, his own allegory of the Isle of Tomtoddies in *The Water-Babies*, where all the people have been turned into turnips and mangold wurzels because their foolish parents have made them work unremittingly at their lessons, was written only a few years before *Madam How*. When one of the turnips asks Tom, 'Can you tell me anything at all about anything you like?', his voice sounds suspiciously like a question from *Madam How* (p. 166). Kingsley revived the over-educated turnip caricature in a lecture given towards the end of his life, combining it with his ever-present fear of the wrong sort of education driving men to drink. In 'The Science of Health' (1872) which makes a case for setting up what he calls a 'public school of health,' with lectures given by women as well as men, he warns that a child educated in ignorance of the laws of nature could end up 'with a huge upright forehead like that of a Byzantine Greek filled with some sort of pap instead of brains, and tempted alternately to fanaticism and strong drink.'[38]

Ultimately, whatever his views about the mother's centrality in the child's upbringing and emotional life, Kingsley was a controlling father, whose benevolence was mediated through an energetic encouragement of all children, including his own, to interrogate the surrounding natural world by asking him a barrage of questions. The three books written for his own children, though apparently very different in subject matter, all demonstrate a model of learning and teaching, with the adult figures facilitating the children's access to knowledge and forming their moral outlook as well as their understanding of science. His is a moral mythology of mistakes made and punishment inflicted, a system of repentance for the damage done by men to nature, as his insistent voice in the narrative urges: 'I want you to look and think. I want every one to look and think. Half the misery in the world comes first from not looking, and then from not thinking' (*Madam How*, p. 188).

Though he invites his children to participate in this process, they are conscripted learners, whose spontaneous curiosity needs to be prompted, and though his letters show that he was keen to interest his daughters in natural science, his model of educational fatherhood ultimately sidelines the female members of his family. Read in the context of his own 'gender trouble' – his uncertainties over whether mothers or fathers were the better teachers and offered boys the more fitting role-model – Kingsley's children's books show him overcompensating for his absent fathers with his own pervasive, fatherly–teacherly presence, which overrides the voices of women scientists and motherly fairies. By the time he wrote *Madam How*, there was no place in the manly dialogue of father–teacher and 'little man' for the distracting presence of the 'kind pussy mammas' of *The Water-Babies* (p. 114), or the 'little maid' with her power to shame the proud professor and evade the huntsman squire.

Notes

1. C. Kingsley, *Charles Kingsley: His Letters and Memories of His Life*, edited by his wife, 5th edn, 2 vols (London: Henry S. King, 1877), I, p. 209.
2. Ibid., I, p. 418.
3. Ibid., II, p. 176.
4. Ibid., II, p. 21.
5. Ibid., II, p. 137.
6. J. S. Mill, *Autobiography*, 1873, ed. by Jack Stillinger (Oxford: Oxford University Press, 1969), pp. 5–6.
7. T. Copley, *Black Tom: Arnold of Rugby: The Myth and the Man* (London: Continuum, 2002), p. 69; A. C. Benson, *The Life of Edward White Benson*, 2 vols (London: Macmillan, 1899), I, p. 242; E. Gosse, *Father and Son* (Harmondsworth: Penguin, 1983), p. 146.
8. B. Masters, *The Life of E. F. Benson* (London: Chatto and Windus, 1991), p. 27.
9. Benson's *Life of Edward White Benson*, I, p. 188.
10. F. Dolman, ' "Lucas Malet at Home": A Chat with the Daughter of Charles Kingsley,' *The Young Woman: A Monthly Journal and Review*, 4 (1896), p. 148.
11. Kingsley, *Letters*, II, p. 7
12. Ibid., II, pp. 205–6.
13. Dolman, ' "Lucas Malet at Home" ', p. 148.
14. Kingsley, *Letters*, II, p. 245.
15. Ibid., II, p. 252.
16. S. Chitty, *The Beast and the Monk: A Life of Charles Kingsley* (London: Hodder & Stoughton, 1974), p. 280.
17. C. Kingsley, 'The Science of Health,' in *The Works of Charles Kingsley, Vol. XVIII Sanitary and Social Lectures and Essays* (London: Macmillan 1880), p. 35.
18. C. Kingsley, *Madam How and Lady Why: First Lessons in Earth Lore for Children* (London: Macmillan, 1899; orig. pub. 1870), p. 178.
19. D. Rosen, 'The Volcano and the Cathedral: Muscular Christianity and the Origins of Primal Manliness,' in D. E. Hall (ed.), *Muscular Christianity: Embodying the Victorian Age* (Cambridge: Cambridge University Press, 1994), p. 31.
20. Ibid., p. 32.
21. L. Fasick, 'The Failure of Fatherhood: Maleness and its Discontents in Charles Kingsley,' *Children's Literature Association*, 18.3 (1993), p. 106.
22. L. Fasick, 'Charles Kingsley's Scientific Treatment of Gender,' in Hall (ed.), *Muscular Christianity*, p. 100.
23. A. Rauch, *Useful Knowledge: The Victorians, Morality, and the March of Intellect* (Durham, NC and London: Duke University Press, 2001), p. 51.
24. R. Mangnall, *Historical and Miscellaneous Questions for the Use of Young People* (ed. Rev I. Cobbin, London: Fisher, Son & Co., 1840; orig. pub. 1800) Preface.

25. Mrs Marcet, *Conversations for Children; On Land and Water* (London: Longman, Orme, Brown, Green, & Longmans, 1838), p. 176.
26. C. Kingsley, *Alton Locke, Tailor and Poet: An Autobiography*, 1850 (Oxford: World's Classics, 1983), p. 8.
27. Kingsley's 'The Air-Mothers', in *Sanitary and Social Lectures and Essays*, p. 135.
28. C. Kingsley, *The Water-Babies: A Fairy Tale for a Land-Baby* (Oxford: World's Classics, ed. B. Alderson, 1995; orig. pub. 1863), p. 13
29. Kingsley, *Letters*, II, p. 161.
30. Ibid., II, p. 163.
31. C. Nelson, *Boys will be Girls: The Feminine Ethic and British Children's Fiction, 1857–1917* (New Brunswick, NJ and London: Rutgers University Press, 1991), p. 152.
32. Fasick, 'The Failure of Fatherhood,' p. 107.
33. *Jane Eyre* (1847) is a female *Bildungsroman* more than a study of Rochester's dilemma as possible father of Adèle; *The Tenant of Wildfell Hall* (1848) is ultimately more concerned with Helen Huntingdon's motherhood than her husband Arthur's fatherhood. Dickens's David Copperfield (1850) does not become a father until the end of the novel, and *Little Dorrit* (1857) is more the daughter's story than the father's.
34. C. Kingsley, *The Heroes; or Greek Fairy Tales for my Children* (London: Macmillan, 1892; orig. pub. 1856), p. xi.
35. Preface to 'Town Geology' in C. Kingsley, *Scientific Lectures and Essays* (London and New York: Macmillan 1890), p. 18.
36. Kingsley, 'Heroism,' in *Sanitary and Social Lectures and Essays*, p. 246.
37. I am grateful to Trev Broughton for coining this term at the 'Father Figures' conference, July 2003.
38. Kingsley, 'The Science of Health,' p. 37.

Part 2
Patterns of Involvement

Father as Mother: The Image of the Widower with Children in Victorian Art

Terri Sabatos

In 1876, Sir Luke Fildes exhibited *The Widower* at the Royal Academy annual summer exhibition. Fildes's inspiration for the scene, he later recalled, was an incident that occurred while he was working on his better-known *Applicants for Admission to a Casual Ward*, exhibited at the Royal Academy in 1874. According to Fildes, he was painting in the fellow standing against the wall when the model became tired of standing. The artist suggested that the man, who was modelling with his child, take a rest while Fildes went on to work on another section of the canvas. After a while, Fildes peered behind the screen where the man had been sitting and saw the tableau which prompted *The Widower*. The artist related what he saw to the *Strand* magazine: 'The child had fallen asleep, and there was this great, rough fellow, possibly with only a copper in the world, caressing his child, watching it lovingly and smoothing its curls with his hand.'[1]

In *The Widower*, Fildes reframes the scene as domestic tragedy. The artist depicts a humble cottage interior where several children sit at a small table on the left and finish their evening meal, while the youngest child crawls playfully after a toy behind them. They all appear blissfully unaware of the tragedy unfolding at their side. Their father sits on the right cradling another child and grasping her small hand to his lips.[2] The child lies limp in her father's embrace; her curly head is slumped over her father's arm, probably in death. An older daughter, who is setting out bread and dishes on the table, realizes what has occurred and presses her apron to her mouth in despair.

For those familiar with Victorian genre painting, this scene does not seem out of the ordinary. In general, the Victorian middle-class art viewer (and buyer) was attracted to narrative, especially narrative that related to the home and family, and genre scenes such as these, focusing on the life of the working classes, would have been familiar images for most of the Victorian era. In the early nineteenth century, David Wilkie, inspired by the paintings and prints of

Illustration 2 Sir Luke Fildes, *The Widower* [1874], 1902.
Courtesy of the Walker Art Gallery, National Museums, Liverpool

seventeenth-century Dutch artists and the poetry of his countryman Robert Burns, became enormously popular depicting the lives of the rural Scots. Encouraged by Wilkie's success, artists such as Thomas Faed, who came from a family of artists, followed suit and painted domestic scenes full of gentle humour and quiet pathos.[3] Scenes of the poor, especially the rural poor, were particularly popular at exhibitions and with art collectors, and continued to appear throughout the century.

However, while the effects of poverty were clearly suggested in these scenes, its harsher consequences, such as death and disease, were generally glossed over or ignored altogether. Beginning in the 1840s, artists such as Richard Redgrave attempted to inject a stronger element of realism into academic paintings of the poor. His *The Sempstress* (1844), highlighting infamous abuses in the dressmaking industry, shows a needlewoman alone in her garret room stitching far into the night. Although his depiction still contains a liberal dose of sentiment, by tackling a current social problem Redgrave brought a new immediacy to representations of the poor.[4] Redgrave's generation was followed in the 1870s by the so-called social realists, among whom Sir Luke Fildes was prominent. Fildes, together with fellow artists Frank Holl and Hubert von Herkomer, often shocked exhibition-goers with their more gritty brand of realism: disease, death, drunkenness and crime were all often graphically depicted on large-scale canvases rather than on the smaller scale normally considered appropriate for genre scenes. Fildes and Holl eventually abandoned social realist art for the more lucrative field of portraiture, but other artists such as Thomas Kennington, Eyre Crowe and Walter Langley continued to image the lives of the poor into the new century.[5]

Although visual representations of working-class life were thus fairly familiar, Fildes's *The Widower* is relatively unusual. It is not the tragic theme that is uncommon, as scenes of grieving widows, funeral processions, and dead and dying children were popular throughout the latter half of the nineteenth century. This image is unusual because it depicts a widower caring for his children. Of the many extant scenes that deal with death, mourning or fatherhood, there are very few that deal with the Victorian widower, and even fewer that portray widowers with children. Significantly, of those that show the widower actively taking care of his children, many focus specifically on the working-class father.[6] Three such images will be discussed here: Sir Luke Fildes's *The Widower* (1874), Thomas Faed's *Worn Out* (1868) and Arthur Stocks's *Motherless* (1883).

Besides their obviously similar subject matter, all these images were shown at public exhibitions: those by Fildes and Faed at the Royal Academy annual summer exhibition, which was arguably the most prestigious venue in the Victorian art world; and that by Stocks at the autumn exhibition of the Walker Art Gallery in Liverpool. These canvases, then, were offered to the thousands of predominantly middle- and upper-class viewers who attended exhibitions each year.[7] What kind of resonance could these representations of the working-class father have had for their audience? This essay will examine these images of fathers caring for their motherless children and discuss the ways in which they participate within Victorian controversies concerning the father's role within the domestic sphere, as well as in related debates about masculinity and the ethics of work. Where literary scholar Joseph Kestner argues that these images work to expose the conflicts within the ideal of the Victorian paterfamilias, I shall suggest that these paintings may actually function to include the working-class father within acceptable norms of class and gender.[8]

As is well known, the ideal Victorian middle-class family was organized around an ideology of 'separate spheres' which was at its most insistent by mid-century.[9] According to this formulation, a woman's supposedly more passive and nurturing temperament suited her to the protected environment of the domestic sphere where she raised her children, created a comfortable home for her husband, and acted as the moral anchor for her family. A man's nature was considered more active and aggressive; he was thus expected to be better able to negotiate the public world of work and business. However, while his occupation might take him outside the home, domesticity, as John Tosh and Claudia Nelson have demonstrated, had an important role to play in defining middle-class masculinity.[10] While ideally a man's proper arena was the public sphere, he was also supposed to draw part of his identity from marriage and the domestic sphere. Home not only provided comfort and solace away from the harsh, often inhumane environment of the workplace, it was also an arena in which the Victorian male could enact the privileges of his gender. As Tosh explains, 'To form a household, to exercise authority over dependants and to shoulder the responsibility of maintaining and protecting them – these things set the seal on a man's gender identity.'[11]

However, as Nelson explains, while the responsibility of providing for the home and family was unquestionably the male's prerogative, his role within the home was not always clear. As the century progressed, as the mother's role grew in significance and men's occupations, rather than their association with domesticity, became a more conclusive marker of masculinity, questions concerning the exact role that the father was to play in the home became more insistent.[12] Throughout the second half of the nineteenth century, while few critics denied that the mother's influence was vital to raising children and to maintaining the proper moral domestic environment, many cast doubt on the nature and extent of the father's influence. Some argued that his prolonged absences from home precluded any sort of sustained impact on it; others that men's 'natures' made them incapable of providing any sort of nurturing environment. None the less, some commentators believed that men should attempt to cultivate those qualities that were considered more feminine, such as tenderness and patience. These qualities would not only make fathers more caring and involved parents, but would also cleanse them of the harsher aspects of their character. However, this idea had its opponents too, as many feared that redomesticated fathers would become effeminate and would raise a generation of weak and ineffective young men – clearly an undesirable outcome for a mighty empire-building nation such as Britain.[13]

Such discussions took on particular force in the case of the fathers in these images. What should happen if the mother died and the father were literally

Illustration 3 Thomas Faed, *Worn Out*, 1868.
Courtesy of Christie's Images Inc. © Christie's Images Ltd, 2006

forced to adopt the role of care-giver and nurturer? Ideally, his elder daughter or sister would step into the breach and assume the mother's role.[14] But what if this were not practical or possible? Would the same anxieties about male effeminacy apply? Kestner reads *The Widower* in conjunction with the similar image by Thomas Faed, *Worn Out,* which also shows a labourer, presumably a widower, who has been awake all night caring for his sick child.[15] Evidence of the father's tender care is strewn about the room: the half-eaten bowl of food; the dog-eared book from which the man has been reading to console or distract his son; the father's coat laid neatly over the child for extra warmth. Unlike Fildes's image with its dark, gloomy palette and indications that the child has died, Faed's is a visually and emotionally lighter narrative. Faed employs much brighter colours and includes elements of quiet humour, such as the mouse nibbling on a scrap of food near the father's chair; and the father's ungainly pose as he succumbs to exhaustion. The less serious tone and the more luminous colour allow the viewer to surmise that the crisis has passed and that the child will recover. Despite their differences, Kestner contends that images such as those of Fildes and Faed assist in exposing the cracks in the Victorian masculine ideal, because it is specifically within the paradigm of the paterfamilias that its contradictions become manifest.[16] Unlike other patterns of Victorian male behaviour, such as the military, the patriarchal male must interact within a space that is not exclusively homosocial. According to Kestner, it is within this heterosocial family group that, despite prevailing ideologies, the limits of male power are probed. Kestner argues that within this domestic space 'the dominant fiction and patriarchal paradigm were frequently exposed as fallible, untenable, dependent and ambiguous under the pressure of economic, sexual, political and class constraints that revealed the male's vulnerable rather than empowered condition'.[17]

Fildes's and Faed's images, Kestner suggests, disclose the contested nature of the paterfamilias by demonstrating that, under class and economic pressures, these fathers are unable to participate within the hegemonic masculine ideal. Their obvious poverty signals their inability to act as provider, and this in turn feminizes them. Kestner claims that 'For many middle-class artists ... lower-class males assume traits generally associated with the feminine: marginality, dependence and passivity.'[18] Kestner's reading chimes with the fears of those Victorian commentators who predicted that men forced to take on domestic duties would also take on feminine characteristics. In other words, by showing their fathers as nurses, a role normally reserved for the mother, Faed and Fildes subvert norms of masculinity and blur gender roles.

While Kestner identifies the way in which such images encapsulate tensions within the monolithic ideal of Victorian manliness, his discussion does not explicitly consider why the working-class male is depicted as the nursing father more frequently than the middle-class one.[19] Middle-class fathers are often depicted playing or interacting with their children, as in the painting *Many Happy Returns of the Day* by William Powell Frith (1854), but they are seldom, if ever, shown as nurses or comforters.[20] This is undoubtedly due, in part, to the fact that many middle-class and certainly upper-class families employed others to care for their children. However, while these working-class fathers do take on the role of nurse and are undoubtedly poor, rather than signalling their removal from the hegemonic masculine ideal, as Kestner contends, these images actually attempt to include him within it, and thereby to assuage some of the anxieties that the middle classes felt about the working classes. Rather than revealing tensions between masculinity and the domestic sphere, these images, I shall argue, actually work to incorporate these 'humble' fathers back into middle-class ideology by suggesting that the respectable working classes might share the values and priorities of the middle classes.

The working classes, especially those of the most impoverished strata, held a particular fear and fascination for the Victorian middle and upper classes throughout most of the nineteenth century. As Peter Keating observes, 'Victorian attitudes to the poor . . . were built around a series of unresolvable paradoxes.'[21] Early in the century, despite their numbers and clear visibility, they were discussed as if they inhabited an alien world and were hidden from view, unknown to the upper reaches of the social scale. Yet from roughly 1830 onward they were perhaps the most closely studied and analysed group in British society.[22] Many books, and hundreds of articles in the popular press, chronicled their often desperate living and working conditions. Among the many problems that poverty engendered, according to the philanthropists, missionaries and social explorers, was the impossibility of proper 'family life' in such wretched conditions. The poor were thus often depicted as inhuman and abusive parents, too drunk to care for their children. Although many critics sought to blame the effects of grinding poverty rather than the parents themselves, the results were the same: the working classes were seen as incapable of responsible parenting.[23]

It is in mitigating these dark images for their predominantly middle-class audience that the paintings of Fildes, Faed and Stocks may come into play. These fathers, despite their poverty, exhibit a gentle, loving demeanour that belies much of the contemporary criticism of their sex and class. To heighten the emotional appeal of the scenes, Fildes and Stocks draw attention to their subjects' widower status in their titles; Stocks goes further, poignantly placing the man and his child at the mother's graveside. While it is not clear if Faed's father figure is a widower, we may be fairly certain that there is no constant female presence in the home: the father is acting as nurse and there are no overtly feminine domestic markers such as frilly curtains, pictures on the wall, or knick-knacks that might serve to indicate a woman's touch. In so far as a mother's influence was considered vital to the moral well-being of the family, which in turn was revered as a sacred institution, her death represented both a personal loss and a threat to the social fabric. All three widowers are faced with a twofold responsibility: to learn to care for their children and to maintain the integrity of their families.

Images such as these, featuring the lives of the working classes and reinforcing normative behaviour and values, would have had specific resonances for the middle- and upper-class viewer. As Lynda Nead has argued, exhibitions were public sites 'which bound bourgeois society together in a nexus of shared tastes and values'.[24] While Nead is discussing images that worked to define middle-class codes of sexuality and respectability, more general notions of class and gender

Illustration 4 Arthur Stocks, *Motherless*, 1883.
Courtesy of the Walker Art Gallery, National Museums, Liverpool

propriety were also played out on the walls of the Royal Academy and other exhibition halls. While the most impoverished members of the working classes were commonly assumed to operate outside respectable middle-class conceptions of domesticity, these fathers, despite their poverty, are exhibiting the love and care that all fathers should provide. If, as Nead suggests, such images 'worked to negotiate and displace contradictions of class' then Fildes, Faed and

Stocks offer assurance that segments of the working class could participate within the dominant middle-class value system.[25]

Furthermore, by emphasizing the protagonists' widower status, these artists at once place these scenes within the contemporary debates on the father's role in the domestic sphere, particularly as it relates to his role as caregiver, and begin to diffuse anxieties about male feminization. As widowers they evidently have no choice but to adopt the role of nurse to their children. This role was thrust upon them, not by wives who have abandoned their natural domestic duties and thus subverted proper gender roles, but through the tragedy of death. It is significant, therefore, that Fildes's and Faed's widowers are both shown within the home. While the meagre furnishings of their homes attest to the poverty of the inhabitants, small elements hint at the care which both fathers have taken to provide not just shelter but a true home for their families. In *Worn Out*, Faed includes a vase with green leaves sprouting from the top; a rough curtain has been pushed back from the window to allow light in; a violin hangs near the window, its shiny exterior suggesting that it is played frequently; perhaps most importantly, the tiny hand of the sick child clutches his father's shirt, indicating a wish to keep him close by. There is little sign here of the malfunctioning household or intemperate, abusive father so often deplored in temperance and philanthropic iconography. As death once again strikes his home, the plight of Fildes's father figure is particularly desperate. The artist, however, is equally careful to render the widower's attempts at homeliness: the cottage, though simple, is neat, and some care has been taken to adorn it with pictures and trinkets on the chimney mantle. Food is visible on both the main table and the small table where the other children eat; they all exhibit the round cheeks and sturdy limbs of the well-fed. A puppy eagerly awaits a scrap from the children and he, too, looks healthy and ready to play. Note also that the eldest daughter is setting the table, taking up, in the approved Victorian manner, the role of substitute mother as she struggles to keep the domestic construct whole.

While Stocks's father is not depicted in the home, he too is participating in important domestic rituals. His black mourning neckcloth and the mound of virtually bare earth announce that his bereavement is fairly recent. He balances his child on his knee and gently kisses her forehead as he attempts to plant a geranium on his wife's grave.[26] Attending to the grave of a family member was among the Victorian rituals of mourning and remembrance, and for the middle-class viewer would have indicated that the husband was performing his proper duties to his deceased wife.[27] His care for his child is evident in her pink cheeks, healthy limbs and his loving caress. Though her white apron displays a small tear and the hem is slightly ragged from wear, she is nevertheless neatly and cleanly dressed and sports a ruffled pink bonnet.

As we have seen, Kestner claims that Fildes and Faed adopt a kind of feminine visual vocabulary to depict these men forced to take on the role of mother. Fildes's father sits hunched over the body of his child and clutches the tiny hand to his mouth in an overt display of grief. Faed's father is also seated, but he is stretched out, overcome by exhaustion, with his head thrown back passively in sleep. Both men, according to this view, are caught in weak, feminized postures, a result of their forced appropriation of female gender roles. Kestner asserts that this is an attempt by the middle-class artist visually to equate the poverty of the working-class father with the feminine, thus exposing the reality that many men, because of economic circumstances, could not provide for their families and were not able to operate within the 'patriarchal constructions of masculinity'.[28] Certainly question marks hang over Victorian representations of the working man in repose. In *Men at Work: Art and Labour in Victorian Britain*, Tim Barringer notes the impact of the writings of Henry Mayhew and Thomas Carlyle on Ford Madox Brown's famous canvas *Work* (1852–65). Following Carlyle, Brown believed that honest manual labour, backbreaking but necessary work such as that done by the navvy in *Work*, was 'a moral, even religious act in itself, being a contribution . . . to economic and civic progress.'[29] The physical value of work is made visible in the navvies' sinewy arms and broad chests; their healthy bodies connote the strength and vigour of the British nation. Manual labour also carried with it particular markers of masculine identity. As Barringer notes, in *Work*, Brown contrasts the navvies' robust bodies with that of the flower seller, visually marginalised to the left of the canvas. The flower seller has not been taught a useful occupation, it is implied, and thus inhabits more feminine dress and a less muscular body. For Brown, Barringer claims, 'The absence of work results in the erasure of masculinity.'[30]

In the case of the images under discussion here, however, another reading is possible. As Tosh has noted, physical strength played a key role in constructing a distinctively working-class masculinity, while at the same time connoting certain manly values which crossed class divisions.[31] Since, as Barringer observes, social conventions prohibited the middle-class body (other than hands and heads) from being revealed, the working-class body became the key site where muscularity, masculinity and work could legitimately intersect.[32] By depicting 'great, rough' bodies, and by extension indicating that these fathers make their living by some type of manual labour, Fildes, Faed and Stocks encode their figures with an 'essential' masculinity that works to diffuse the visual relation to the feminine.

The fathers depicted by Fildes and Stocks are both holding their children, creating a strong visual contrast between their smaller bodies and the fathers' larger ones. Fildes's father hunches over his child as he cradles her in his lap. His broad shoulders and long arms envelope the child while the father's large hands support one small shoulder and clutch a much smaller hand. The father's knees, encased in rough work trousers, jut out from beneath the child, and large-booted feet sit squarely on the earthen floor. Although he is positioned slightly to the viewer's right of centre in the composition, he nevertheless dominates it through sheer proportion: he is so much bigger than the child, and indeed almost everything else in the room. Stocks likewise creates a sharp contrast between the body of the father and that of the child. The father, dressed in corduroy work clothes and heavy boots, balances his small charge on his knee with a large work-roughened hand, while the other hand holds a spade, a masculine tool that counters the child's more feminine bonnet and apron. His head, with its shaggy, awkwardly combed hair and weather-beaten face, presses close to his child's, his much coarser features highlighting her softer ones. Faed deploys similar contrasts in *Worn Out*. The father's heavily bearded face is on the same sight line as his child's smaller, angelic one, and the child's tiny hand grasps the father's shirt, very near the father's much larger hand. Stretched across its centre, he, too, dominates the composition. Dressed in work clothes and heavy boots, his bulky frame almost overwhelms the small chair in which he sits. Where the other artists provide few concrete clues to the fathers' occupations, Faed underlines his subject's artisan status by including a carpenter's bag and tools in the lower right corner. Although they may be operating within the domestic sphere, these fathers are anything but feminine, and exhibit all the breadth of body and masculine attributes of Brown's navvies. Rather than displacing these fathers, all three artists actually work to keep them within accepted visual codes of masculinity.

Given their historical moment, such visible displays of active fathering on the part of poorer citizens may have had a directly political dimension: Fildes's and Faed's images were produced in the wake of debates around the 1867 Reform Act. As Keith McClelland has demonstrated, and as Matthew McCormack elaborates in this volume, discussions over whether or not the working-class male should be granted the vote were often centred on ideas of 'dependency'.[33] Reformers such as John Bright sought to distinguish the 'respectable' working-class man from those he labelled the 'residuum' – the class which lived in the most abject poverty and which was almost entirely dependent on the Poor Law or charity.[34] The distinction between the respectable worker and the residuum hinged in part upon the Victorian concept of domesticity. As McClelland notes, 'Virtue became attached, not least, to the cultivation of domesticity in which a man was independent and respectable by means of being able to maintain a dependent wife and children within the household.'[35] Men of the working class who could maintain their families without relying on charity were deemed worthy of the vote. The dependency Kestner finds in Fildes's and Faed's bereaved fathers does not, I would argue, compromise their implied independence as providers. While the homes in the paintings are humble, both fathers are able to offer loving care, food and shelter, and have made some attempt to create a domestic environment. Stocks's widower, although not shown in the home, is clearly providing for his child. He, along with the men in Fildes's and Faed's paintings, are portrayed as accepting their responsibilities as fathers and managing their households and their dependants. While they have had to become both mother and father to their children, their willingness to take up these additional duties, according to the reformist rhetoric, does not dislocate them from the patriarchal hegemony; rather, it strengthens their claims to participation within it.

Fildes's *The Widower* was perhaps the best known of these images during the Victorian era, and critical reactions to this canvas are in many ways typical of responses to this type of scene. While many critics were harsh with Fildes for attempting a genre scene on a scale usually reserved for History or High Art images, it was the affective content of the painting that triggered the strongest reaction.[36] *The Times* was not pleased with the intense emotion, claiming 'the painter, we submit, is under a mistake who brings big dirty boots, squalling and scrambling children, parental and sisterly love, into such contact'.[37] The critic rehearses the prejudices of many social reformers and others who believed that tender emotion and abject poverty could not coexist. (Remember, though, that Fildes himself reported a similar reaction when he first saw the impoverished model holding his child in the studio.[38]) The very juxtaposition of poverty and domestic affection impressed other critics, however. An anonymous reviewer, acknowledging the emotional impact of the scene, dismissed any connotations of femininity either on the part of Fildes or the image itself: '"In whatever manner the painter wishes to be read, his beautiful picture may be hailed as a manly, conscientious, and soulful piece of work, unstrained, undefaced by maudlin sentiment, but exquisitively touching."'[39] Here the critic not only points out the emotional qualities of the scene, but also brings them firmly into the arena of masculine propriety. The *Athenaeum* ascribed to the painting's central group 'the truest force of pathos, never better designed, and in its rough way never better'.[40] The *Art Journal* was the most lavish in its praise, and after a lengthy description concluded:

> Such is the scene depicted by Mr Fildes and after all, some may say, it is only genre on a life-size scale; and this may be true; but the genius of the painter has lifted it into the region of High Art. The man kissing his dying child is but of lowly kind; but the love in that kiss, and the yearning in that look, place him on a level with the lordliest on the earth.[41]

Explicitly highlighting the father's lowly class, the critic suggests that it is his very ability to express his love for his child in an overt way that elevates him not just to respectability but to nobility. Rather than excluding this working-class father from the middle-class hegemonic masculine ideal, Fildes, a decidedly middle-class artist, actually works to contain him within the domain of bourgeois respectability not in spite of, but through, the father's gentle behaviour.

Implicit in these positive critiques is an assumption that the painting's success depends in part on the capacity of an attentive viewer to empathize with the emotional quality of the scene. Reviewing the genre of domestic narrative painting, a writer for the *Art Journal* in 1863 claimed that such images functioned to erase class divisions by awakening a common sense of humanity within the viewer:

> From the prince to the peasant, from the palace to the cottage, the range in rank is wide; yet the same sentiments – love to God, charity to neighbours, duties of parents and children, sympathy ready to mourn with those who mourn; or to rejoice over those who are glad in heart – these principles and emotions, the outcomings of our universal humanity, have found earnest and literal expression through domestic pictures.[42]

It was in other words, more than simply a matter of recognizing common human experiences across class lines; it was equally important to be able to connect to the sentiments involved. This is echoed by a reviewer for *The Morning Post* who claimed, '"the man who could view the picture [*The Widower*] without emotion would not be a desirable person to know."'[43] Empathy is a desirable quality, the journal suggests, in 'persons'. Neither in

Fildes's construction of the scene nor in the male viewer's response to it is there any suggestion of unmanly sentimentality.

Such images, it is important to concede, probably did little to alter the way in which many middle- and upper-class viewers regarded the poor. Although, as Julian Treuherz observes, the so-called social realist artists did succeed in bringing an influential strain of realism to academic representations of the poor, they were not intended as a call to social activism. They worked best at stirring awareness in their viewers as to the plight of the less fortunate.[44] They also worked to reassure the public that although working-class domesticity was precarious, it was also precious: even when it was thrown into disarray by the death of the wife and mother, gender boundaries might remain intact and the respectable working-class father might assume his patriarchal duties by taking care of his family.

Victorian discourses on fatherhood offered few watertight prescriptions for family life, and doubtless few Victorian fathers, regardless of class, lived up to any of these ideals for very long. Contemporary critics debated these matters anxiously and offered a variety of ways to consider and solve the perceived disjunction between manly independence and domestic unity. The canvases discussed here illustrate the ways in which visual culture engaged, and attempted to negotiate with, these concerns. Whether or not these canvases offer an 'accurate' picture of the Victorian working-class father in distress is questionable (though Julie-Marie Strange's chapter in this volume proposes some new points of access to this issue). No doubt many working-class widowers were loving parents who toiled tirelessly to provide for their families, just as there were undoubtedly many who were abusive and uncaring. Though they do not represent, in any simple way, the experience of working-class fathers, these images offered ways for their Victorian audience – and for us – to frame important questions about fatherhood, masculinity and class.

Notes

I offer sincere thanks to the editors Trev Broughton and Helen Rogers for their assistance and patience, and to friends who read and commentated on the chapter: Dr Kathryn McDaniel, Dr Marie Secor, Patricia Smith-Scanlan, Lauren Keach Lessing, Capt. Tammy Gant and Capt. Timothy Lynch.

1. *Strand Magazine*, 1893, 124; quoted in J. Treuherz, *Hard Times: Social Realism in Victorian Art* (London: Lund Humphries; and New York: Moyer Bell, with Manchester City Art Galleries, 1987), p. 85. See also L.V. Fildes, *Luke Fildes, RA, A Victorian Painter* (London: Michael Joseph, 1968), pp. 24–5, 38–43.
2. *Art Journal*, June 1876, p. 189. Although the child's sex is unclear, the *Art Journal* refers to the child as a female.
3. M. McKerrow, *The Faeds, A Biography* (Edinburgh: Canongate Press, 1982).
4. The word 'sentimental' is highly charged and has, as J. Treuherz notes, 'come to mean self-indulgent and excessively emotional'. But, for Victorian art critics, it could be an important component of an artist's ability to arouse sympathy in the viewer: see Treuherz, *Hard Times*, p. 12.
5. For Victorian realist painting, see H. Rodee, *Scenes of Rural and Urban Poverty in Victorian Painting and their Development 1850–1890*, Ph.D. Dissertation, Columbia University, 1975; and Treuherz, *Hard Times*.

6. This claim is based on the number of images relating to death and mourning in research at the British Library and the Witt Library at the Courtauld Institute, London; T. R. Sabatos, *Images of Death and Domesticity in Victorian Britain*, Ph.D. Dissertation, Indiana University, 2001.
7. See P. Gillett, *Worlds of Art: Painters in Victorian Society* (New Brunswick, NJ: Rutgers University Press, 1990), pp. 193–241. According to Gillett, the annual yearly attendance at the Royal Academy Summer Exhibition during the 1880s and 1890s was 355,000. Although the exhibition drew viewers from a wide range of social classes, the majority came from the middle classes, and the upper tier of the labouring classes.
8. J. Kestner, *Masculinities in Victorian Painting* (Aldershot: Scolar Press, 1995).
9. For debates over 'separate spheres' see Davidoff and Hall, *Family Fortunes*; L. Nead, *Myths of Sexuality: Representations of Women in Victorian Britain* (Oxford: Blackwell, 1988); E. Langland, *Nobody's Angels: Middle Class Women and Domestic Ideology in Victorian Culture* (Ithaca, NY: Cornell University Press, 1995); C. N. Davidson and J. Hatcher (eds), *No More Separate Spheres: A Next Wave American Studies Reader* (Durham, NC: Duke University Press, 2002).
10. Tosh, *A Man's Place* and Nelson, *Invisible Men*.
11. Tosh, *A Man's Place*, p. 108.
12. Nelson, *Invisible Men*, pp. 14–15.
13. Ibid., pp. 41–72.
14. Davidoff and Hall, *Family Fortunes*, pp. 346–8.
15. While the man's marital status is unclear, Faed intended the viewer to understand that the father alone nursed the child. Faed wrote to William Hepworth Dixon, 'The picture represents a working man who has been watching his little boy far through a *restless* night. The child, holding his father's shirt sleeve has fallen asleep.' Quoted in McKerrow, *The Faeds*, p. 115.
16. Kestner, *Masculinities in Victorian Painting*, pp. 141–77.
17. Ibid., p. 142.
18. Ibid., p. 143.
19. As Kestner demonstrates, other images, such as Fildes's *The Doctor* (1891) and William Quiller Orchardson's *Mariage de Convenance* (1883), problematize middle-class and upper-class masculinity. See Kestner, *Masculinities in Victorian Painting*, pp. 164–166, and 168–169.
20. See, for example, William Powell Frith's *Many Happy Returns of the Day* (1854), reproduced in Lionel Lambourne, *Victorian Painting* (London: Phaidon, 1999), plate 201. Although the father does not gaze directly at the birthday girl, as Lambourne notes, a scene of a family gathered together for a meal was 'an enduring symbol of happy domestic life', p. 173. For an image of a middle-class father actively playing with his children, see 'A Happy Home', *My Sunday Friend*, February 1888, p. 13.
21. P. Keating, 'Words and Pictures: Changing Images of the Poor in Victorian Britain', in Treuherz, *Hard Times*, p. 126.
22. Ibid., pp. 126–30.
23. Nelson, *Invisible Men*, pp. 173–200.
24. Nead, *Myths of Sexuality*, p. 190.
25. Ibid., p. 190.
26. The child's sex is unclear, but will be referred to as female for convenience.
27. P. Jalland, *Death in the Victorian Family* (Oxford: Oxford University Press, 1996), pp. 291–5.
28. Kestner, *Masculinities in Victorian Painting*, p. 143.

29. T. Barringer, *Men at Work: Art and Labour in Victorian Britain* (New Haven, CT and London: Yale University Press, 2005), p. 40.
30. Ibid., p. 55.
31. J. Tosh, *Manliness and Masculinities in Nineteenth-Century Britain: Essays on Gender, Family and Empire* (London: Pearson Longman, 2005), pp. 37, 95. C. Wolkowitz, 'The Working Body as Sign: Historical Snapshots', in Katherine Backett-Milburn and Linda McKie (eds), *Constructing Gendered Bodies* (Basingstoke and New York: Palgrave, 2001), pp. 85–103.
32. Barringer, *Men at Work*, p. 50.
33. K. McClelland, '"England's Greatness, The Working Man"', in Hall, McClelland and Rendall, *Defining the Victorian Nation*, pp. 71–118.
34. *Hansard*, 3rd ser., Vol. 186, cols 626–42, 26 March 1867; cited in J. Harris, 'Between Civic Virtue and Social Darwinism: The Concept of the Residuum', in D. Englander and R. O'Day (eds), *Retrieved Riches: Social Investigation in England 1840–1914* (Aldershot: Scolar Press, 1995), p. 74; cited in McClelland, '"England's Greatness,"' pp. 97–8.
35. McClelland, '"England's Greatness,"' pp. 100–1.
36. The *Athenaeum* criticized the size of the canvas: 'It is a large picture; in fact much larger than was required by anything shown in the design or the painting, undoubtedly the latter would have looked better on a canvas one-eighth the size of this one' (13 May 1876), p. 672.
37. *The Times*, 8 May 1876, p. 9.
38. Linkages between the lower-class male (as both subject and audience) and more tender emotions predated these works. In 1857, Clark exhibited *The Sick Child* at the Royal Academy. While no image is available, the reviewer for the *Athenaeum* describes a scene roughly similar to Fildes's *The Widower*: 'a rough countryman in a large fustian jacket holds a sick child in his lap'. This man is not a widower (his wife is also shown attempting to coax the child to take a bite of food). The reviewer praised the work, especially the devoted concern exhibited by the father: 'The father's profile indicates such tender anxiety and such sadness that the roughest man might not be ashamed to shed a tear to see it.' *Athenaeum*, 23 May 1857, p. 668.
39. Quoted in Fildes, *Luke Fildes*, p. 40.
40. It should be noted that the *Athenaeum* disliked almost everything else about the painting except for the figure of the widower and his child (13 May 1876), p. 672.
41. *Art Journal*, June 1876, p. 189.
42. *Art Journal*, June 1863, p. 110, as quoted in Nead, *Myths of Sexuality*, p. 18.
43. As quoted in D. Croal Thompson, 'The Life and Work of Sir Luke Fildes, RA', *Art Annual: Supplement to the Art Journal*, Christmas 1895, p. 8.
44. Treuherz, *Hard Times*, p. 13.

Hands-on Fatherhood in Trollope's Novels

Margaret Markwick

When the child care guru Benjamin Spock died in 1997, his son John in a post-obit interview commented, 'He was very Victorian. He's never been a person who gave me a hug. He wouldn't kiss me.'[1] In describing the cold detachment of his father as 'Victorian', he fed into a nexus of assumptions and associations that people commonly make about Victorian men in general and fathers in particular. Anthony Trollope, for his part, has largely been viewed as the chronicler of men wielding their power in their vestries, in their ministries and on their estates. There has been little focus on his portrayal of their domestic milieu. This is a sad oversight, for when we set to examine his men round the hearth, remarkable and stereotype-challenging detail emerges. Trollope's novels advance a consistent theme of masculinity, within which men achieve their true potential by embracing their feminine side. This is not the anachronism that it might seem, since in *Phineas Redux* Laura Kennedy writes to Phineas Finn for news about how her brother and sister-in-law are shaping as parents: 'You have enough of the feminine side of a man's character to tell me how they are living.'[2] Phineas Finn (whose affections have all the constancy of a butterfly) is thus identified as a man who knows his own nurturing side, and is observant about other men as parents. Early on in *Phineas Redux* he has written to these friends asking, 'Does Oswald make a good nurse with the baby?' (Vol. 1 p. 18). When he goes to stay with them we read, 'he rode Lord Chiltern's horses, took an interest in the hounds, and nursed the baby' (Vol. 1 p. 26). Trollope's men push the pram, nurse the baby, change the nappies and put the children to bed. Indeed, men such as Phineas who philander their way through the novels still get to marry the girl if they are seen to nurse a baby along the way.

The moral ambiguity of this sits teasingly with Trollope's self-professed high purpose as a novelist; as he says in *An Autobiography*, 'The novelist, if he has a conscience, must preach his sermons with the same purpose as the clergyman, and must have his own system of ethics.'[3] Earlier he has said, 'I think that no youth has been taught that in falseness and flashness is to be found the road to manliness; but some may perhaps have learned from me that it is to be found in truth and a high but gentle spirit.'[4] In reconciling the disparities of principle and entertainment, Trollope is never polemical. It is in his storyline and the occasional authorial aside that we learn his credo that men will find a richer happiness in their lives by expressing their affections openly, in both words and actions. This contrasts with recent studies of Victorian masculinities, which have perceived the domestic hearth as the focus of men's power, not their emotional literacy.[5]

Trollope achieves this while not disrupting his persona as a writer of fiction for men. The times he was writing in were distinguished by a surge of interest in economic theory in the face of the social upheavals caused by the industrial revolution. The commentators on the emerging industrial economy formulated their views in a discourse that turned away from addressing the individual and focused on a wider macrocosmic field of study. Malthus's essays on population, Bentham and his utilitarianism, and Ricardo's theories of the mechanics of capitalism all fostered a discursive environment depleted of sentiment.[6] This helped to promote a growing anxiety about the marketplace. How could a man keep his integrity and succeed in business? Was it indeed possible to combine integrity and financial success? Such challenges were explicitly addressed by the ethical asceticism of Carlyle and the populist writings of Samuel Smiles, both of whom, none the less, defined men in their public sphere. In spite of his caustic lampoon of Carlyle as Dr Pessimist Anticant in *The Warden*,[7] Trollope shares many of his convictions about the lack of principle at large in public life. They form the underlying premise of many of his novels. *The Three Clerks* (1858), *Rachel Ray* (1863), *The Struggles of Brown, Jones and Robinson* (1870) and *The Way We Live Now* (1875): these are all satires on the corruption of capitalist thinking when it is allowed to float free from a moral grounding.

Despite Trollope's scepticism about political economy, Malthusian theory and the newly emerging science of demography are regularly woven into his texts. In *Doctor Thorne*, Frank Gresham junior twits his aunt with a joke she doesn't understand:

> 'No I won't be plucked. Baker was plucked last year . . . he got among a set of men who did nothing but smoke and drink beer. Malthusians we call them.'
> 'Malthusians?'
> '"Malt", you know, aunt, and "use", meaning that they drink beer.'[8]

This joke is not just at the expense of his aunt and female ignorance of contemporary economic debate. It is also a joke about class, about the working man with his tobacco and beer and his position in the marketplace, and the parallels for Frank in the marketplace of marriage. It may very possibly, for Trollope, have held reverberations of the debate about birth control, as it does for us, since Malthusian theory was and is often spuriously connected with the advocacy of contraception,[9] and Trollope regularly urges his heroines to marry, have two children and live happily ever after. The new demographers instigated censuses and their continual refinement, from the blunt head count of 1801 to the 1851 census that recorded ages, civil condition, occupation, birthplace and infirmities, with a separate census of education and religious attendance. The results drawn from these censuses generated great interest (particularly the religious attendance census), and their findings influence Trollope's presentation of his fictional communities. Instances of Trollope's interest in economics, statistics and censuses regularly creep into the novels, though it is in his travel books that his enthusiasm is given its fullest rein.[10]

The 1861 census shows that 1 in 5.5 families was headed by a single parent.[11] Stone has pointed out the similarity with the social structure of modern times, where divorce plays the role so arbitrarily taken by death in the nineteenth century,[12] but there was a critical difference: in 1861, one in three of these single parents were men. This compares with a UK incidence in 2000 of one in four families headed by a single parent, with lone fathers heading only one in eight of these.[13] Step-parenthood, therefore, was common, though there were more stepmothers than stepfathers.[14] Because Trollope places his characters very precisely in their domestic context, it is possible to conduct our own census of Trollope's fictional, though largely monoclass, society. If we confine ourselves to the novels set in England and Wales, and if we consider families involved in the main actions of the plots where their operation as a family has a significant bearing on the story, we have a cohort of 52 two-parent families, and 54 single-parent families. Of the two-parent families, 8 are step-families. There are 29 women, and 25 men bringing up children on their own. Thus Trollope's communities have equal numbers of two- and one-parent families, and nearly half his lone parents are men. His men on their own are particularly prone to render their daughters vulnerable. Emily Wharton (*The Prime Minister*) needs a mother's advice and guidance, as does Alice Vavasor (*Can You Forgive Her?*), though Mr Wharton makes a better fist of it than does Mr Vavasor. One significant factor here may be that Alice's mother dies soon after she is born, whereas Mrs Wharton dies only two years before the start of the novel. Mr Amedroz fails Clara in *The Belton Estate*, and Admiral Blackstock fails his daughter Lizzie Eustace in *The Eustace Diamonds*. That our census reveals Trollope's statistically skewed relish for relationships under stress should be no surprise since, as we shall see, examining the extra vulnerability of men in their closest relationships leads to some of his most interesting plots. Lone fathers with problems are counterbalanced by the sensitive parenting of Dr Thorne, bringing up his niece in *Doctor Thorne*, and Septimus Harding, raising two girls on his own in *The Warden*. Mr Harding 'had that nice appreciation of the feelings of others, which belongs of right exclusively to women',[15] which suggests that, like Phineas Finn, he was in touch with 'the feminine side' of his nature. Squire Newton also incorporates these feminized skills into the model of manliness that shapes the parenting of his illegitimate son in *Ralph the Heir*.[16]

Being kind and gentle with children was part of the chivalric duty of every preux chevalier, but Trollope's heroes go further and take real pleasure in their hands-on contact with children. We have already seen Phineas Finn nursing the Standish baby. Harry Clavering is equally comfortable in a domestic, child-centred setting when he visits the Burtons and kisses the children in their cots. Much is made of Harry's propensity for the discourse of the hearth. Theodore's invitation to him when his quandary over his two fiancées is making him ill is to 'come once more to Onslow Crescent, and kiss the bairns, and kiss Cecilia too, and sit with us at our table, and talk as you used to'.[17] Similarly, John

Caldigate, when he has done with his wild oats, enjoys the practicalities of child care when his son is born: 'Then he took the child very gently, and deposited him, fast asleep, among the blankets. He had already assumed for himself the character of being a good male nurse.'[18] The implication of 'good male nurse' would seem to be that John Caldigate changed the nappies.

Phineas Finn, John Caldigate and Harry Clavering have this in common: in spite of their rakish pasts, they openly acknowledge the pleasure and satisfaction of close involvement in the nurturing of babies and children, and in their stories this is the common signifier of their sterling qualities that cancels out their shortcomings when judged by a more conventional code. When one starts looking more widely for textual indicators of character based on how men behave with children, the pointers are everywhere. Henry Grantly takes his baby girl out in her pram.[19] Lady Albury, pleading Jonathan Stubbs's cause with Ayala, says, 'See him with children!',[20] Burgo Fitzgerald, the rake and wastrel who nevertheless has redeeming features, is described as 'soft and gracious with children'.[21] Conversely, criticizing Sir Hugh Clavering, his uncle the Reverend Henry Clavering says, 'He is a hard man; the hardest man I ever knew. Who ever saw him playing with his own child?'[22] All are significant comments on the masculinity of these men. The men who take pleasure in the physical care of children, and understand children, are the men who can be trusted to make good husbands; they can be relied on to be gentle and considerate; they will be good providers, with their pleasures focused on their hearths.

As children grow up, the open love of fathers becomes mutually enriching. In *Doctor Thorne*, Frank Gresham, father and son, have a warm and loving relationship which continues into Frank junior's manhood. Both father and son are free with physical demonstrations of their affection for each other, and neither will brook criticism of the other from any quarter. We are told that Mr Gresham loved his son 'with the tenderest love' (p. 400), while Frank 'loved his father truly, purely, and thoroughly, liked to be with him, and would be proud to be his confidant' (p. 55). Mr Gresham expresses his love physically: 'He put his hand on his son's shoulder, and half caressed him' (p. 79). That this is commonly how he demonstrated his feeling for his son is reflected in Frank's readiness in his turn to reassure his father of his love for him with physical touch: 'Frank drew near to his father, and pressed his hand against the squire's arm, by way of giving him, in some sort, a filial embrace for his kindness' (p. 601).

In another passage, quite remarkable for what it implies about the discourse between the two men, Frank has been declaring that his love for Mary transcends anything that he could learn about her birth, and both men have been undissimulating in acknowledging the world's skewed values in allowing money to outweigh the disadvantages of lowly birth. Frank hotly defends Mary's suitability as a bride for him, saying that he does not give a straw for what other people think. His father reads more deeply into his son's heart: 'What you mean is that . . . you value your love more than the world's opinion.' He recognises the integrity of his son's protestations. This is not without its own particular pain for him. He knows, and acknowledges, that money is only an issue because of his own poor stewardship. Frank sets out his plans for earning his own living. His father reflects on the import of his son, his heir, seeking work. The two men, in trust and respect, offer their hearts for inspection: 'Frank . . . I wonder what you think of me? . . . Yes, what you think of me for having thus ruined you. I wonder whether you hate me?' The invitation to give voice to unspoken angry feelings is immediately rebuffed: 'Frank, jumping up from his chair, threw his arms round his father's neck. "Hate you, sir! How can you speak so cruelly. You know that I love you . . . But father, never say, never think that I do not love you!"' (p. 515). This is the dialogue of two men who understand their hearts, and value the capacity for the expression and exchange of feeling. Frank has grown up secure in his father's love for him – 'his father, whose face was always lighted up with pleasure when the boy came near him' (p. 54).

There are other such relationships in the novels where the warm, loving feeling which flows freely between father and son is regularly expressed in an embrace. In *Ralph the Heir*, Squire Newton and his illegitimate son Ralph, against all cultural odds, have just such a relationship. For the Squire, 'His boy was as dear to him as though the mother had been his honest wife' (Vol. 1, p. 128). 'There had never been a more devoted father, one more intensely anxious for his son's welfare' (Vol. 2, p. 38), while of Ralph we read, 'He could only take his father's arm, and whisper a soft feminine word or two. He would be as happy as the day is long if only he could see his father happy' (Vol. 1, p. 273).

The ironic antithesis of this in George Bertram's relationship with his father in *The Bertrams* emphasizes the point. Lionel Bertram, notable by his absence on any plane from his son's childhood, agrees to meet George, now a young man, in Jerusalem. George, whose relationship with his father is perhaps based on a fantasy untempered by reality, endows his father with all the parenting qualities he so patently lacks, and responds to him as though they were tied by bonds as firm as those between the Greshams: 'the son was half holding, half caressing his father's arm. Sir Lionel, to tell the truth, did not much care for such caresses, but under the peculiar circumstances of this present interview, he permitted it.'[23] The idealized father/son relationship that George aspires to, and perhaps observed between Arthur Wilkinson and his father when he was growing up, is warm and physical. His own father's heart is cold, calculating and manipulative. Just as the good rapport between Arthur Wilkinson and his father is implicit in the text, so one might make similar assumptions about the father/son relationships of other young men who show a marked aptitude for tenderness in parenthood. Mark Robarts, Jonathan Stubbs, Theodore Burton, Harry Clavering, Phineas Finn, perhaps all learn to find pleasure in children's company by being cherished by their fathers.

But it is his men bringing up children alone who reveal Trollope as the herald of the new man. Dr Thorne, a bachelor who brings up his niece, 'had a great theory as to the happiness of children. He argued that the principle duty which a parent owed a child was to make him happy. He delighted to talk to children and to play with them.' No wonder he was popular in the Gresham nursery: 'He would carry them on his back, three or four at a time, roll with them in the gardens, invent games for them, and contrive amusement in circumstances which seemed quite adverse to all manner of delight.' And he held advanced views on corporal punishment: 'Why struggle after future advantage at the expense of present pain, seeing that the results were so very doubtful?' When he is challenged on the need for control and correction for children, he counters that he also needs control and correction but manages not to steal his neighbour's peaches or make love to his neighbour's wife without recourse to the rod.[24] In *The Last Chronicle of Barset*, Henry Grantly's wife has died in childbirth, and he brings up his baby daughter alone (though with the full panoply of Victorian upper middle-class nursemaids). Two years later he falls in love with Grace Crawley, daughter of an impoverished and disgraced clergyman. The text makes it clear that he is physically and emotionally very involved in his baby daughter's care. When he spends Christmas with his parents, special arrangements are to be made for father and baby: 'Anything that he wanted for Edith was to be done' (p. 218). We see him taking Edith out in her pram and when, on a day of male bonding with his friends, he becomes downhearted at their pessimistic reflections on the Crawley family, he chooses to go home to be there for Edith's bedtime rather than stay and dine with his companions (p. 135). When he falls in love, Grace's suitability as a mother to his child is paramount. He is primarily concerned about the quality of love and affection his little girl needs. Before he declares his love, he makes opportunity both for him to observe Grace with his little girl, and for her to examine her feelings about Edith. He lets her stay overnight in Grace's charge. When he asks Grace to marry him, it is a dual proposal: 'I have come here, dearest Grace, to ask you to be my wife, and to be a mother to Edith' (p. 298).

Each time Henry examines his feelings about Grace, his feelings about Edith guide his thoughts. When he discusses with Miss Prettyman how he should proceed in pressing his suit, he says, '[I have been] wondering whether I was too old for her, and whether she would mind having Edith to take care of' (p. 64). He pours out his heart to Mrs Thorne, the former Martha Dunstable, and tells her of the warnings men have given him about Edith's interests (p. 139). While he reveals less of the vulnerability of his heart when talking to his mother of his love for Grace and his determination to marry her, Edith is central to his argument. The words that Henry uses in these dialogues reflect his emotional literacy: ' I know what my feelings are. I do love her with all my heart,' he says to Miss Prettyman (p. 64).

It is Septimus Harding, his grandfather and the eponymous Warden, who shows Henry the way to mend the rift that has opened between him and his father over his plans to marry Grace. Mr Harding, who 'had that nice appreciation of the feelings of others which belongs of right exclusively to women' noted earlier, says to Henry, 'Be gentle with him – and submit yourself' (p. 629), and as Henry reflects on this, he realises that 'it might be becoming in him to forgive his father' (p. 687). Henry knows that, through taking on his grandfather's precepts, he shows that he is a bigger man than his father. Two men who have had to be mother and father to their children, and who have risen to the challenge, show that masculinity becomes truly strong and worth striving for when it encompasses nurturing qualities. Plantagenet Palliser's journey to recognise this truth in *The Duke's Children* is a much rougher ride.

The Duke's Children opens with the family, newly returned from a year on the continent, plunged into grief by the sudden death of Glencora, the Duchess of Omnium. The Duke, Plantagenet Palliser, is bereft: 'It was as though a man should suddenly be called upon to live without hands or even arms.'[25] While he loves his children, his expression of his love is hindered by his misconceptions of his role as parent; instead of promoting and sharing their welfare, he becomes a block to their happiness. His trajectory from misguided and pessimistic attempts to exercise control to the articulation of pleasure in the choices his children make of partners and way of life is the discourse of this novel; the road he has to travel is hard, and his shoes often rub, but he can finally look honestly into his heart and find words to express the feelings he acknowledges are there. He was an absent parent when his children were small. His eldest son, aged perhaps three, sitting on his great uncle's knee in *Phineas Finn*, says 'Papa is very well, but he almost never comes home.'[26] This has some sadness for Plantagenet. In *The Prime Minister*, he says, 'I am always dreaming of some day when we may go away together with the children, and rest in some pretty spot, and live as other people live.'[27]

Plantagenet's tragedy in *The Duke's Children* is that he has to learn how to be a mother and a father to his children from a heart that has feelings, but no capacity to express emotions. His quarrel with Mrs Finn over his daughter's engagement to Frank Tregear festers because he cannot talk through the situation beyond his anger: 'As he thought of it, he became hot, and was conscious of a quivering feeling round his heart' (p. 119). A man's tendency to be inarticulate about his feelings is a common theme in the novels. In *Kept in The Dark*, Trollope says, 'That which we call reticence is more frequently an inability than an unwillingness to express itself. The man is silent, not because he would not have the words spoken, but because he does not know the fitting words with which to speak.'[28] Men who fail to learn to locate their feelings accurately, Trollope is saying, are led to pursue false trails, with no insight into how they damage that which they most love, or how to repair it. It is a fine description of that emotional illiteracy often identified as the root of men's problems today, articulated over a hundred and twenty years earlier.

Plantagenet has no facility for articulation as the book opens. His view of his task as the parent of a 19-year-old young woman is restrictive and fettering: 'How was he to decide whom she should or whom she should not marry? How was he to guide her through the shoals and rocks which lay in the path of such a girl before she can achieve matrimony?' (p. 4). His rhetorical questions form an ominous indicator of things to come, as he mistakes the place of duty and obedience in his task of encouraging his children to be confident and make independent choices about their future.

His problems with Mary start almost immediately when he discovers that she has pledged herself to Frank Tregear, a commoner without means. Plantagenet entirely fails to recognise his sterling qualities, and sees only an arrogant adventurer after his daughter's money. In trying to browbeat his daughter, he merely succeeds in denying himself the comfort of her love and embrace at his own time of greatest need The discussion with Mrs Finn while they are on holiday in Austria marks the beginning of Plantagenet's change of heart, though it is a slow and painful process. He knows he must finally concede when he recognizes that his future happiness hangs on a warm, tender and physically affectionate relationship with his daughter, and when he realises that his stance has been a barrier to this:

> He put his arm round her and kissed her, – as he would have had so much delight in doing, as he would have done so often before, had there not been this ground of discord . . . It was sweet to him to have something to caress. Now in the solitude of his life, as years were coming on him, he felt how necessary it was that he should have someone who would love him. Since his wife had left him, he had been debarred from these caresses by the necessity of showing his antagonism to her dearest wishes. (p. 528)

The shift in his relationship with his sons, particularly his heir, Silverbridge, is a similar journey of revelation for him. Though it has always been a source of sadness that Plantagenet's political life has forced him into the role of absent parent, it is as much the nature of the man as his career in life that keeps them apart: 'He was a man so reticent and undemonstrative in his manner that he had never known how to make confidential friends of his children' (p. 44). Fortunately for the well-being of his children, they had a warm, close and supportive relationship with their mother: 'In all their joys and in all their troubles, in all their desires and in all their disappointments they had ever gone to their mother. She had been conversant with everything about them, from the boys' bills and the girl's gloves to the innermost turn in the heart and disposition of each (p. 3).'

Now he has to learn to name his feelings, and then act on them, and Silverbridge puts Plantagenet through something like a refiner's fire, where each time that he seems to learn to take pleasure and pride in his son's demonstration that he is his own man, the temperature rises and he has to face the challenge of an even tougher ordeal, until he finally emerges to enjoy unalloyed pleasure in his children.

Plantagenet's first conflict with Silverbridge is over his son's insistence on holding his own and dissenting opinion over politics: 'The Pallisers have always been Liberal. It will be a blow to me, indeed, if Silverbridge deserts his colours' (p. 37). He continues, 'I trust you will consider it . . . that you will not find yourself obliged to desert the school of politics in which your father has not been an inactive supporter, and to which your family has belonged for many generations' (p. 57). An exchange about philosophical positions becomes personalized: 'Then you refuse to do what I ask?' Silverbridge never rises to the bait, to retort in anger. His joke about the Radicals habitually calling the Conservatives fools, and his modest assessment of himself as a fool, pushes his father into petulance: 'He was tempted again and again to burst out in wrath and threaten the lad, – to threaten him as to money, as to his amusements, as to the general tenure of his life. The pity was so great that the lad should be so stubborn and so foolish' (p. 57–8). The repetition of 'lad' emphasises that Plantagenet undervalues his 22-year-old son's maturity. He denies him man's estate, as he contemplates denying him his financial independence. When Silverbridge is returned to Parliament, he writes a letter, beginning 'My Dear Father', which is open, honest and true. This facilitates Plantagenet's reply: 'I am able to congratulate you as a father should a son, and to wish you long life and success as a legislator' (p. 121). As his son settles into the harness of parliamentary life (though not as assiduously as his father might wish), Plantagenet experiences a common ground between them, which fosters the growth of respect. After listening to a debate together, Silverbridge invites his father to dine with him at his club, 'anxious to make things pleasant for his father'. Plantagenet 'liked the feeling that he was dining with his son'. The combined effect of the efforts of the son and the increasing confidence of the father to believe that his gesture will be well received brings about a watershed in Plantagenet's development as an effective parent to his son: 'He put out his hand, and gently stroked the young man's hair. It was almost a caress, – as though he would have said to himself, "Were he my daughter, I would kiss him"' (p. 208). A physical embrace marks the resolution of his next ordeal with Silverbridge, when he is swindled out of a fortune in a shady horse-racing deal: 'Then the father came up to the son and put his arms around the young man's shoulders and embraced him. "Of course, it makes me unhappy . . . But if you are cured of this evil, the money is nothing"' (p. 364).

When Plantagenet goes into the fire a third and final time, when Silverbridge insists he will marry the woman he loves, a commoner and an American, he needs the wisdom of all the experience he has accumulated over the previous months. Hearing that his son's choice is Isabel Boncassen, he cries, 'Is there to be no duty in such matters, no restraint, no feeling of what is due to your own name, and to others who bear it?' (p. 485). Isabel is the loved and cherished daughter of parents who are loved and respected in their turn, but Plantagenet wishes his son to marry Lady Mabel Grex, the daughter of a man he knows to be 'a wretched unprincipled old man, bad all round . . . But the blue blood and rank were there' (p. 391). He hankers after the glory of the match, and disregards the pitfalls of a dysfunctional family, while his son, with better-honed articulacy in emotional matters, follows his heart in choosing a young woman sincere, honest and open in her love, with no guile, who will love him and their children in the same fashion.

But while Plantagenet's immediate reaction seems to be as entrenched as his earlier responses to Silverbridge's espousal of the rival cause, his passion for horse-racing, and his daughter's commitment to her love, the shifting of his position now seems to cause him less anguish than he felt at the outset of this chronicle. All the plot lines converge for a final resolution. Gerald dissipates a younger son's portion; his manly repentance must be recognized, and himself forgiven; Tregear must be accepted into the family fold; Silverbridge's political career must be acknowledged as a source of pride, and finally, he must accept Isabel Boncassen as 'bone of his bone'. This he does with grace, affection, honesty and deep feeling, when he gives her a diamond ring, the first present he ever gave to Glencora: 'You shall be my child,' he says, 'And if you will love me, you shall be very dear to me . . . I must either love [my son's] wife very dearly, or else I must be an unhappy man' (p. 510).

As Plantagenet settles into his new-found land, his demeanour changes in other ways, equally radical for him. He makes a joke of his son's change of political heart: '"I suppose it is your republican bride-elect that has done that", said the Duke, laughing' (p. 623). And at his daughter's marriage, 'perhaps the matter the most remarkable . . . was the hilarity of the Duke' (p. 632–3). It is clear from the closing paragraphs that, while the memory of his suffering stays with him, there is a confidence there that he is now better equipped to face his new world. It is Silverbridge's assimilation of nurturing qualities from his close relationship with his mother that enables him to parry his father's poorer personal skills with warmth and humanity. In learning to value such qualities, and to incorporate them into his own behaviour, Plantagenet learns the fulfilment of knowing his 'feminine side'. From a cold, harsh, distant, judgmental, patriarchal stand, Plantagenet moves to a parental position that allows him to take pleasure in his children's pleasure and to express that physically. Denied by death the warm comforts of his wife, in learning how to be father and mother to his children, he also begins to heal the wound of Glencora's loss.

As we have seen, Trollope makes clear his didactic purpose as a novelist in *An Autobiography*. He presents as his heroes men who extend the parameters of masculine behaviour into territory more usually defined as female. At the same time, he reflects men behaving in a manner not unusual for the times in which he lived. I have found no evidence of a contemporary critic charging Trollope with a distorted representation of men's lives;[29] no voice says there is anything unusual about Theodore Burton putting the children to bed,[30] or Henry Grantly pushing the pram. J. A. and O. Banks in their still unrivalled series of studies of Victorian domestic life draw on Trollope for accurate evidence of the way we lived then,[31] and Henry James wrote that, in the novels, Trollope's characters 'do, in short, very much as the reader is doing out of them'.[32] I suggest we take these as serious indicators that Trollope offers us an historically plausible account of men's aptitude for child care, and consider whether hands-on fatherhood was not, in fact, more of a Victorian ideal than we usually acknowledge. For this is the untold history of Victorian fathers, where men, so many of whom were forced by circumstance into lone parenthood, learn that close involvement with the minutiae of children's lives offers life-long satisfactions.

Notes

1. 'Growing up the Hard Way', BBC2, 11 June 1997, 9.00 p.m., dir. by Ella Bahaure.
2. A. Trollope, *Phineas Redux*, 1873 (Oxford: Oxford University Press, 1983), Vol. 1, p. 57.
3. A. Trollope, *An Autobiography*, 1883 (Oxford: Oxford University Press, 1980), pp. 221–2.
4. Trollope, *Autobiography*, p. 146.
5. For instance, Tosh, *A Man's Place*, particularly Introduction and Ch. 3, but compare this with Davidoff and Hall, *Family Fortunes*, Ch. 7.
6. This discourse, often regarded as masculinist, did not invariably exclude women. Florence Nightingale was taught advanced mathematics by her father, and Harriet Martineau wrote *Illustrations of Political Economy*, tales to popularize the theories of Smith, Ricardo, Malthus and Bentham, first published in 1833, but still in print in the 1880s.
7. A. Trollope, *The Warden*, 1855 (Oxford: Oxford University Press, 1991).
8. A. Trollope, *Doctor Thorne*, 1858 (Oxford: Oxford University Press, 1980), p. 72.

9. Y. Charbit, 'The Fate of Malthus's Work: History and Ideology', in J. Dupaquier *et al.* (eds), *Malthus Past and Present* (London: Academic Press, 1983).
10. For instance, in *The American Senator* (1876), Trollope says, 'At every interval of ten years, when the census is taken, the population of Dilsborough is found to have fallen off in some slight degree.' (Oxford: Oxford University Press, 1986) p. 2, and in *The Vicar of Bullhampton* (1869), Frank Fenwick speaks of only a quarter of London's population going to church, a statistic established by the religious census of 1851 (Oxford: Oxford University Press, 1988), p. 493.
11. Figures taken from Census of England for the year 1861, Vol. 2 (London: Eyre and Spottiswood, 1863) xx, Table V: Civil or conjugal condition of the people.
12. Stone, *Road to Divorce*, p. 410.
13. J. Haskey, 'One-Parent Families – and the Dependent Children Living in them – in Great Britain', *Population Trends* 109, Autumn 2002, p. 53.
14. M. Drake, 'The Remarriage Market in Mid-Nineteenth Century Britain', in J. Dupaquier *et al.* (eds), *Marriage and Remarriage in Populations of the Past* (London: Academic Press, 1981).
15. A. Trollope, *Barchester Towers*, 1857 (Oxford: Oxford University Press, 1996), Vol. 2, p. 265.
16. A. Trollope, *Ralph the Heir*, 1871 (Oxford: Oxford University Press, 1990).
17. A. Trollope, *The Claverings*, 1867 (Oxford: Oxford University Press, 1986), p. 276.
18. A. Trollope, *John Caldigate*, 1879 (Oxford: Oxford University Press, 1993), p. 232.
19. A. Trollope, *The Last Chronicle of Barset*, 1867 (Oxford: Oxford University Press, 1980), p. 68.
20. A. Trollope, *Ayala's Angel*, 1881 (Oxford: Oxford University Press, 1986), p. 505.
21. A. Trollope, *Can You Forgive Her?*, 1864 (Oxford: Oxford University Press, 1982), Vol. 1, p. 365.
22. Trollope, *Claverings*, p. 203.
23. A. Trollope, *The Bertrams*, 1859 (London: Penguin, 1993), p. 23.
24. Trollope, *Thorne*, pp. 41–2.
25. A. Trollope, *The Duke's Children*, 1880 (Oxford: Oxford University Press, 1991), p. 2.
26. A. Trollope, *Phineas Finn*, 1869 (Ware: Wordsworth Editions, 1996), p. 543.
27. A. Trollope, *The Prime Minister*, 1876 (Oxford: Oxford University Press, 1983) Vol. 2, p. 104.
28. A. Trollope, *Kept in the Dark*, 1882 (Oxford: Oxford University Press, 1992), pp. 158–9.
29. On the contrary, see D. Smalley (ed). *Anthony Trollope: The Critical Heritage* (London: Routledge and Kegan Paul, 1963), *passim*, particularly p. 110, '[Trollope's novels are] just as real as if some giant had hewn a great lump out of the earth, and put it under a glass case, with all its inhabitants going about their daily business' (Nathaniel Hawthorne to Joseph M. Field, 11 Feb. 1860).
30. Trollope, *Claverings*, 295.
31. J. A. Banks, *Prosperity and Parenthood: A Study of Family Planning among the Victorian Middle Classes* (London: Routledge and Kegan Paul, 1954); J. A. and O. Banks, *Feminism and Family Planning in Victorian England* (Liverpool: Liverpool University Press, 1965).
32. H. James, review 'The Belton Estate', *Nation* (New York) 4 Jan 1866, Vol. ii. pp. 21–2.

6

Father(ing) Christmas: Fatherhood, Gender and Modernity in Victorian and Edwardian England

Neil Armstrong

Scrooge was better than his word. He did it all, and infinitely more; and to Tiny Tim, who did NOT die, he was a second father.[1]

In popular perception, the Victorian Christmas has come to epitomize an authentic vision of the Christmas festival centred on the family and the domestic hearth. Its seminal text, *A Christmas Carol* (1843), celebrates the familial affections of Christmas, but also the obligations of giving and the duties of paternal care. Scrooge's transformation from miser to fountain of benevolence finds special resonance in his relationship with Tiny Tim, sanctifying fatherhood at the spiritual core of Christmas. Later in the Victorian period, the link between Christmas and fatherhood became reified through the dissemination of Santa Claus rituals of gift-giving, with particular emphasis on Christmas stockings. Such rituals are not without wider significance for the nineteenth-century family. Scholars such as John Gillis have argued that, during this period, Christmas and other holidays became symbolic occasions where families, particularly of the middle classes, celebrated idealized conceptions of themselves.[2] Within this scheme a study of the Christmas festival can add to our understanding of the nature of the father–child relationship in the Victorian and Edwardian periods. In what follows I draw upon a wide social range of evidence from memoirs and private family papers to explore the shifting attitudes and fathering practices during the Christmas festival. While the emergence of Santa Claus rituals gave fathers a more structured role, it complicated their symbolic authority as patriarchs, particularly in the gift relationship. These rituals are also considered in relation to the public iconography of Santa Claus, who had become a major feature of Christmas commercial and philanthropic campaigns by the beginning of the twentieth century. Representations of Santa Claus were frequently aligned with images of aircraft and motor cars that epitomized a consciously modern age, and, though humorous in tone, they may hint at a masculine ambivalence towards the Christmas festival and the broader trends of modern society.

While historians have debated the extent to which Victorian Christmas customs represent an 'invented tradition',[3] there can be no doubt that the celebration of Christmas expanded in complexity during the Victorian period. One aspect of this, the celebration of Christmas in the home, became increasingly dependent upon material culture, elaborate rituals of gift-giving and forms of play and theatricality, often centred around the children of the household. Leslie Bella and William Waits have identified this process as a feminization of Christmas, whilst in a broader context the physical and emotional labour of holidays has largely been defined as women's work.[4] What role did fathers play in this feminized space? Did the reliance on female labour in the home, which in middle- and upper-class households might also be reinforced by a largely female workforce of servants, serve to reinforce patriarchal authority, or did the involvement of fathers in such feminized environments prove problematic for contemporary models of masculine identity? Gillis found no such problems for the middle-class male of the mid-nineteenth century, arguing that, for men, Christmas was a time of considerable licence, a time of dressing up and joining in children's play. In this gendered scheme, Christmas is made by women but performed by men.[5] John Tosh has also identified Christmas as a time when Victorian fathers were licensed to play, and identifies the emergence of the modern Santa Claus in the 1870s as representing a shift in the 'spiritual underpinnings of paternal authority' from the 'judging, watchful father of Evangelical tradition' to the 'source of material largesse' in the form of Christmas presents.[6]

Tosh is keen to stress that the evangelical father figure was not incompatible with a playful interaction between father and child.[7] Equally, evangelical fathers of the early and mid-nineteenth century could feel a keen sense of emotional satisfaction from the Christmas reunion with their children. One such example is the Bedfordshire squire, John Thomas Brooks of Flitwick (1794–1858). Brooks's diary entries in the 1830s and 1840s reveal the happiness he derived from the Christmas family reunion that took place when his children returned home from school. Whilst this happiness was framed by evangelical seriousness, it did not preclude him attending Christmas tree events and dances, though he did reserve the right as a father to opt out. On New Year's Eve 1846 he noted in his diary, 'Domestic: pressed to go tonight with Dawsons to see a Christmas Tree for the children, escaped.' In terms of gift-giving, Brooks employed the widespread practice of giving his children Christmas shillings.[8] Whilst twentieth-century social theory has emphasized the depersonalized nature of currency as a gift,[9] children did not necessarily view it in this way. For the children of Charles Wood, the 1st Viscount Halifax (1800–85), receiving Christmas shillings was noteworthy enough to be mentioned in correspondence with other relatives. Charles Wood's political career meant that time with his children was very limited. During Christmas 1851, for example, when Wood was Chancellor of the Exchequer, he arrived to see his children on Christmas Eve. A snapdragon[10] was held, and shillings were distributed. On Christmas morning the children had a walk with their father after church, following which he departed. As his son, Charles Lindley Wood (1839–1934) recorded, 'Papa went away yesterday, we were all very sorry for him to go as it is a long time since we have seen him.'[11] The available evidence suggests that early-Victorian fathers could enjoy the opportunity for interaction with their children which the Christmas festival offered, but which was not considered to be compulsory.

It is possible to detect a shift in Christmas fathering practice in the generation of men born in the 1830s. Charles Lindley Wood, who became the 2nd Viscount Halifax in 1885, was much more involved in the household Christmas than his father. His diaries of the 1870s and 1880s contain references to being busy with decorations, practical aspects of theatricals, wrapping presents and the writing of Christmas cards and letters. He corresponded with his wife on the topic of Christmas presents, and shopped for them himself whilst in London. Most importantly, he played a significant role in entertaining children at Christmas, including reading ghost and adventure stories, staging elaborate ruses, leading trips to the pantomime, and rearranging furniture to facilitate the children's 'great romps' around the hall.[12] David Roberts has commented on the way in which the absent father of the Victorian governing classes could 'appear at Christmas and Easter', and that '[a]mong the landed families papas were indeed great fun. They dispensed gifts, took their sons hunting, their daughters to ducal balls, and the whole family to the Alps.'[13] For the children of such fathers, Christmas might linger long in the memory, and provide stories that captured the essence of their relationship with a parent during childhood. Charles Lindley Wood's son Edward (1881–1959), subsequently the 1st Earl of Halifax, recalled in his memoir an instance from a childhood Christmas when the 2nd Viscount made his gardeners pretend to be gypsies out to kidnap a young boy, and another occasion when his father burst into the room dressed as Gagool from *King Solomon's Mines*, which was being read to the children that Christmas.[14]

Not all aristocratic fathers performed the role of the delightful papa, however. At Lyme Park in Cheshire, Thomas Wodehouse, the 2nd Lord Newton (1857–1942), whose Edwardian Christmases were recorded in a memoir by his daughter Phyllis, is described as either disliking or pretending to dislike Christmas. The father's importance to the family Christmas is demonstrated by Wodehouse's influence on his elder children, who became a 'little blasé' about Christmas. Because of this attitude, Wodehouse's symbolic authority was disseminated amongst other prominent members of the household, including the upper servants. His wife opened the ball and led the servants' beef distribution, whilst the decoration of the Christmas tree and the presentation of gifts to estate employees was performed by the butler. During Christmas, fathers who were less than enthusiastic could also open up performative space for uncles to engage with children and become central to the intimate atmosphere. Phyllis described her Uncle William as entering 'most whole-heartedly into the Christmas revels. He loved them because he not only loved children but was a child himself at heart.'[15]

Wodehouse was particularly irritated by the term Santa Claus,[16] a name he would have heard with increasing frequency throughout his adult life, with the consequence that the housekeeper performed that role at Lyme Park in the Edwardian period.[17] The myth and iconography of Santa Claus was largely forged in America from elements of European ancestors, including Saint Nicholas of Myra, the English Father Christmas, the French *Père Noël*, the Dutch *Sinterklaas*, and the German *Christkindlein*, who through mispronunciation became known as Kris Kringle in the United States.[18] Aiding the dissemination of Santa Claus rituals were Clement Clarke Moore's poem, 'A Visit From St Nicholas', first published in 1822 (though not in England until 1891), and Susan Warner's *Carl Krinken: Or, the Christmas Stocking*, which was published three times in London in 1854 and 1855, and went into several later editions.[19] It is probable that knowledge of Santa Claus rituals was only slowly disseminated in England. Both Tosh and John Pimlott have emphasized Edwin Lee's contribution to *Notes and Queries* in 1879, in which he highlighted a 'Santiclaus' custom in the West country, as the first evidence of this occurring in England.[20] However, this evidence may have obscured a wider dissemination, since Santa Claus was mentioned in a *Daily Telegraph* editorial as early as 1873.[21] By the 1890s and 1900s, oral and autobiographical accounts of childhood Christmases indicate that elements of the Santa Claus myth had been incorporated into household Christmas practice, particularly amongst the middle classes. In many cases this caused considerable excitement and anticipation on the part of the child, as William Fryer Harvey (b. 1885) recalled:

> On Christmas Eve we hung up our stockings . . . and tried in vain to sleep. How slowly the hours dragged! There are steps on the landing and voices whispering. The steps retreat. Whoever the steps belong to has decided that it is not safe to enter yet. They are going to give us another half an hour. It is hard to go to sleep; it is harder still to keep awake. And then before we realise it the room is no longer black but grey, and hanging on to the bed is a beautifully distorted stocking with a fascinating bulge in the region of the calf . . . What time is it? . . . Half past six, because somebody is already moving about downstairs, and that means there is still thirty minutes before we can go into father's and mother's room to show them the contents of our stockings . . . Bertha [the nurse] comes in to light the gas and pandemonium breaks out as we examine at leisure the contents of the stockings.[22]

By its very nature, this account is ambiguous regarding parental involvement, but it seems to suggest that the performance of the Santa Claus role was undertaken by both parents, and not specifically the father. Another factor is the extent to which the child had an active knowledge of the source of largesse. Harvey implies that he knew that his parents were filling his stocking, though this impression may be attributable to hindsight. Because sources for the history of childhood tend be written about children rather than by children, the psychological world of the child is hard to recreate and interpret. Occasionally sources survive in which both father and child address the issue of Santa Claus. In December 1909 Auberon Kennard was aboard the SS Plassy, and wrote to his son Denys: [O]ur best love and wishes for a very happy Christmas. I wonder whether Santa Claus will come and put anything in your stocking.' This stratagem may have been employed to overcome the awkwardness of the separation of parent and child during a period that had become synonymous with family gatherings. The following year, Denys wrote to his grandfather stating, 'I had a very happy Christmas. Such a lot of toys and a big stocking from Father Christmas.'[23]

A common theme that emerges from recollections of childhood Christmases in the late-Victorian and Edwardian periods is the differentiation between gifts provided in stockings and other, larger forms of Christmas present, with the implication that stocking gifts were from Santa Claus but larger presents were from the parents. This raises questions concerning the wider symbolic purpose of Christmas presents for children. This was a period in which male breadwinner hegemony was the ideal, and it could be argued that giving Christmas presents to children represented a display of patriarchal authority: the gifts would not be materially reciprocated in any meaningful way, and the children's act of reciprocity lay in their continued performance of obedience and respect. It may have also been a mechanism for extracting emotional gratification from children. Elsewhere I have outlined a theory of 'Christmas intimacy', describing the heightened emotional state that the gathering of family and friends during the festive season can stimulate, and it became increasingly recognized in the nineteenth century that children were central to the unlocking of the Christmas festival's fullest emotional potential.[24] It should also be recognised that obedience and emotional gratification were closely bound up with one another. This scheme of gift exchange could be complicated, however, when considering the intermediaries that played a role in the gift relationship between father and child. First of all, even though she was economically and legally subordinate to her husband, the wife also demanded obedience and respect as a parent, as well as requiring a similar source of emotional gratification from her children through participation in domestic rituals. Whilst by no means universal, the acts of purchasing and wrapping Christmas presents were more likely to have been undertaken by mothers or other female relatives. Finally, there were also any number of unseen intermediaries in the gift relationship, including household servants, shop assistants, advertising agents, distributors, wholesalers and manufacturers.

These intermediaries may have served to dilute the symbolic potential of the Christmas present from father to child, leaving a psychological void which the modern Santa Claus icon attempted to fill. By having a separate stocking full of gifts from Santa Claus, the bonds between the child and the family patriarch could be reconnected. The mysterious and magical qualities of Santa Claus helped obscure the intermediaries in the gift process.[25] Yet the attempt was not entirely convincing. It made sense that the father would be physically transformed at Christmas, just as the domestic interior of the home was transformed with decorations, adding to the emotionally heightened atmosphere by creating an environment which was simultaneously different and the same. It should not automatically be assumed, however, that all fathers donned the grandfatherly beard and robes of Santa Claus, as evidence of fathers actually dressing up as Santa Claus is rare. It can also be argued that fathers did not need to dress up in order for the connection between paterfamilias and Santa Claus to be made clear in children's minds, since the usage of the term 'father' made the association plain. However, although the names Santa Claus and Father Christmas were used interchangeably in late-Victorian and Edwardian England, the former was far more common. Furthermore, there is evidence to suggest that children perceived Santa Claus to be a very remote being. Herbert Palmer, who grew up in Preston in the 1880s, remembered 'being puzzled about his ubiquitous personality, for he was even stranger than God (who, after all, was an unseen spirit) in being able to visit tens of thousands at the same time'. Consequently, Palmer tried to sleep with his head under the bedclothes, so as to avoid being startled and scaring Santa Claus away.[26]

For a considerable portion of the population, many elements of the Santa Claus ritual would have been beyond their means. Nevertheless, evidence does exist of working-class children receiving Christmas stockings in the late-Victorian and Edwardian periods. John Blake (b. 1899) and Grace Foakes, both of whom produced memoirs of Edwardian working-class childhoods in the 1970s, recorded having Christmas stockings. These accounts, however, do not make strong connections between fathers and the stocking ritual. Blake recalled that it was his mother who 'used to gather up little items . . . and some sweets and fruits and nuts, and wrap them up in fancy paper' for the Christmas stocking.[27] Foakes recalled that her father took her and her brother, significantly the two eldest children, to Smithfield Market on Christmas Eve, where he purchased a turkey, oranges, nuts and sweets. Foakes remembered that her father was in regular employment during this period of her life, and always saved for Christmas. In the evening of Christmas Day the family would gather round the fire whilst Foakes's father roasted chestnuts.[28] Whilst the thoughts and feelings of Foakes's father cannot be recaptured, what emerges in her narrative is a pride in her father's knowledge of the Christmas markets and in his ability to get the best goods he could afford. Equally important, though, is Foakes's account of the Christmas preparations that took place within the physical confines of the home. The task of preparing the food lay with her mother, leaving her father to indulge in the more playful and seasonal activity of roasting chestnuts, that symbolized a fatherly competence.

It is possible that Foakes's father was drawing upon a tradition of domesticated working-class manhood that went as far back, at least, as the Chartist movement and had become part of mainstream trade-union rhetoric by the 1870s.[29] It is also the case that there were some working-class families where domestic life was dominated by the mother, and the father was excluded from the 'emotional currents of the family'.[30] For example, none of the working-class interviewees involved in both Paul Thompson's *The Edwardians* and Thea Thompson's *Edwardian Childhoods* revealed any distinct roles in the family Christmas for their fathers.[31] Domestic violence could also be an issue, though not one restricted to the working classes alone. Jose Harris highlights how, in the late-Victorian and Edwardian periods, bank holidays became known as the 'saturnalia of beaten wives', whilst Robert Roberts described how 'Christmas or bank holidays could leave a stigma on a family already registered "decent" for a long time afterwards'.[32] Recalling her Edwardian childhood in the Potteries, Alice Towey noted how the Christmas period was characterized by fighting between her parents.[33]

There were some working-class children whose Christmas experience was framed almost entirely within philanthropic contexts, and by the Edwardian period there was the possibility of receiving Christmas provisions or presents from Santa Claus himself. Philanthropy was one of the contexts in which Santa Claus emerged as a public icon, and may have represented a civic form of paternalism. Charity had been a part of Christmas since the festival's earliest origins, and this charity in turn had always been concerned with the weakest and most vulnerable members of society, including children. In the mid-Victorian period, prevailing attitudes towards childhood decreed that the basic necessity of a child during the Christmas period included not only sustenance but also a Christmas present, and charity appeals began to appear in the press to foster this. In 1879, readers of the *Truth* were subscribing to an annual exhibition of toys to be distributed amongst children in London hospitals and workhouses.[34] By the Edwardian period, provincial newspapers had launched their own Christmas charity appeals. In 1909, for example, the *Yorkshire Evening Post* distributed 30,000 Christmas presents to poor children in Leeds. At the suggestion of readers, the *Yorkshire Evening Post* employed a Santa Claus to distribute the presents at various schools throughout Leeds, recognizing that Santa Claus was a useful intermediary in the gift relationship when the donor was necessarily anonymous.[35] This anonymity may have served to mask the power relationship inherent in what was ultimately a class-based form of paternalism. In *A Christmas Carol*, part of Scrooge's transformation relies on his whispered promise of philanthropy to the charitable collectors whom he had previously dismissed. The authority of the father depended upon fulfilling obligations in both the public and the private Christmas.[36]

Because of the logistics of the *Yorkshire Evening Post's* enterprise, Santa Claus was only able to appear in the motor car that conveyed the Christmas to the various schools.[37] The appearance of Santa Claus in a motor car within the logistics of mass philanthropy is suggestive of the way in which Christmas embraced elements of a self-consciously modern age, particularly in terms of new transport technologies.[38] From the 1890s onwards, images appeared in the public domain placing Santa Claus in the vanguard of these developments. In the 1890s, images of Santa Claus in airships begin to appear on Christmas cards, whilst by 1910 an illustration by C. T. Hill appeared in Cassell's *Trips to Storyland*, featuring Santa Claus flying an aeroplane.[39] Christmas cards depicting Santa Claus driving a motor car began to appear is about 1902. Sean O'Connell highlights how the technology and physical aspects of early motoring facilitated the alignment of the car with masculinity,[40] and may have acted as an affirmation of Santa Claus's masculine traits. Santa Claus's adventures in the modernity of new transport technologies were not without problems, however. An illustration by S. J. Cash in the 1904 edition of *Partridge's Children's Annual* featured Santa Claus attempting to fix a motor car that had broken down in the snow, whilst, in a 1907 edition of the *London Magazine*, Charles Crombie depicted Santa Claus crashing an airship whilst attempting to deliver Christmas presents. These representations used humour to 'send up' Santa Claus, betraying the sense in which he was an anachronistic throwback in the modern age. Whilst these images mainly conveyed a sense a fun, they may

Illustration 5 S. J. Cash, 'Why Santa Claus Was Late', *Partridge's Children's Annual*, 1904.
Courtesy of the Mary Evans Picture Library

also have hinted at a wider ambivalence concerning the modernity of new transport technologies.[41]

The iconography of Santa Claus rapidly penetrated the illustrated forms of advertising that came to dominate the national and provincial press from around 1900 onwards. Co-opted to sell a wide range of commodities, the commercial representation of Santa Claus drew upon a range of masculinities.

Illustration 6 Charles Crombie, 'Santa Crashing an Airship', *London Magazine*, Vol. 36, 1907.
Courtesy of the Mary Evans Picture Library

Chocolate manufacturers, particularly Cadburys, were keen to portray Santa Claus in domestic settings, handing gifts to children. As one advertisement from 1908 commented, 'Santa Claus has no gift that will delight the children more than Cadbury's Chocolates.'[42] In other advertisements, Santa Claus's rugged masculinity was confirmed by association with products such as Cope's Bond of Union tobacco and Marston's Burton ale.[43] However, Santa Claus's

Illustration 7 Williams' Shaving Soap, *Illustrated London News*, Christmas Number, 1901.
Courtesy of the J. B. Morrell Library

difficulties of existing in the modern world were again highlighted in humorous terms by an advertisement for Williams's shaving soap that appeared in the *Illustrated London News* in 1901. This advertisement recognised that Santa Claus's appearance was out of step with the fashionable modern man; the drastic remedy to this situation was to remove Santa Claus's beard.[44]

By the Edwardian period, Santa Claus was living both apart from and within the modern, commercial, urban world. In the discourse of philanthropy, Santa Claus resided in fairyland, the binary opposite of the urban squalor experienced by many poor children. In the late-Victorian and Edwardian periods, however, fairyland increasingly appeared once a year in the department stores. Bill Lancaster attributes the first Santa's grotto to J. R. Roberts' store in Stratford, London, in December 1888.[45] The creation of shopping arenas for children at Christmas spread rapidly in the 1890s and 1900s, and can only have aided the dissemination of Santa Claus rituals in society. They featured elaborate in-store displays that emphasized modernity. At one Leeds department store in 1905, a scene featured a snow-covered old English village at Christmas, interrupted by the appearance of Santa Claus in a motor car.[46] At Peter Robinson's, Oxford Street, in 1913, in what the *Lady's Pictorial* termed the 'children's dreamland realised', the spectacle began with a miniature recreation of Hendon Aerodrome, where airships delivered presents. This was followed by the 'children's dream train' which took them 'off on a tour through an enchanted land, and round a great golden Spanish galleon laden with treasures. A stop was eventually made at a castle door, which opened, disclosing none other than Father Christmas himself.'[47] Erika Rappaport has demonstrated how the department store was constructed as a feminized space in the nineteenth century.[48] Whilst the technological aspects of the in-store Christmas displays may have acted as a masculine stronghold in an otherwise feminine environment, there is the possibility that the department store Santa Claus complicated the performance of masculine fatherhood within the home. Whilst Christmas had given men a licence to play since at least the mid-Victorian period, a licence that signalled a masculinity at ease with domesticity and fathering, the masculinity offered by the department store Santa Claus became increasingly infantilized, owing much to the spirit of *Peter Pan*, 'the boy who never grew up', of which the theatre production became a central part of the West End's Christmas in Edwardian London.[49] Furthermore, the existence of a department store Santa Claus, that children could visit, loosened the connection between fathers and Christmas paternal benevolence.

According to press discourse, real fathers suffered the same mishaps in modernity as the visual representations of the Edwardian Santa Claus. Christmas shopping was another feature of this period's modernity, because of the large crowds it drew into urban environments, which again provoked an ambivalent response. Mark Connelly has drawn attention to the incident outside Swan and Edgar in London during Christmas 1909, when the police had to be called because crowds at the windows on the corner of Great Malborough Street and Regent Street had blocked the road, bringing traffic to a standstill.[50] Equally, the press often described the excitement provoked by the Christmas crowds. In 1908 the *Daily Mail* described the 'Christmas crowd' as 'the crowd that enjoys itself', whilst in 1910 the *Lady's Pictorial* commented on how women were 'not likely to abate one jot or tittle of the exquisite delight of Christmas shopping', where 'there [would] be just the same exciting and excited crowds in the shops'.[51] Often, however, this enthusiasm did not extend to the male Christmas shopper. Christopher Hosgood has demonstrated how the late-Victorian and Edwardian press perpetuated the notion that the male

Christmas shopper was hapless and hazard-prone, utterly incapable of choosing a suitable gift. Hosgood compares this with the representations of female Christmas shoppers, who were temporarily cast in a virtuous light, selflessly providing for their families, before their participation in the New Year sales restores the usual trope of the female shopper as vain, selfish and aggressive.[52] Whilst, as Hosgood argues, the gendered representation of Christmas shopping can be partially understood in terms of the Christmas tradition of role-reversal, the spectacular displays and crowded streets of the Christmas shopping environment were another central feature of the modern age, and men's travails in the field of Christmas shopping can be read as a critique of their performance in the developing consumer world.

The press discourse of men as failed Christmas shoppers is not evidence that men were bad at Christmas shopping, though the trope has been enduring enough to be fairly familiar to a twenty-first-century audience. It does, however, point to wider anxieties about men's role in the celebration of Christmas, and might be linked to prevailing models of masculinity at this time. At least for the middle classes, Tosh highlights the late-Victorian and Edwardian period as one in which the dominant model of masculinity was incompatible with domesticity, based upon homosocial association and a raised imperial consciousness.[53] Equally, other contemporary models of masculinity, such as the aspiring middle-class businessman, might have been ill-suited to fathering. A satirical article appearing in the *Daily Mail* in 1908 under the headline 'Holiday Problem, "What shall we do with the children?"', advised fathers to adopt a businesslike strategy of getting to know their children's tastes and interests.[54] This suggests, as Tosh does, a dominant code of manliness hostile to emotional expression.[55] The Edwardian period witnessed a flight from the celebration of Christmas in the home, with Alpine and Mediterranean holidays becoming increasingly popular over the Christmas period, and many families choosing either to stay in London hotels or seaside resorts or to eat Christmas dinner at London restaurants. Some press commentators considered what was perceived to be the traditional Victorian Christmas of the home to be incompatible with the demands of modern living, and in particular the problems of retaining reliable servants. This led some to question whether the family Christmas would survive. There is no doubt that the press exaggerated the extent to which the family Christmas was in danger, and it is also clear that the desire to escape it crossed gender lines, but it is likely that some of men's anxieties regarding Christmas derived from the incompatibility of a feminized Christmas and the prevailing models of masculinity, which were not always well attuned to dealing with father–child interaction.

It is hard to generalize about the role of fathers in the Victorian and Edwardian Christmas. Amongst men of all classes, it is possible to demonstrate a range of responses from active engagement to utter indifference. At times, father's responses to Christmas were aligned to contemporary masculinities based upon class, occupation and income, though masculine Christmas performances could vary significantly within any of these categories, and other factors, such as religion, could also be important. It is possible, however, to suggest certain trends. Each successive generation of fathers in the nineteenth and early twentieth centuries was more likely to make a greater effort to interact with their children during the Christmas season, as the stern evangelical father figure declined, and romanticized beliefs concerning the nature and meaning of childhood became increasingly popular. The emergence of Santa Claus rituals in the later part of the nineteenth century provided a greater structure for the father–child relationship in a festive context. It is no coincidence that the Santa Claus icon emerged at a time when the Christmas festival was perceived to have been feminized, and a dominant form of masculinity rejecting domesticity had coalesced around homosociality and imperial adventure. Santa Claus placed the father figure at the heart of the domestic Christmas as material provider. Yet Santa Claus was also a public icon of commerce and philanthropy. Any suggestion of a conflation of the role of real fathers and the myth and iconography of Santa Claus must be problematic. Yet, by the beginning of the twentieth century, it is possible to discern that Santa Claus's misadventures in modernity reflected a wider ambivalence concerning a father's role in the celebration of Christmas and modern society in general. As a Christmas shopper, the modern man was ruthlessly parodied as hapless and hazard-prone, while, in the domestic context, the emergence of Santa Claus unsettled the father's position as patriarch, disrupting the gift relationship. The emergence of Santa Claus not only shaped fathering practice during the Christmas festival but also reflected the shifting models of fatherhood and masculinity in Victorian and Edwardian England.

Notes

1. C. Dickens, *The Christmas Books* (Oxford: Oxford University Press, 1988), p. 90.
2. Gillis, *A World of Their Own Making*.
3. N. Armstrong, 'Christmas in Nineteenth-Century Britain and America: A Historiographical Overview', *Cultural and Social History*, 1 (2004). pp. 118–25.
4. L. Bella, *The Christmas Imperative: Leisure, Family and Women's Work* (Halifax, Nova Scotia: Fernwood, 1992), Ch. 3; W. B. Waits, *The Modern Christmas in America: A Cultural History of Gift Giving* (New York: New York University Press, 1993), Ch. 6; M. Di Leonardo, 'The Female World of Cards and Holidays: Women, Families, and the Work of Kinship', *Signs*, 12 (1987), pp. 440–53.
5. J. R. Gillis, 'Ritualization of Middle-Class Family Life in Nineteenth-Century Britain', *International Journal of Politics, Culture and Society*, 3 (1989), p. 230.
6. Tosh, *A Man's Place*, pp. 4–7, 88, 147–9, 195.
7. Tosh, *A Man's Place*, p. 88.
8. R. Morgan (ed.), *The Diary of a Bedfordshire Squire* (Bedford: Bedfordshire Historical Record Society, 1987), pp. 6, 12, 55, 78.
9. C. Burgoyne and D. A. Routh, 'Constraints on the Use of Money as a Gift at Christmas: The Role of Status and Intimacy', *Journal of Economic Psychology*, 12 (1991), pp. 47–69.
10. Defined by T. G. Crippen in the following terms: 'A quantity of raisins, or other dried fruit, is placed on a broad, shallow dish, brandy is poured over it, and set on fire. The company in turn snatch the fruit out of the blaze . . . It is usual to extinguish all the lights in the room while the game is in progress. T. G. Crippen, *Christmas and Christmas Lore* (London: Blackie and Son, 1923), p. 133.
11. Borthwick Institute for Archives, University of York, Hickleton Papers, A2.87, Charles Lindley Wood to Mary Wood, 25 December 1851, 26 December 1851.

12. Borthwick Institute for Archives, University of York, Hickleton Papers, A7.5, diaries of Charles Lindley Wood; A2.124, Agnes Wood to Charles Lindley Wood, December 1875, 10 December 1878, 6 December 1879; A2.125, Charles Lindley Wood to Agnes Wood, 11 December 1879.
13. Roberts, 'The Paterfamilias', p. 65.
14. Earl of Halifax, *Fulness of Days* (London: Collins, 1957), p. 32.
15. P. E. Sandeman, *Treasure on Earth: A Country House Christmas* (London: National Trust, 1995), pp. 13–14, 35, 37, 76, 97.
16. Because of the feminized 'a' at the end of Santa, Wodehouse believed that 'Santa means a woman'. Sandeman, *Treasure on Earth*, p. 97.
17. Ibid., p. 99.
18. R. Belk, 'Materialism and the Making of the Modern American Christmas', in D. Miller (ed.), *Unwrapping Christmas* (Oxford: Oxford University Press, 1993), pp. 77–8.
19. J. A. R. Pimlott, *The Englishman's Christmas: A Social History* (Hassocks: Harvester, 1978), pp. 115, 118–19.
20. Pimlott, *Englishman's Christmas*, p. 114; Tosh, *A Man's Place*, p. 148.
21. *Daily Telegraph*, 25 December 1873.
22. W. F. Harvey, *We Were Seven* (London: Constable, 1936), pp. 119–20.
23. Isle of Wight Record Office, Oglander Collection, OG/CC/22810, Auberon Kennard to Denys Kennard, 13 December 1909; OG/CC/2323, Denys Kennard to John H. Oglander, 31 December 1910.
24. N. R. Armstrong, 'The Intimacy of Christmas: Festive Celebration in England, *c.* 1750–1914', unpublished Ph.D. thesis (University of York, 2004).
25. Stephen Nissenbaum has argued that in nineteenth-century America 'Santa mediated magically between parents and child – between the buyer and the recipient of the gifts.' See S. Nissenbaum, *The Battle for Christmas* (New York: Vintage, 1997), p. 175.
26. H. E. Palmer, *The Mistletoe Child: An Autobiography of Childhood* (London: J. M. Dent, 1935), pp. 124–5.
27. J. Blake, *Memories of Old Poplar* (London: Stepney Books, 1977), p. 12.
28. G. Foakes, *Between High Walls: A London Childhood* (London: Shepheard-Walwyn, 1972), pp. 57–8.
29. A. Clark, 'The Rhetoric of Chartist Domesticity: Gender, Language and Class in the 1830s and 1840s', *Journal of British Studies*, 31 (1992), pp. 70–1; K. McClelland, 'Some Thoughts on Masculinity and the "Representative Artisan" in Britain, 1850–1880', *Gender and History*, 1 (1989), pp. 164–77.
30. J. Tosh, 'What Should Historians do with Masculinity? Reflections on Nineteenth-Century Britain', in R. Shoemaker and M. Vincent (eds), *Gender and History in Western Europe* (London: Arnold, 1998), p. 72; C. Chinn, *They Worked All Their Lives* (Manchester: Manchester University Press, 1988); Ross, *Love and Toil*.
31. P. Thompson, *The Edwardians: The Remaking of British Society*, 2nd edn (London: Routledge, 1992); T. Thompson, *Edwardian Childhoods* (London: Routledge, 1981).
32. J. Harris, *Private Lives, Public Spirit: Britain 1870–1914* (Harmondsworth: Penguin, 1994), p. 94; R. Roberts, *The Classic Slum: Salford Life in the First Quarter of the Century* (Manchester: Manchester University Press, 1971), p. 9.
33. Thompson, *The Edwardians*, pp. 306, 310.
34. G. Weightman and S. Humphries, *Christmas Past* (London: Sidgwick and Jackson, 1987), pp. 143–5.
35. *Yorkshire Evening Post*, 13 December 1909, 17 December 1909.

36. Dickens, *Christmas Books*, pp. 11, 87.
37. *Yorkshire Evening Post*, 13 December 1909.
38. Harris, *Private Lives, Public Spirit*, pp. 32–6.
39. J. Comfort et al., *Trips to Storyland: A Picture Book for Boys and Girls* (London: Cassell, 1910).
40. S. O'Connell, *The Car and British Society: Class, Gender and Motoring, 1896–1939* (Manchester and New York: Manchester University Press, 1998), pp. 44–5.
41. M. Daunton and B. Rieger, 'Introduction' in M. Daunton and B. Rieger (eds), *Meanings of Modernity: Britain from the late-Victorian Era to World War II* (Oxford and New York: Berg, 2001), p. 7.
42. *The Times*, 2 December 1908.
43. *Leeds Mercury*, 23 December 1902; *Daily Mail*, 4 December 1908.
44. *Illustrated London News*, Christmas Number, 1901.
45. B. Lancaster, *The Department Store: A Social History* (London and New York: Leicester University Press, 1995), pp. 23–4.
46. *Leeds Mercury*, 11 December 1905.
47. *Lady's Pictorial*, 22 November 1913.
48. E. D. Rappaport, *Shopping for Pleasure: Women in the Making of London's West End* (Princeton, NJ: Princeton University Press, 2000).
49. J. P. Wearing, 'Edwardian London West End Christmas Entertainments 1900–1914', in J. L. Fisher and S. Watt (eds), *When They Weren't Doing Shakespeare* (Athens, GA: University of Georgia Press, 1989), p. 236.
50. M. Connelly, *Christmas: A Social History* (London and New York: I. B. Tauris, 1999), pp. 194–5.
51. *Daily Mail*, 18 December 1908; *Lady's Pictorial*, 26 November 1910.
52. C. P. Hosgood, '"Doing the Shops" at Christmas: Women, Men and the Department Store in England, c. 1880–1914', in G. Crossick and S. Jaumain (eds), *Cathedrals of Consumption: The European Department Store, 1850–1939* (Aldershot: Ashgate, 1999).
53. Tosh, *A Man's Place*, Ch. 8.
54. *Daily Mail*, 18 December 1908.
55. Tosh, 'What Should Historians do with Masculinity?', p. 79.

Part 3

A Different Class?

Father's Pride? Fatherhood in Industrializing Communities

Andrew Walker

The dual role of the father as family man and provider has received surprisingly little attention and, despite recent work on the development and consolidation of the 'breadwinner ideal', there has been little examination of how this ideal was implemented and negotiated within distinctive workplaces.[1] This chapter argues that the sexual division of labour and the role of the father in the home and the workplace were contingent on particularities of specific occupations, labour markets and cultures, and that older patterns of gendered labour were not always displaced. Based on the Sheffield trades and the South Yorkshire mining industry, it explores the reproduction of the paternal role in the workplace, and the relationships between particular patterns of family labour and wider cultural discourses on fatherhood.

Feminist historians have argued that working men campaigned for breadwinner status as a means of securing patriarchal authority in the home and the workplace. Yet the 'complementary ideals of the male breadwinner who earned a family wage and the woman who devoted herself to full-time domesticity', as Sonya Rose points out, 'could not be realised by the majority of working-class married couples'. Even in years of relative prosperity, the households of most industrial workers continued to depend on the supplementary earnings of women and children.[2] The political consequences of the breadwinner strategy have been seen as divisive for the emergent labour movement, undermining the possibility of sexual equality at home and work. As Anna Clark contends, 'the fatal flaws of misogyny and patriarchy ultimately muted the radicalism of the British working class'.[3] At the same time, Judy Lown suggests that there was a coincidence of interest between the patriarchal demands of the male-dominated labour movements and the employment strategies of industrial paternalists who often modelled new lines of production 'on pre-existing family inequalities of status and authority which were presented as "natural" differences'. As an employer, for instance, the textile manufacturer Courtauld was 'motivated to act towards dependants as a father does to his wife, his children and his servants'.[4] In many large units of production where industrial paternalism prevailed, such as Courtauld's 'family firm', the authority and significance of the father figure were clearly articulated to workplace employees. Paradoxically, the 'metafather figure' of the industrial paternalist may have diminished the perceived importance and influence of working-class male householders; indeed, under such paternalist regimes, the adoption of the breadwinner ideal by many trade-unionists may have been a means of reasserting the equal status of male workers with employers and supervisors *as men*.

However, in the early nineteenth century, commentators on working-class family and domestic life tended to emphasize the influence of mothers – and especially the detrimental influence of errant mothers – rather than that of fathers. That mothers should take the principal role in bringing up children is made clear in a telling deposition to the 1843 Children's Employment Commission. A female member of the philanthropic Visiting and Bettering Society in Sheffield thought that there could not be any place where the morals of children of the poorer classes [were] worse than in Sheffield'. She attributed this delinquency to their mothers: '[They are] generally speaking idle and dissolute. They spend their time, whole mornings together, in smoking and gossiping and often in drinking. The children are often dreadfully neglected, dirty and immoral.'[5] No mention is made of the children's fathers. Elsewhere in the same report, children's lack of educational provision is attributed to the ill-advised consumption habits of mothers: 'One woman who was smoking told me that she could not afford to send her children to school . . . she did not appear to look upon education as anything but a superfluous ceremony whilst smoking was, she said, a comfort she could not do without.'[6] Despite the prevalence of the drunken father in temperance literature, linkages between fathers' intemperate spending patterns and their children's lack of education are scarce in the report.

Such claims of poor parenting were countered, however, in the same report. The wife of a Sheffield striker for a table blade forger stated: 'Neither of my boys have had any schooling at all: the eldest can read very well . . . his father has taught him a little on Sundays.'[7] While such testimony points to the range and diversity of working-class experiences of fathering and being fathered, Jelinger Symons's report on Sheffield to the Commission was, in the main, consistently condemnatory of the 'melancholy amount of immorality amongst the children of the working classes in Sheffield', concluding: 'Its proximate cause must be sought in the bad example of the parents.'[8] Whilst some witnesses attributed no blame for poor parenting to either mothers or fathers, a police superintendent stated, 'The habits of the adults confirm the children in their vices. The great bulk of the men habitually spend their evenings in the beer-houses which is a cause of the loose life of the younger branches of their families.'[9]

A recurring concern in the report was the independence enjoyed by children, caused by their tendency to work at an early age for adults outside their immediate family group.[10] Symons recommended that a 'limitation of children's labour' would meet 'with cordial approval . . . and by none would it be more vigorously abetted than by the respectable portion of the working classes themselves'.[11] Similar concerns were expressed in the textile industry in urban centres such as Bradford.[12]

When Sheffield's metal trades were examined again by the 1865 Children's Employment Commission, the report's author J. Edward White found that, since the earlier inquiry, 'on the whole, there seem[ed] to be good reason for hoping that there [was] a decided improvement.'[13] Nevertheless, White complained that excessive drinking prevailed, and that attendance at day-schools and Sunday schools was low, and echoed Symons's concerns about the early independence of children: 'great moral injury results ... from the high wages earned at an early age, making children independent of the control of their homes'.[14] However, these remarks were confined to the 'country districts' around Sheffield rather than to the town itself, where, it seems, children were more inclined to work alongside family members.[15] In Sheffield, the commissioners thought that self-control and self-government were being adopted effectively within the context of the family and reinforced at work and at home.

As White explained, 'most respectable men ... do not take their own or other people's children to work for them until the age of 12 or 13'.[16] Such sentiments were shared by working-class witnesses, such as a Sheffield file grinder who observed that the age of 14 was 'soon enough' to begin working in his trade: 'I have known some put to it by 10 years old but they don't ought. It's their own fathers have put these young ones to it and they (i.e. the boys) have been ruined before manhood.'[17] In this and other instances, the employment of young children was ascribed to the moral failings of the father.

A subtle shift can be detected, then, in the apportionment of criticism for poor parenting between the 1843 and 1865 Children's Employment Commissions. Whereas in 1843 liability for the poor moral and physical condition of children was attributed largely to mothers, by 1865 more attention was paid to the irresponsibility and failings of the fathers. This shift in emphasis is particularly significant in the context of the contemporaneous parliamentary debates about extending the franchise to working men in which, as Matthew McCormack and Helen Rogers show, reformers stressed working men's economic and social responsibilities as respectable, sober and prudent husbands and fathers.[18]

Two burgeoning areas of later nineteenth-century South Yorkshire form the focus of the remainder of this chapter. One is a Sheffield township, Attercliffe, in which the iron and steel industry was growing rapidly at the expense of the more traditional light metalworking industries, such as cutlery, and edge-tool-making. The other is situated about four miles south-east of Barnsley and comprises several coalfield settlements, notably Darfield and Wombwell. Examination of fatherhood in these occupational contexts enables scrutiny of the role of the father in particularly male-orientated employment cultures where opportunities for women were either severely restricted or, in the case of underground colliery working, prevented by law following the 1842 Mines Act.[19] In the 1881 census, in the mining settlements of Darfield and Wombwell, only 6.3 per cent of mining households accommodated women listed as working, compared to 23.4 per cent of non-mining households.[20] The 1881 census enumeration for Attercliffe also reveals the much lower employment of women in families headed by men employed in steelmaking: only 17.6 per cent listed as working compared to 31.8 per cent in households headed by men engaged outside the steel industry.[21] Though census data notoriously underrecorded female productive labour, the relative differences identified here are instructive.[22]

In such environments, it might be expected that 'traditional' gendered boundaries prevailed within the private, domesticated world of women and home, and the public, work-orientated world of males. In fact, plenty of evidence reveals that such gendered models were regularly contravened. Local newspaper reports of incidents in the coalmining district of Wombwell juxtaposed women's engagement in activities associated with the domestic realm with their sociability in the streets and even acts of public confrontation. Typical headlines included: 'Social life at Snape Hill',[23] 'A Departing Salute at Wombwell',[24] and 'Neighbourly Love. Another Episode of Washing Day.'[25] Following violent scenes on a colliery picket line in 1881, in which women were involved, the presiding magistrate declared that the women 'appeared to be more violent than the men . . . they disgraced their sex, which men liked to call the softer sex, by doing so . . . he could not apply a worse epithet to them than to say they were worse than a lot of Irishmen.'[26] Against a background in which bourgeois presumptions of gender roles appeared to be frequently challenged, even within households characterized by low rates of female employment outside the home, it is clearly misleading to assume that the delineation of parenting responsibilities conformed to the generally accepted middle-class ideal, in which mothers were responsible principally for rearing their offspring whilst the main duty of fathers was to provide for their families.

Both of these South Yorkshire districts grew significantly during the second half of the nineteenth century: Attercliffe's population from 4873 in 1851 to 51,807 in 1901; Wombwell's population from 1627 to 13,252 during the same period.[27] Much of this expansion was due to a significant influx of workers. In a sample from the 1871 census for Attercliffe, 75 per cent of household heads had been born outside Sheffield.[28] Shortly after the opening of the Wombwell Main colliery in 1855, 76 per cent of the eponymous settlement's 588 inhabitants had been born outside the parish.[29] The principal reason for moving was invariably to enhance the economic position of the migrants: rural incomers to Attercliffe from Lincolnshire and East Anglia in the 1870s could expect to earn 50 per cent more as labourers in the iron and steel works than by working on the land.[30] Many of the long-distance migrants to the South Yorkshire coalfield district came from existing coalfields, most notably from the Black Country.[31]

The mechanics of migration might point to important aspects of working-class fatherhood. The dislocating act of migration was not to be undertaken lightly, yet census data for the South Yorkshire coalfield suggests that those most inclined to move were young families. In Darfield in 1881, 76 per cent of the migrants from the Black Country were either young adults aged between 20 and 29 years or children aged under ten. Movement into the district of young families from other parts of Yorkshire, Nottinghamshire and Derbyshire was also relatively common.[32] The driving force behind this movement was often the household head, seeking to improve the lot of his family. Whilst migration was frequently prompted by particular local crises, the decision about where to move may have been informed by more long-term considerations on the part of the father, who might identify potential destinations which would offer work not just for himself but possibly (in the middle term) for his offspring and, especially in the case of coalminers, their sons. The experience of those living in Wombwell Main underlines this point. In 1861, five years after the colliery had opened, 76 per cent of its inhabitants had been born outside the parish and yet, over the next twenty years, residential persistence remained high as the owners of Wombwell Main colliery pursued a family recruitment policy.[33] Of 49 household heads at Wombwell Main in 1881 with co-resident working sons, only three heads had no sons working in the coal industry.[34]

Historians and historical sociologists have suggested that by the second half of the century the reconstitution of the family in the workplace through recruitment practices was rare, and, as a consequence, the authority of the male household head was diminished.[35] Others affirm that, by the mid-nineteenth century, although family recruitment within workplaces continued, family groups did not necessarily comprise units of production within the workplace. According to Michael Anderson, where children did work alongside their fathers, it was often for a relatively short period of time, after which the child became economically independent and obtained work elsewhere.[36] Much of the work on nineteenth-century family employment in the workplace has focused on the textile districts in the North-West of England. More recently, however, Marguerite Dupree found that in the Staffordshire Potteries sons tended to follow their fathers' occupations from adolescence and into adulthood, indicating a more prolonged period of fatherly influence over sons than Anderson's analysis of Preston's textile industry reveals.[37] The pattern of male family recruitment to be found in South Yorkshire coalmining districts and the Sheffield township of Attercliffe mirrors Dupree's conclusion that, to a disproportionate extent, sons followed fathers into particular industries. This suggests close economic links between fathers and sons, which could continue after the son's departure from the parental home.

Fatality lists from a mining disaster at Lundhill colliery near Wombwell in 1857, in which 189 men perished, make it clear that a familial approach to recruitment was employed: 62 of the 189 men who died were members of just 28 families.[38] Census enumerators' books for 1871, 1881 and 1891 in three districts from the Darfield and Wombwell area, where large numbers of mining employees lived, indicate the extent of familial working. The figures displayed in column 4 of Table 7.1 demonstrate the tendencies in each settlement of co-resident family members to be employed in the mining industry. In making this calculation, a weighting is given to the proportions of households in each settlement which are headed by mining employees and which accommodate other mining workers, and to the average number of sons who work alongside their fathers.

Whilst the employees of Wombwell Main appeared most likely to work alongside kinsfolk in the eponymous colliery, it seems that in each of the settlements studied, the incidence of familial employment was steadily rising over time. The circumstances of family employment discerned from the Mitchell Main colliery's underground workers' signing-on book suggest that the most

Table 7.1 Household familial employment in colliery settlements

	(1)	(2)	(3)	(4)
1871				
Lundhill	46	18	25	0.755
Low Valley	91	13	18	0.274
Wombwell Main	76	33	46	0.844
1881				
Lundhill	55	11	16	0.423
Low Valley	96	17	27	0.447
Wombwell Main	84	48	79	1.548
1891				
Lundhill	50	17	30	1.059
Low Valley	156	51	87	0.951
Wombwell Main	90	45	83	1.701

Key:
(1) = Number of households headed by colliery employees
(2) = Number of those households with sons working in mining
(3) = Number of sons working in mining
(4) = Total familial index; formed from the product of the figures in the following columns: (3)/(1) and (3)/(2).

Source: Census enumerators' books:
1871: Lundhill – Darfield e[numeration] d[istrict] 4; Low Valley – Darfield e.ds 1 and 5; Wombwell Main – Darfield e.d. 5.
1881: Lundhill – Darfield e.d 7; Low Valley – Darfield e.d. 2; Wombwell Main – Darfield e.d. 6.
1891: Lundhill – Darfield e.d 10; Low Valley – Darfield e.d. 3; Wombwell Main – Darfield e.d. 9.

common arrangement was for a youngster to be employed as a trammer alongside an elder relative, usually the father, who worked as a hewer.

Of the family groups examined in the signing-on book between 1881 and 1886, some 75 per cent of family groups comprised hewers and trammers.[39] During this period, hewers' names appear consecutively alongside several different relatives' names. In many of these instances, it seems likely that the hewer was working alongside sons. At Mitchell Main colliery, where the company was responsible for hiring, the practice of familial recruitment, especially drawing upon male relatives of hewers, was relatively common.

When this evidence is considered together with the census information conveyed in Table 7.1, a somewhat surprising finding emerges: during the later years of the nineteenth century, at a time when it has been assumed that large workplaces were increasingly the site of depersonalizing and routinizing work processes, in the collieries of the Darfield and Wombwell district the dependence upon personal relations in the workplace was, if anything, growing.[40] Similar patterns of familial recruitment occurred in the Sheffield iron and steel industries. This attracted the attention of the 1865 Children's Employment Commission where White concluded, 'It remains as it was formally the general custom for children and young persons to be employed not by the

Table 7.2 Family groupings in signing-on books: Mitchell Main Colliery

1881	Charles Allsopp, hewer, 26
	William Allsopp, trammer, 21
1888	Charles Allsopp, hewer, 29
	Henry Allsopp, trammer, 18
1881–6	William Hodgson, hewer, 52
	John Hodgson, trammer, 19
1887	William Hodgson, hewer, 58
	Walter Hodgson, trammer, 20
1881–4	David Dunn, hewer, 39
	John Dunn, trammer, 18
1884	David Dunn, hewer, 44
	William Dunn, trammer, 20
1885	John Dunn, hewer, 21
	Samuel Dunn, trammer, 16

Source: NCB524, Sheffield Archives

manufacturers, but as apprentices or servants to men who work by the piece or contract.'[41] Of all the households in Amberley Street, Attercliffe, enumerated in 1871 which contained two generations of working males and where the head was employed in the iron and steel industries, at least one male from the younger generation worked in the heavy industries.[42]

Speaking of his own firm's steel-rolling mills and forges in Attercliffe, E. F. Sanderson told the 1865 Commissioners, 'The boys are all employed by the men who are generally their own fathers.' This assertion was corroborated by a 15-year-old tilter: 'All the other boys in this building work for their fathers except one who works for his uncle like me.'[43] The reconstitution of the family in the workplace occurred not only in the small- and medium-sized iron and steel works but also in the largest. One employer stated approvingly, 'We like . . . for the convenience of the workers to keep the same sets working together as the food of a family can then be sent at the same time and altogether it suits their home arrangements better.'[44] The reasons for the encouragement of such family working may have been rather more wide-ranging than this explanation suggested. Sanderson noted, 'The men would not like so well not to have boys under them as men would be less obedient.'[45] Clearly, the employment of boys by workmen facilitated the upholding of discipline in the workplace. However, perhaps equally importantly, the household head's superiority in the workplace could reinforce his authority at home. Twelve-year-old George Ross, for instance, who worked under his father, a steel-roller at Firth and Son's steel manufacturers in Sheffield, was pressured by his father to study at home: 'Father sets me to it sometimes in the evening.'[46]

Thus far, it has been suggested that fathers encouraged co-resident sons to work alongside them, thereby allowing fathers some control over the flow of income into their households and reinforcing their parental authority through their positions within the workplace. Moreover, the occupational influence of fathers over their sons could extend beyond their offsprings' period of co-residency, as indicated by marriage records. Savage and Miles have examined intra-working-class mobility using marriage records, finding that the majority of sons remained in the same skill sector as their fathers throughout the Victorian period. This was particularly the case of sons whose fathers were employed in the skilled sector of the working class. In the period 1859–74, 75 per cent of sons remained in the same skill sector as their skilled fathers.[47] Marriage records for Attercliffe, Darfield and Wombwell reveal that not only were sons inclined to be occupied in the same skill sector as their fathers, but often they were employed in the same occupation as their fathers. Of the registered marriages in Christ Church, Attercliffe, between 1861 and 1871, where the groom's father was occupied in the cutlery or edge-tool trades, known as the light trades, no fewer than 60 per cent of the sons were also involved in these trades.[48] Only 13 per cent of the grooms whose fathers worked in the light trades were occupied in the iron and steel industries at a time when about four times as many workers were employed in Attercliffe in iron and steel than in the light trades.[49] Of 22 bridegrooms over the period 1861–71 who were occupied in the light trades, the bride's father of just one was engaged in the iron and steel industries.[50] When statistically far more job opportunities were available in the iron and steel industry, the occupational continuity across generations prevalent in the light trades suggests the influence of fathers in determining their sons' choice of occupation. However, this marked pattern of occupational generational continuity is not evident in the iron and steel industry: over the same period 66 per cent of bridegrooms occupied in the heavy trades had fathers who were not. This is perhaps partly explained by the relative newness of large-scale iron and steel production in the township, compared to the long-standing employment traditions associated with the light trades.[51]

Paralleling the differences in father–son occupational patterns in Attercliffe, sharp distinctions between colliery surface workmen and underground employees are discernible in the South Yorkshire coalfield. A 25-per-cent sample of marriages registered at Darfield and Wombwell parish churches for the periods 1850–85 and 1864–88 respectively indicates the tendency for underground colliery workers' sons to follow the occupational lead of their fathers.

Table 7.3 Familial colliery employment links discerned from marriage records where bridegroom is an underground mining worker, 1850–85 (%)

Occupation	Father	Father-in-law
Surface workers	2.6	3.1
Underground workers	47.5	38.7
Other	49.9	57.9
Total	100.0	100.0

Note: A total of 665 marriages were considered, of which 307 included bridegrooms who were recorded as colliery underground workers.

Sources: Darfield All Saints Parish Church, Parish Register, 1850–85; Wombwell St Mary's Parish Register, 1864–88.

Table 7.4 Familial colliery employment links discerned from marriage records where bridegroom is a surface worker at a coal mine, 1850–85 (%)

Occupation	Father	Father-in-law
Surface workers	21.9	9.6
Underground workers	6.8	21.9
Other	71.3	68.5
Total	100.0	100.0

Note: A total of 665 marriages were considered, of which 27 included bridegrooms who were recorded as colliery surface workers

Sources: Darfield All Saints Parish Church, Parish Register, 1850–85; Wombwell St Mary's Parish Register, 1864–88.

As shown in Table 7.2, of bridegrooms who were employed underground, 47.5 per cent of their fathers were similarly employed, whilst only 2.6 per cent of their fathers worked as colliery surface workers at a time when one third of colliery employment comprised surface work.[52] An examination of the Darfield and Wombwell Anglican marriage records reveals that where the father of the groom was an underground worker, more than nine times out of ten his son also worked below ground.[53] The same marriage records relating to men occupied in colliery surface work reveals a somewhat different picture. In instances where grooms were surface workers, as Table 7.4 demonstrates, only 21.9 per cent of their fathers also worked at the pit bank.[54]

Within some occupational groups which were considered to be skilled and which necessitated a period of formal or informal apprenticeship, a steady pattern of sons following their fathers' occupational footsteps can be discerned. Occupational links between fathers and sons, then, suggest the important economic relationship between these family members, which may imply the existence of close social relations as well, especially in the coal industry, where the networks of work and leisure were intimately connected. Amongst these groups of workers were hewers at the coalface, and cutlers and iron founders who prided themselves on their relatively high levels of workplace autonomy, defended in part through formal or *de facto* apprenticeships. Ideals of respectability were valued by such workers and demonstrated in their campaigns for active citizenship, not least through the formation of trade unions.[55]

The economic linkage between fathers and daughters is, inevitably, rather more difficult to establish. What does seem evident is that fathers' relationships with daughters could become geographically more distant than with sons. In the coalmining district of South Yorkshire during the later part of the century, employment opportunities for sons were relatively plentiful, as testified by an 1898 Wombwell School Board minute which noted ruefully that boys 'were able to get employment in the pits at 12 years of age' when they should have been at school.[56] In the case of adolescent girls, it is clear that for many it was necessary to obtain work away from home. Census enumerators' books for the Wombwell district indicate clearly the disproportionate absence of adolescent girls from the area.[57] The most persuasive explanation for this is the tendency to put out miners' daughters into domestic service, a phenomenon which continued into the 1930s, as Winifred Foley's autobiography memorably indicates.[58]

Even in the households of skilled workers, it was always advisable to be reliant on more than one source of income. In many of the areas examined here, this generally occurred once offspring reached the age when they could be found employment. The importance of the family economy, with significant income being contributed by a number of household members, persisted within the homes of skilled labourers largely without compromising the status of the father figure. This was achieved partly through the non-public, domesticated earning strategies of daughters and wives. Perhaps more clearly, however, it was accomplished through the influence of fathers over sons in the securing of employment, with sons often working as *de facto* apprentices to their fathers, either employed directly by them in the case of Attercliffe's light trades and in the skilled employment within iron and steel works, or indirectly through family-friendly employers such as Wombwell Main colliery.

Far from patterns of employment threatening the family form, and indirectly the role of the father figure, as suggested by Neil Smelser and to a lesser extent Anderson, it seems, in the case of skilled labour at least, that links between fathers and sons at the workplace in the later nineteenth century continued to be of considerable significance, both economically and no doubt socially and culturally, in industrial South Yorkshire. Intergenerational occupational links and the championing of the male breadwinner are emphasized in one instructive local newspaper report in 1891. An account of a dinner enjoyed by family groups and organized at Wombwell Main by the miners' union branch reports how union leaders addressed boys sitting alongside their fathers. As one official urged, he 'hoped they would get the lads in the union'. The speech of another official memorably describes how the ideal of husband and father as breadwinner and provider was mobilized by working-class movements: 'He should like to impress upon wives to keep their homes nice and clean. Make their homes so that their husbands will feel pleasure in coming home to them when they have done their day's work.'[59] The notion of the family wage, the centrality of the home, the significance of the father's role within it, and his influence in regenerating the workforce, all feature prominently in the rhetoric of working-class organizations within later nineteenth-century South Yorkshire.

Notes

1. In studies of working-class life, fatherhood is often elided with the role of husband, as in Carl Chinn's *Poverty Amidst Prosperity* (Manchester: Manchester University Press, 1995) where the index refers interest in 'fathers' to 'husbands'.
2. Rose, *Limited Livelihoods*, pp. 15, 16, 78.
3. Clark, *The Struggle for the Breeches*, p. 271.
4. Lown, *Women and Industrialization*, p. 98.

5. Parliamentary Papers (hereafter PP), Children's Employment Commission, 10, 1843, p. e8.
6. Ibid., p. E31.
7. Ibid., p. e24.
8. Ibid., p. E13.
9. Ibid., p. e7.
10. Ibid., p. E14.
11. Ibid., p. E32.
12. Ittmann, *Work, Gender and Family in Victorian England*, pp. 148–9.
13. PP, Children's Employment Commission, 4th Report, Volume XX, 1865, p. 10.
14. Ibid., p. 10.
15. Of fourteen children referred to in the 1865 report of children's employment at Sheffield grinding wheels, seven were reported to work alongside family members – four fathers, two grandfathers and one uncle; in seven cases no details were given. Ibid., pp. 15–22.
16. Ibid., p. 10.
17. Ibid., p. 17.
18. See also McClelland, 'England's Greatness', in Hall et al., *Defining the Victorian Nation*.
19. J. Humphries, 'Protective Legislation, the Capitalist State and Working-Class Men: The Case of the Mines Regulation Act', *Feminist Review*, 7, (1981), pp. 1–33; and A. John, *By the Sweat of Their Brow* (London: Croom Helm, 1980).
20. 1881 census: Darfield enumeration district 1. Of 201 households not headed by a male occupied in the coalmining industry, 47 contained women recorded as employed. Only 10 of the 158 mining households contained women recorded as working.
21. These figures are derived from the consideration of a sample of streets in Attercliffe township, comprising Amberley Street, Heppenstall Lane, Swallow Row and Washford Road. The census data is drawn from 1881 Darfield enumeration districts 3, 5, 8, 10 and 16. Fifteen of 85 households headed by a male employed in steel-making accommodated at least one recorded working female; 27 of 85 households not headed by a male steelworker housed female workers.
22. S. Rose, *Limited Livelihoods*, pp. 80–2; and E. Higgs, 'Women, Occupations and Work in Nineteenth-Century Censuses', *History Workshop Journal*, 23, (1987), pp. 59–80.
23. *Barnsley Chronicle*, 16 March 1867.
24. Ibid., 17 June 1871.
25. Ibid., 24 January 1891.
26. Ibid., 5 March 1881.
27. D. Hey, *A History of Sheffield* (Lancaster: Carnegie, 1998), p. 147; W. Page (ed.), *The Victorian History of the County of York* (London, VCH, 1913), Vol. 3, pp. 542–4
28. Census Enumerator's Book (hereafter CEB), Attercliffe enumeration district 5, 1871. A total of 115 of 152 households surveyed had heads born outside the borough of Sheffield.
29. CEB, Darfield enumeration district 5, 1861.
30. The wages of a steel labourer were reported as 21 shillings in 1872 by 'one of the largest steel manufacturers in Sheffield', in E. Young, *Labor in Europe and America* (1875), p. 295. Fourteen shillings was the average weekly wage of 'the farm labourer of the Wisbech District' in Cambridgeshire, according to *The Spectator*, 18 January 1873.

31. G. Barnsby, 'The Standard of Living in the Black Country During the Nineteenth Century', *Economic History Review*, 24, 2, (1971), pp. 220–39; R. Lawton, 'Population Movements in the West Midlands, 1841–61', *Geography*, 43, (1958), pp. 172; and M. Rowlands, *The West Midlands from A.D. 1000* (London: Longman, 1987), p. 256. In 1871, 79 of 369 males resident in the colliery community of Low Valley had been born in the West Midlands. CEB, Darfield enumeration district 1, 1871.
32. In 1871, 71 West-Midlands-born men and women aged 20–9 years and 54 children aged under ten years lived in Snape Hill, Darfield village and Low Valley, constituting 76 per cent of the total of migrants from Shropshire, Staffordshire, Warwickshire and Worcestershire in the district; CEB, Darfield enumeration district 1, 1871.
33. Of 407 persons resident at Wombwell Main in 1881 aged ten years or over, 172 had been resident in the settlement in 1871. CEB, Darfield enumeration district 5, 1871 and Darfield enumeration district 6, 1881.
34. CEB, Darfield enumeration district 6, 1881.
35. N. Smelser, *Social Change in the Industrial Revolution* (London: Routledge and Kegan Paul, 1959).
36. M. Anderson, 'Sociological History and the Working-Class Family: Smelser Revisited', *Social History*, 3, (1976), pp. 317–34.
37. M. Dupree, *Family Structure in the Staffordshire Potteries, 1840–1880* (Oxford: Oxford University Press, 1995), especially pp. 157–67.
38. *Barnsley Times*, 28 February 1857.
39. Of 229 family groups – identified as such by the fact that the individuals shared the same surname and signed on consecutively – 173 groups comprised hewers and trammers. NCB524, Sheffield Archives, Mitchell Main signing-on books, 1881–6.
40. See H. Braverman, *Labour and Monopoly Capital* (New York: Monthly Review Press, 1974).
41. PP, Vol. XX, 1865, p. 3.
42. In Amberley Street in 1871, 23 men in 9 such family households were employed in the iron and steel industries. CEB, Attercliffe census enumeration districts 3 and 4.
43. PP, Vol. XX, 1865, p. 33.
44. Ibid., pp. xvi–xvii.
45. Ibid., p. 33.
46. Ibid., p. 27.
47. M. Savage and A. Miles, *The Remaking of the British Working Class, 1840–1940* (London: Routledge, 1994), p. 35.
48. From the Christ Church, Attercliffe, marriage records, 1861–71, of 23 marriages in which the bridegrooms' fathers were occupied in the light trades, 14 of the sons were also occupied in these trades. Only 3 of the 23 grooms had jobs in the iron and steel industries.
49. Census returns for four sample streets in 1871 (Swallow Row, Washford Road, Heppenstall Lane and Amberley Street) reveal that of 125 occupied males, 25 worked in the light trades and 100 were employed in the iron and steel industries. CEB, Attercliffe enumeration districts 3, 4, 5 and 9, 1871.
50. From the Christ Church, Attercliffe, parish records, 1861–71.
51. From the Christ Church, Attercliffe, marriage records, 1861–71, of 53 grooms occupied in the iron and steel industries, 35 had fathers employed in other trades.
52. The figures are based upon a 25-per-cent sample of marriages recorded in Darfield parish church, 1850–85 and Wombwell parish church, 1864–88. The number of grooms who were employed as mining workers below ground totalled 307, of

whose fathers, 8 were employed as mining surface workers and 146 were also employed below ground.
53. From a 25 per cent sample of marriage records recorded in Darfield and Wombwell parish churches between 1850–85 and 1864–8 respectively, where the bridegroom's father was employed as an underground mining worker, 119 grooms were also employed below ground and 10 grooms were employed as surface workers.
54. The figures are based upon a 25-per-cent sample of marriages recorded in Darfield parish church, 1850–85 and Wombwell parish church, 1864–88. The number of grooms who were employed as mining surface workers totalled 37, of whose fathers 8 were also surface workers.
55. See S. Pollard, *A History of Labour in Sheffield* (Liverpool: Liverpool University Press, 1959), pp. 72–7 on the development of trade unions in the cutlery industry and light trades. See F. Machin, *The Yorkshire Miners: A History* (Barnsley: National Union of Mineworkers), pp. 277–92 on the formation of a South Yorkshire Miners' Association.
56. SB6/6, Barnsley Archives, Wombwell School Board Minutes, 6 June 1898.
57. In 1881, of 410 people enumerated between the ages of 10 and 19 years in Snape Hill, Low Valley and Wombwell Main, only 149 (36 per cent) were female; CEB, census enumeration districts 1, 2, 5 and 6.
58. W. Foley, *A Child in the Forest* (Cheltenham: Thornhill Press, 1991).
59. *Barnsley Chronicle*, 7 November 1891.

8

'First in the House': Daughters on Working-Class Fathers and Fatherhood

Helen Rogers

Conventionally, and in contrast to memoirs by mothers, autobiographies by Victorian men disclose little about their experiences of parenthood, though they often detail their relationships with parental figures in childhood.[1] Consequently, our understanding of the father–child bond in the nineteenth century has been refracted through the perspectives of sons and daughters and, above all, through the accounts of the antagonistic filial bond foregrounded in early twentieth-century psychology, fiction and memoirs. Modernism's debunking of the Victorian paterfamilias can be read as a revolt of gender and of generation and as evidence of 'the end of paternal deference' and 'the flight from domesticity' that John Tosh detects from the 1870s onwards.[2] Yet the authoritarian and reticent Victorian papa characteristic of modernist writing bears the traces of a historically distinctive family form – that of the professional, mercantile and well-to-do middle classes. Though the father figured very differently in other social classes, few scholars have responded to Carolyn Steedman's call for 'a reading of history that reveals fathers mattering in a different way from the way they matter in the corpus of traditional psychoanalysis [and] the novels that depict the same familial settings'.[3]

This chapter turns to alternative constructions of the filial bond in the writings of three women from the working and lower-middling classes in the second half of the nineteenth century. Unlike the fraught filial relationships depicted by 'the moderns', their writings emphasized mutuality between family members, and parents as exemplary role models for their children. They found an audience for their ideas in the mid-Victorian popular periodicals which were so influential in the promotion of cross-class ideals of self-improvement, and which aimed above all at the working man. As Terri Sabatos notes in her chapter, the working-class father was becoming the subject of considerable anxiety in this period, as male alcoholism, desertion, domestic violence and indigency were seen to mark off the undeserving poor from the respectable classes, defined increasingly by the independent status of the male householder and family man.⁴ These concerns were shared by the writers here who, while they engaged with mid-century discourses on the family and gender respectability, also eulogized older conceptions of the labouring family. In the early century, social and political radicals had sought to defend the integrity of the artisanal 'cottage economy' from the onslaught of mechanized production by calling for the 'family wage' that would enable a man to keep his wife and children in the home. According to some feminist historians, the appeal to a 'natural family order' before the factory system was little more than a myth and masked the history of women's productive work, while calls for the breadwinner wage strengthened men's authority in the workplace and diminished the earning power of women.⁵ But for the writers examined here, the 'cottage economy' was no mere rhetorical device, for it spoke to their experience of the artisanal household; they sought to adapt that model for the newly established manufacturing communities. Tracing their delineation of the paternal role in prescriptive writing and autobiographical recollections, this chapter investigates how fathers *mattered* to them. Yet precisely because the father mattered, he was more easily rendered as an ideal: their texts are as illuminating in what they do not, or cannot, say about the father.

Janet Hamilton (1795–1873), the daughter of agricultural workers, was born in the village of Carshill in Lanarkshire. From the age of seven, she kept the house, spun yarn, and learned to work the tambour from her mother, an occupation she maintained throughout her life. Hamilton's father established a shoemaking business and at the age of 13 or 14 she married his apprentice and raised ten children in Coatbridge, near Edinburgh. Taught to read by her mother, Hamilton only learned to write in her fifties when the first of her many essays, sketches and poems were published in Cassell's *Literature for the Working Man*.⁶ In the first half of the century, Coatbridge grew from a parish with under 6000 inhabitants, employed mainly in spinning and weaving, to one of Scotland's principal industrial towns built especially on iron-smelting.⁷ Addressing the manners and morals of the new working class that she saw emerging around her, Hamilton's writing sought to instil the values of the pious, Presbyterian, peasant household exemplified by her ancestral family. Her anecdotes of Scottish peasant life drew on family histories, many of which were related by her grandfather who lived in her mother's home before his death in 1800, aged 97. By reaching back to the pre-industrial era, these stories emphasized familial obligation that extended beyond kin: Hamilton's grandfather had provided a home for an orphan girl, and when later she was seduced and abandoned by her employer's son, he welcomed the mother and illegitimate child back into the family.⁸

In Hamilton's youth, no householder who neglected family worship was considered 'respectable'. But the labour discipline of the new manufacture placed pressure and constraints on working-class families, especially since men's work now took them away from their homes, leaving women as 'wife, nurse, and servant-of-all-work'. This lent Hamilton's conception of fatherhood an acute consciousness of class difference. Where the wealthier classes could 'with advantage to their children, transfer their parental responsibilities' to servants and tutors, working men were compelled to spend most of their time at work, even on the sabbath, and thus their time for fathering was tightly – and for Hamilton, unfairly – restricted. Consequently, fatherhood was exercised most fully on the sabbath: 'Working-father – this is not only God's day, but it is also peculiarly yours.' He should lead family prayer, read from the Scriptures and take the children to church while mother nursed the baby and made dinner. Domestic labour was shared more equally on the sabbath, when father was at rest from paid work. Returning from church, mother should question her children on the sermon and, after dinner, father should take his family for a ramble, carrying his baby and instructing his children in the bounty of God's nature. While mother put baby to bed, the children would repeat their school lessons to father who, finally, should read from the family bible: 'What a blessed home is this, however lowly, especially when the father is actuated by the same spirit and motives as the mother!'[9]

Though Hamilton saw parenting as a gendered activity, she did not exempt men from domestic labour and she expected her sons as well as her daughters to perform household work before they were old enough to learn a trade. Hamilton positioned both spouses as 'heads of families', implying a partnership in which they were responsible to their children, their God, and to the public purse that bore the cost of parental neglect. While viewing parents as joint heads of household, Hamilton's conception of Christian partnership was framed by the father's 'impartial' role as judge and arbiter of rewards and punishments.[10] In her temperance writings she compared this Protestant and patriarchal model of paternal authority with male delinquency, manifested in drunkenness, domestic violence and paternal neglect – a pervasive theme of contemporary temperance literature.[11]

Though the upright artisan was expected to attend to his family, Keith McClelland suggests that radical reformers were keen to establish homosocial spaces away from the home where men could express respectable masculinity.[12] For many philanthropists, however, rational recreation and amusement were the means of securing working people's attachment to the home and family in place of the political meeting and the public house, an ideal shared by Hamilton.[13] She was forthright in her condemnation of the previous generation of political reformers, arguing that the agitators of 1819 had been men careless of family as well as property.[14] Though a supporter of John Bright, the Liberal champion of manhood suffrage in the 1860s, she did not refer directly to contemporary working-class political movements but instead advocated the moral and intellectual advancement of her class primarily through education.[15] While promoting mechanics institutes, she insisted that self-improvement should not be acquired at the expense of family obligations. In particular, the content and delivery of education had implications for the conduct of fathers. Though practical training in engineering and mechanical sciences would improve a man's 'position both in his family and in society', Hamilton warned against focusing exclusively on the 'education of the mind' and 'neglecting the culture of the heart': 'But nowhere is the want of the culture of the heart so apparent as in one who is a husband and father.' If a father neglected his home, his children would not seek his kisses, his wife would become 'awe-struck and constrained before him' and neighbours would comment on how the mechanics institute made him 'a proud, sulky fellow'. Self-help was compatible, therefore, with the mutual advancement and thorough education of both sexes, though in ways differentiated by gender. Expanding Pope's proposition that 'the proper study of mankind is man', Hamilton instructed that 'the proper study of womankind is woman'. Her own literary pursuits were supported by her husband, who procured material from local libraries to satisfy her voracious appetite for reading.[16] The influence of evangelical strictures on paternal duty and affection in the delineation of a middle-class domestic manliness in the early nineteenth-century has been noted, but Hamilton's insistence on the cultivation of men's hearts – a sentimental discourse often reserved for women – suggests both the attractions of such discourses beyond evangelicalism and the middle class, and their adaptation within labouring communities.[17]

Where Hamilton rooted working-class improvement in the family home, the schoolmistress Mary Smith (1822–89) believed, by contrast, that self-help and mutual instruction would be the basis of a regenerated public and civic life, open to both sexes. As a teacher and activist, she contended that men and women of all classes had to be educated for duty and independence, virtues originally instilled in her by her father, 'the best man whom I have ever known'. Unlike Hamilton, she rejected marriage as incompatible with her desire to become a poet and, in her early twenties, left her paternal home in Oxfordshire to support herself as a governess and later as a teacher in Carlisle.[18] In defining herself as an independent working woman and a reformer, Smith continued to view her father as her most important role model and it was his manly qualities, demonstrated in public and in private, that she sought to promote among the working men of Carlisle.

The daughter, like Hamilton, of a shoemaker, Smith grew up in an artisan household in the village of Cropredy, where women as well as men were valued as vital contributors to the family economy. Her mother died when Smith was eight years old – an instructive lesson in the importance of women's productivity, for the family never recovered the loss of her 'superior business skills' as a grocer. Though he married his housekeeper, who became a devoted wife and stepmother, Smith's father William remained her formative parent.[19] In the shoemaker's home, the worlds of labour and of parenting and nurture were not clearly segregated as they were supposed to be in the middle-class house. Listening to the journeymen in William's workshop, Smith acquired her earliest education; this was where she 'soon learned the difference between man and man'. On winter evenings she held the lamp for her father while he cut leather and talked to her about her schooling: 'Blessed times they always were, full of instruction!' Their relationship was intimate and affectionate: he carried Smith home from dame school on his shoulders, full of 'childish talk to his little "wench"'.[20] William encouraged her passion for literature, finding her books and taking her part when his wife complained that her daughter neglected chores for reading. He took an active interest in her schooling, persuading her teacher to give his child lessons in arithmetic and, as a devout member of the Independent Baptists, reprimanded the teacher when his daughter was made to copy the church catechism: '"Popery! Popery! Please don't let the child learn this!"', he wrote in her school book. Smith partly acquired her love of verse from her father, who composed rhymes with his children. He also sought, to no avail, to protect his daughter from the contaminating influence of popular culture: against his instruction, she listened to the washerwoman's songs which were to be the other early influence on her verse. In 1860, the publication of Smith's first volume of poetry was marred for her by her father's recent death – 'the only eyes which would have looked kindly on my verses' – and she consoled herself by paying for his gravestone, inscribed with two of her own lines.[21]

Tosh suggests that, in middle-class families, fathers often permitted themselves more openly tender relationships with their daughters than with their sons, for sons had to learn the self-control and emotional distance that would enable them to follow in their fathers' footsteps, carry on his name and, often, his line of business or profession. The closeness of such father–daughter relationships was predicated, however, on the assumption that the daughter might remain within the family home as carer for her parents, or would re-enact the filial bond in her husband's house as a devoted and dutiful wife.[22] But while duty-bound on both sides, Smith's relationship with her father was based on a friendship in which her father recognized her fierce sense of individuality, speaking to her 'rather as a woman than as a girl; quite aware of [her] odd ways'.[23] He may have sought in his daughter the affinity he had enjoyed with her mother; certainly their filial relationship contained many of the elements of the rational companionship that contemporary feminists believed should underlie the marital union. Notable figures in the Victorian women's movement shared the political and intellectual commitments of their fathers who initiated them into the worlds of philanthropy or reform.[24] With her father, Smith likewise attended sermons by Nonconformist divines and he took her to hear the celebrated anti-slaver William Knibb: a defining moment in the life of a girl who was to commit herself to emancipationist principles.[25]

William's public conduct provided Smith with an enduring model of integrity and authority: 'One of the first things I discerned in my early childhood was, that my father was not like other men'. Neither drinking, swearing, nor getting into 'towering passions', he was 'at all times, a sober, sensible, gentle, and patient man.' He was hounded by village youths who mocked dissenters as 'queer folk', but his forbearance and 'calm and determined manner' always subdued the 'rough multitude'. Smith saw her father's Christianity – based on brethrenship and fellowship – as egalitarian and democratic, and contrasted his embodiment of Christian manliness with the autocratic power and privilege of the state church and its village incumbent, a man she vehemently resented for badgering her father to baptize his children. Yet Smith could not replicate her father's equanimity. She delighted in refusing to curtsey to the Anglican lady school visitors who treated her as an 'alien': 'I did not learn this from my father, who ever spoke in the most respectful and conciliatory manner to any of them.' Though she continued to see her father as an exemplary figure, she did not defer absolutely to his authority; rather, her dissent moved beyond her father's Nonconformist quietism to include political radicalism. Yet she dared not confess to her father that she had attended a rally at the height of the early Chartist agitation to hear Henry Vincent, a lecturer who appealed to Chartist women by urging them to raise their children as 'little democrats'. Quitting Oxfordshire involved separation and independence from her father, who was reluctant for her to leave. In 1842 she won his permission to go to Westmorland for three months, though she felt she would never fully return.[26] The extent of Smith's subsequent political and cultural activism in Carlisle, remarkable for a woman of her class, was probably achieved because of her distance from her paternal home.

Until her death in 1889 Smith participated in the radical-liberal, Nonconformist and improvement circles in Carlisle, giving readings to working men, lecturing poor women on the moral and physical training of children, and providing educational classes for factory girls. Working behind the scenes with the 'élite' of the city's working men in the temperance movement, the Liberal Club and the Committee of Non-Electors, Smith campaigned for the enfranchisement of the working man. The promotion of domestic manliness became a feature of working-class independence in Carlisle as reformers repudiated the militancy of earlier popular protest, as illustrated by an article on 'domestic felicity' in a periodical by and for the city's working men which, in 1863, described the good family man as he

> who takes pains to cultivate his moral and intellectual nature, to improve at the same time his social condition, and to make the comfort and welfare of his wife and family his constant care, [who thus] will reap the richest reward that a beneficent providence can bestow, or a human enjoy. Though he may not be appreciated by the world, he has a little world of his own where his good qualities pass at their full value.[27]

In a pamphlet written for the Liberal Party during the 1868 General Election, the first held under the expanded franchise, Smith invoked the same scene of proletarian 'domestic felicity' under the fictional guise of Mrs Susan Trueman, wife of a Methodist working man:

> I've a lot of little 'uns, and the great aim of Trueman and myself is to keep them decent and give them a decent education, and very hard we both work for it – I at home and he at the shop – and, bless him he's a good man, he neither takes beer nor 'bacco, nor ever spends a farthing wrongfully, but brings it home to me, just keeping a few pence for a paper or two which he sits by the fire and reads at nights.

Exhorting the women of Carlisle to take an interest in the election, Mrs Trueman has acquired her liberalism from her husband, a good father who patiently nurses the baby while she composes her letter. Despite Smith's commitment to the political equality of the sexes, she envisaged the husband and father presiding over his family; yet if the home 'belonged' to the male householder, as in many working-class communities, Mrs Trueman held the family purse.[28] For Smith, as for Hamilton, the ideal family was modelled on partnership and complementarity.

Mrs Trueman's home-spun truths about domestic and civic duty were depicted by Smith as the product of rational companionship within the

Christian family. Yet, unlike her fictional alias, Smith remained single to pursue her ambition of becoming a poet. She was deeply conscious of the precarious position of self-supporting women. As for many working-class children whose parents arranged their early employment, her father brokered her move to Westmorland as companion to a Baptist minister's wife, but he overlooked the terms of her employment. Conscious of his years of financial difficulties, Smith wrote cheerfully to her father, concealing her treatment by these employers as little more than a very poorly paid servant.[29] In her teaching she strove to show how a woman could be 'a lady without money' and she endeavoured with some limited success to extend rational improvement to women. In 1869, and with support from working men and temperance activists, she formed the Carlisle Women's Suffrage Society. While she reminded men who had recently won their enfranchisement to support women's political rights, like many contemporary reformers she appealed to men's paternalism by calling on 'fathers of families' and 'brothers of pure, loving sisters' to guard women without protection, especially those driven by desertion and destitution to prostitution – a demand that she and other activists repeated in the campaign against the Contagious Diseases Acts.[30]

Despite insisting on female independence, in her autobiography, written at the end of her life, Smith deferred to the ideal of filial duty:

> But whatever I did, I always felt that my father was right, and what he did not allow or approve was wrong . . . and perhaps the real worth of religion to nations as well as to individuals, might be found in the true love of the family. In fact, true religion constrains loving allegiance, as it did in our home; all of us being united in common love toward our father.[31]

For Smith, as for many mid-Victorian feminists, the recognition of paternal authority was compatible with commitment to women's attainment of full selfhood, including citizenship. Likewise, the Baptist teacher and writer, Marianne Farningham, née Hearn (1834–1909), promoted the education and welfare of girls and women, yet contended that the growing focus on individual rights risked undermining the father's rightful position as head of household. In 1869, when Smith established the Carlisle Women's Suffrage Society, when John Stuart Mill published *The Subjection of Women*, and when a bill giving women voting rights in local elections went through Parliament, Farningham expressed reservations about the prevalence of rights-based discourses in her Sunday School book *Home Life*: 'We hear a great deal about women's rights, but there are some men's rights which fare worse still, among which are too many fathers'.' The 'great fuss in the world about everyone having "his rights"', she implied, promoted self-interest at the cost of reciprocal obligation that should underpin family relationships. Echoing the warnings of conduct writers such as Mrs Ellis that too many wives and daughters neglected the father's welfare (see Introduction), Farningham regretted that too often 'he has scarcely a voice in family affairs'. 'The most important person in the household', she reminded her readers, 'is the head of the family' and though his work meant he spent the least time at home, their own comfort depended on the 'breadwinner's' wages and 'on that active brain and those busy hands'. The father should be consulted in all family matters, his pleasure should come first, and his wishes should be law. While conceding that each member of the Christian family had rights to respect, support and attention, she proclaimed, 'The father's rights are first in the house, so long as he live.'[32]

Home Life was printed shortly after Farningham became a professional writer for the religious publisher James Clarke. It drew, like much of her prescriptive literature, on her experience of growing up in a Baptist household – her father was a tradesman and village postmaster – but also from bible classes she ran for girls and young women working in the Northampton shoe factories. Yet Farningham's autobiography, published in 1907, betrays a far more complicated and troubled emotional relationship with her own father than the idealized paternal model advocated in her Sunday-school writings.[33] The memoir hints at conflicts and compromises involved in reconciling the rights and obligations of family members that were so categorically delineated in *Home Life*.

Reflecting on her strict Calvinist upbringing in the Kent village from which she took her *nom de plume*, Farningham noted that 'the family was all important, and the obligations of children and parents received stern and unfailing attention'. Patriarchal authority was firmly enforced: 'The father was the master and judge of the household' and '"Spare the rod and spoil the child" was a frequently quoted axiom'. Contrary to her deferral to paternal authority in *Home Life*, however, Farningham's own family life, she suggested, was happy because her mother's temperament was the presiding influence in the house: 'We got on better than most, because our mother was our minister, and the lessons we had on Sunday evenings were those of love.' If the adult Farningham recognized the father as head of household, as a girl she had seen her mother as 'so much more to us than our father' and as her mother lay dying when she was 12 years old, she passionately prayed, '"O Lord, if you must have one, please take our father to heaven, and leave us our mother"'. Following her death, Farningham wished that her father would remarry, considering it better to have 'an unsympathetic step-mother' than to be motherless, though intriguingly the autobiographer did not comment on the two wives he subsequently married. 'I was very bitter and naughty at that time,' she confessed, 'I did not pray, and was not anxious to be good.' Perhaps to appease his daughter, her father bought Farningham Sunday-school magazines. Based entirely on boys, however, these only increased her frustration. Her autobiography recalls but does not reflect on a number of put-downs by her father. In family prayers he asked God to give Farningham special favour because she was 'so much more plain-looking and uninteresting' than her siblings, a view she internalized, reconciling herself to spinsterhood.[34]

While Farningham alludes tentatively, therefore, to the traumatic loss of her mother that could not be filled by either stepmother or paternal substitute, the tensions and frustrations in her relationship with her father do not lead in the autobiography to explicit criticism of the patriarchal model. Rather, Farningham's differences with her father are signalled by her break from his conception of the Christian life and mode of teaching. Farningham followed both her parents in becoming a Sunday-school teacher. The education provided by the Sunday-school movements and their voluminous literature offered instruction in Christian parenting and filial obligation through fiction and Bible stories illustrating good and bad parenting, dutiful and errant children. But Sunday schools can also be seen as having established models of social parenting in which student teachers learned to care for the spiritual and moral welfare of their pupils and to lead worship in ways they would later practise in their own families. As a Christian instructor (and in common with Hamilton and Smith), Farningham modulated the stern, patriarchal tone of her Calvinist upbringing by preaching a more ecumenical, non-sectarian and evangelical Nonconformism that emphasized nurture and influence rather than strict authority and obedience. Significantly, Farningham's own conversion was at the instigation of a female Sunday-school teacher, rather than her father. Her ministry might be seen, therefore, as promoting a feminized or maternalist version of Calvinism, inspired by the teachings of her mother, her Sunday-school teacher and Christian activists that she met in adult life, such as Mary Carpenter, Clara Lucas Balfour and Frances Power Cobbe, who argued that single women could lead an active public life through the social mothering of the poor.[35]

Although Farningham's memoir hints at childhood struggles with her father, their relationship was intimate and supportive: 'he was always bright and kind, and full of fun and jokes'. While Farningham helped her father as village postmaster by sorting letters, he undertook domestic labour often performed by females, cleaning the shoes, which he did not consider girls' work, and making the fire in the morning. While Hearn could not afford for his daughter to attend school full-time, he agreed to her going part-time if she paid her keep by shoe-binding.[36] Like many young women, Farningham entered full-time employment because her father was experiencing financial difficulties. She left home at 18 to work as an assistant schoolmistress in Bristol and, after a number of teaching positions, became the head of the infant department of the Nonconformist British and Foreign School in Northampton. Though her father was proud when his daughter was offered a salary as a professional writer, she said '[he] had grave doubts as to whether I was wise in giving up my school, and very little confidence that I could make money by my pen'. Given his financial struggles, he may have felt threatened by his daughter earning more than he did. Yet if his 'uncomplimentary doubt' characterized their relationship, so too did her ability to conciliate; she moved home for the summer and there her happiness persuaded him of her choice. Through negotiation and respectful consideration, Farningham found that the loving Christian family could accommodate the competing claims of individual aspiration and mutual obligation; perhaps it was because of their successful resolution that Farningham could retain her deference to paternal authority. She attributed her success as a lecturer to divine recognition of her father's prayer that she receive God's favour, despite her 'plain face and shy manners'. Nothing gave her more pleasure, she recalled, than to hear of one girl resolving after her lecture, '"I will go home and be thick with me feyther"'.[37]

The model of the industrious Christian family advocated by Hamilton, Smith and Farningham drew on their membership of loving and supportive families.

This was a very particular experience of family life where deference to paternal authority was combined with a sense of the partnership between husband and wife and filial obligation between parent and child. It was certainly not an experience shared by all working-class children, and those abandoned, neglected, exploited or abused by fathers and paternal substitutes may have drawn on quite different discourses and genres in their representation of the filial relationship.[38] Indeed, the writers examined here acknowledged that not all families met the standards they set and they contrasted their ideal with the family strained by alcoholism and violence. In their public work, Smith and Farningham learned that not all social problems could be solved through the family. Towards the close of the century, Farningham was deeply alarmed by the NSPCC's revelations about cruelty to children and welcomed public discussion about the role of the state in undertaking responsibility for the welfare of children neglected by 'lazy good-for-for-nothing' parents. She still maintained, however, that poverty was at the root of many family problems and could be alleviated by securing men's position as breadwinner, whereby 'every man willing to work be given work to do at a living wage, and be able to provide necessaries for his own family'.[39]

If the Reform Act of 1867 confirmed the political independence of the working man as a family man, in its aftermath the rights and duties of paternity came under considerable pressure, especially in debates over married women's property, sexual exploitation, domestic violence, and the female suffrage. While animated by many of these concerns, Hamilton, Smith and Farningham retained respect for, and even deference to, the 'good father'. Their understanding of the family assumed the active presence of the father within family and household life. Drawing on their membership of productive, nurturing families where men's and women's work were still closely integrated within the household, they promoted the artisanal family as a viable model for the newer operative communities where work and home were more clearly segregated. The artisanal model could accommodate women's economic independence, creative expression and cultural activity outside the home. As such, their model of domesticity cannot be dismissed as nostalgic myth, even if it bore little relation to the lives of those who lacked parental protection. Their writings on fathers as nurturers and home-workers as well as wage-earners remind us that the separation of home and work was an uneven process and that the organization of domestic labour and child-rearing in lower-class families was influenced by a wide range of occupational and cultural practices and constraints, as well as by individual family dynamics and circumstances. The writings of these working women signal, therefore, neither the end of paternal deference nor the flight from domesticity, but rather the desire to regenerate the dutiful and mutually supportive Christian family.

Notes

1. D. Vincent, *Bread, Knowledge and Freedom: A Study of Nineteenth-Century Working-Class Autobiography* (London: Europa, 1981); Doolittle, 'Missing Fathers'.
2. See introduction; Tosh, *A Man's Place*, pp. 145–94.

3. C. Steedman, *Landscape for a Good Woman: A Story of Two Lives* (London: Virago, 1986), pp. 18–19.
4. See also K. McClelland, 'England's Greatness', in Hall et al., *Defining the Victorian Nation*.
5. Rose, *Limited Livelihoods*; Clark, *The Struggle for the Breeches*.
6. J. Hamilton, *Poems, Essays, and Sketches: Comprising the Principal Pieces from her Complete Works* (Glasgow: James Maclehose, 1880), p. 24.
7. http://www.monklands.co.uk/coatbridge
8. Hamilton, *Poems*, p. 444.
9. Ibid., pp. 443, 397, 386–8, 398.
10. Ibid., pp. 27, 398, 482–500.
11. Maidment, 'Domestic Ideology and its Industrial Enemies'.
12. K. McClelland, 'Masculinity and the "Representative Artisan" in Britain, 1850–80', in Roper and Tosh (eds), *Manful Assertions*, pp. 74–91.
13. H. Rogers, *Women and the People: Authority, Authorship and the Radical Tradition in Nineteenth-Century England* (Aldershot: Ashgate, 2000), pp. 124–60.
14. Hamilton, *Poems*, pp. 456–64.
15. Joseph Wright, *Janet Hamilton and Other Papers* (Edinburgh: R. & R. Black, 1889), pp. 9–10.
16. Hamilton, *Poems*, pp. 456–7, 371, 378–9, 380, 32–3.
17. Davidoff and Hall, *Family Fortunes*; Tosh, *A Man's Place*.
18. M. Smith, *The Autobiography of Mary Smith, Schoolmistress and Nonconformist* (London: Bemrose, 1892), pp. 136 and 196–7. For Smith, see Rogers, *Women and the People*, pp. 241–82.
19. Smith, *Autobiography*, pp. 4–5.
20. Ibid., pp. 14–15 and 41.
21. Ibid., pp. 39–40, 27, 31, 49, 43–4, 22–4 and 215.
22. Tosh, *A Man's Place*, p. 115.
23. Smith, *Autobiography*, p. 41.
24. S. Pedersen, 'Eleanor Rathbone 1872–1946: The Victorian Family Under the Daughter's Eye' in S. Pedersen and P. Mandler, *After the Victorians: Private Conscience and Public Duty in Modern Britain* (London: Routledge, 1994), pp. 105–25; H. Rogers, 'In the Name of the Father: Political Biographies by Radical Daughters', in D. Amigoni, *Technologies of Life Writing and Identity Formation in Victorian Culture* (Aldershot: Ashgate, 2007), pp. 196–219. Hamilton is said to have acquired her interest in public questions and moral welfare from her father, 'an ardent reformer'; see Hamilton, *Poems*, p. 27.
25. Smith, *Autobiography*, pp. 41–3.
26. Ibid., pp. 6–7, 10, 48, 25–6, 147–8, 71–4. For female Chartists and Vincent, see D. Thompson, *The Chartists: Popular Politics and the Industrial Revolution* (New York: Pantheon Books, 1984), pp. 122–50.
27. *Border City*, November 1863, pp. 59–61.
28. For wives as managers of household budgets, see C. Chinn, *They Worked All Their Lives: Women of the Urban Poor in England, 1880–1939* (Manchester: Manchester University Press, 1988), pp. 51–6.
29. Smith, *Autobiography*, pp. 89–91.
30. *The Ulverston Mirror*, 12 June 1869. Walkowitz, *Prostitution and Victorian Society*; Rogers, *Women and the People*, pp. 197–240, 267–8.
31. Smith, *Autobiography*, pp. 27–8.
32. M. Farningham, *Home Life* (London: James Clarke, 1869), pp. 13, 104, 11, 13–14, 104–5.

33. M. Farningham, *A Working Woman's Life: An Autobiography*, (London: James Clarke, 1907).
34. Ibid., pp. 33–4, 40–1, 43–4.
35. Ibid., pp. 34, 40, 44–6, 53–8, 65, 236–39. For 'social mothering', see E. Yeo, *The Contest for Social Science: Relations and Representations of Class and Gender* (London: Rivers Oram, 1996).
36. Farningham, *A Working Woman's Life*, pp. 12, 16, 43, 46–50. In *Boyhood* (London: James Clarke, 1870), Farningham instructed boys to help mothers with heavy work and not to expect to be served by their sisters. The pattern of labour in the Hearn home confirms Lummis's claim that working-class males frequently took part in domestic work, though the sexual division of household labour tended to be shaped by the demands of particular male occupations; see Lummis, 'The Historical Dimension of Fatherhood'.
37. Farningham, *A Working Woman's Life*, pp. 144–5, 170, 159.
38. For instance, Ellen Johnston avoided Christian prescription in her poetic and autobiographical representations of the working-class family and cast her own experience of paternal abandonment and abuse at the hands of her mother and stepfather within romantic and melodramatic conventions: see E. Johnston, *Autobiography, Poems and Songs of Ellen Johnston, The 'Factory Girl'* (Glasgow: William Love, 1867 and 1869); H. G. Klaus, *Factory Girl: Ellen Johnston and Working-Class Poetry in Victorian Scotland* (Frankfurt: Peter Lang, 1998).
39. Farningham, *A Working Woman's Life*, p. 254. For the growing preoccupation with child protection in this period, see H. Hendrick, *Child Welfare: England, 1872–1989* (London: Routledge, 1994).

9
'Speechless with Grief': Bereavement and the Working-Class Father, c. 1880–1914

Julie-Marie Strange

Many working-class families from the middle of the nineteenth century were typified by a sexual division of labour. It is unsurprising, then, that the historiography of working-class family life has tended to privilege the relationship between mothers and their children.[1] Within this framework, the working-class father has featured primarily as a wage-earner whose livelihood defined the status of his dependants. For instance, Karl Ittman's *Work, Gender and Family in Victorian England* (1995) approached the working-class father and husband through the lens of his occupational status, examining how the identity of the 'provider' shaped and interrelated with a political and trade-union consciousness. Ittman does not remove fathers entirely from a domestic sphere, noting that the working-class family cannot be reduced to an economic unit when so little is known about how work and family interact. None the less, fathers feature little in his analysis of the interpersonal dynamics of working-class life beyond a conception of paternal duty: discipline and breadwinning.[2]

This chapter questions the supposedly peripheral role of fathers within the emotional life of the working-class family. In particular, it examines masculine sensibility in respect of death and bereavement. Disease and mortality were common features of working-class life, especially given the high infant and child mortality rates that persisted among the urban labouring population into the twentieth century.[3] Yet the working-class culture of death has, until recently, been interpreted as an exercise in social snobbery and status-seeking, rather than a period of intense emotional strain. This chapter analyses records of the responses of adult men to the deaths of their children or spouses to argue that masculine emotions were often articulated through the role of provider. Such expressions of feeling were inseparable from conceptions of what masculinity meant and how it should be performed. Often reticent and oblique, working-class masculine emotions were no less meaningful for seeming obscure to the middle-class external observer. Indeed, the chapter concludes that men were far from peripheral to the interpersonal dynamics of working-class family life, but, rather, could enjoy a rich emotional life through the symbolic expression of feeling.

Clearly, some fathers (and mothers) had neglectful and, in some cases, abusive relationships with their offspring. Some children expressed open antipathy to their parents in adulthood: Jack Martin (born c. 1905) berated his father for drunken cruelty; Alice Foley (born 1891) derided her father as a vicious and 'open-mouthed braggart of an Irishman'; Pat O'Mara (born c. 1900) portrayed his father as violent and self-centred; and the entire biography of George Acorn (born 1885) stood as a bitter diatribe against his unfeeling and grasping parents.[4] How far these examples can be applied beyond the confines of single family units is, however, highly questionable. Even within individual life stories, conflicting emotion is rife: notably, George Acorn's narrative can, in places, be interpreted as a painful attempt to reconcile himself to his parents' shortcomings and is not entirely devoid of flashes of forgiveness and affection. Likewise, it would be unfair to assume that fathers who did not fulfil the role of provider had no affection for their offspring; sentiment could be expressed through quiet pride in the simple achievements of children, frustration with life's inequities, or subscription to certain codes of behaviour, such as never using violence against a child.[5] Like many dichotomies, representations of 'good' and 'bad' fathers overlook the wealth of diversity and difference that lay in between. As Eleanor Rathbone noted in 1913, one could not judge the poorer classes from extreme examples of 'really bad' parents. The vast majority were 'good in intention'; they tried their best in circumstances which were, arguably, stacked against them.[6]

I

The historiography of death and bereavement in the Victorian period has, until recently, concentrated on particular subjects: cultures of grief among the 'much biographed' élite; the demographics and economic hardships of widowhood; high infant mortality rates; and the respectable funeral and antipathy to pauper burial within working-class culture.[7] To an extent, this bias reflects the dominant concerns of nineteenth-century élites and the limited accessibility of historical resources. For instance, Pat Jalland's *Death in the Victorian Family* (1996) took a peculiarly narrow definition of 'the Victorian' with a deliberate focus on the educated and evangelical élite. In contrast to the dearth of personal testimony from the working classes, Jalland's élite wrote extensively about their lives and, importantly, their feelings in condolence letters, diaries, memorial (or 'mausoleum') books, tracts and sermons, all of which highlighted a rich and deeply moving culture of grief and sympathy.[8]

Within this culture, Jalland drew attention to the special predicament of the widow. Dependent on men for her chief identity, even the widow in élite society faced economic insecurity. Moreover, unless she was among a small minority (beautiful, rich and still young enough to bear children) who remarried, the most common fate of the widow was to spend the rest of her days being defined by the death of her spouse. In comparison, working-class widows often remarried, especially if their children had left home. Most widows with young families, however, faced tremendous economic pressures.[9] As Jack London asserted in his social commentary *People of the Abyss* (1903), the death of the male breadwinner was the worst disaster that could befall a family: 'The thing happens, the father is struck down, and what then? A mother with three children can do little or nothing . . . There is no guarding against it . . . A family stands so many chances of escaping the bottom of the Abyss, and so many chances of falling plump down to it.'[10]

Working-class widows were typically forced to turn to the Poor Law for outdoor relief or indoor assistance. The situation was particularly difficult for widows with small children who had to juggle child care with paid employment. Moreover, such widows were overwhelmingly concentrated in low-status and low-paid occupations such as charring, hawking and box-making.[11]

Anxieties concerning the predicament of the working-class widow tended to elide with fears that charity would encourage dependency. Such apprehension hints at the negative stereotypes underpinning Victorian philanthropy. Indeed, the complex web of ideas linking poverty, character and morality were magnified with reference to the problem of high infant mortality rates. General mortality rates were in steady decline from the 1870s onwards but infant deaths remained stubbornly high, provoking extensive medico-legal debate over the causes of, and potential cures for, what sensationalists liked to call the 'slaughter of the innocents'.[12] Again, this preoccupation is reflected in the historiography. Infant mortality dominates the critical literature associated with death in working-class culture and encompasses works concerned with infanticide, environment, medical reform and innovation, and the emerging science or 'craft' of motherhood.[13]

Reviewing the historiography of death in Victorian and Edwardian Britain highlights the particular visibility of women. Much of this bias rests on the assumptions of contemporaries and historians: the historiography of grief is a history of love and longing, emotions that have tended to be associated with femininity and domesticity. That the Victorian family unit was thought to represent a triad of the male with dependent wife and children has also centred critical attention on the economic difficulties of widows. Likewise, concentration on women as the primary carers (and potential abusers) of children has prompted mothers to take centre stage in the literature concerning infant and child death. Given the prominence of the male subject in much of the history of the nineteenth and early twentieth centuries, the comparative obscurity of masculine cultures of death is curious. For Jalland, male cultures of grief within the élite became less visible with the waning of Romanticism. With the emergence of muscular Christianity, men became increasingly reticent or guarded about expressing their emotions. This is not to suggest that men became unemotional, but, rather, that the ways in which feeling was verbalized and acted out were increasingly subtle, particularly within public contexts where masculinity was shaped by qualities of strength, fortitude and bravery. Jalland demonstrates how social and cultural etiquette supported masculine restitution from loss, with, for instance, widowers being encouraged to return to work speedily following bereavement and, in many cases, to remarry.[14]

Within working-class culture, however, masculine emotional responses to death and bereavement have received little analysis. Within a culture of loss, men feature primarily as the economic mainstays of funeral custom; it was their wages, after all, that (along with the household management of a wife) often determined whether or not a family could afford a respectable funeral (that is, a burial in a family grave as opposed to a pauper grave).[15] Likewise, men's funerals have attracted critical attention because, in many ways, they represented the values of the skilled-male working classes: thrift alongside pride in work and community, attributes that were embodied by the participation of workmates, trade-union and friendly-society members in mourning and burial custom.[16]

In his pioneering attempt to extrapolate the emotional life of the Victorian and Edwardian working-class man from relatively few surviving autobiographies, David Vincent observed that, despite experiencing bereavement on a regular basis, labouring men were notably silent on matters of loss and feeling. Vincent attributed this, first, to the absence of a sophisticated vocabulary for emotion and, secondly, to a capacity to restrain emotion in the context of material insecurity and high mortality rates. Moreover, he noted, most working-class autobiographies were shaped by a desire to chart a political, educational and occupational career where narratives of sentiment may have been deemed inappropriate. Vincent drew particular attention to the extraordinary case of a father abandoning work on the death of his child; it was exceptional, he concluded, because so few fathers could afford the 'luxury' of 'pure' grief. Concepts of pure grief and luxurious bereavement are problematic, however, not least because they imply an ideal state of loss against which everything else falls short. Moreover, there are dangers, as Vincent acknowledged, in equating a literary containment of grief with resilience and recovery in an experiential context. Finally, whilst acknowledging that his analysis rested almost exclusively on men, Vincent was reluctant to pursue the notion that representations of grief, like love, were gendered (although, of course, this was typical of historical literature written in the late 1970s).[17]

This chapter, then, revisits Vincent's themes with reference to the working-class father in the light of recent shifts in the historiography of gender. Primarily, however, it examines working-class men's experience of bereavement using a more flexible interpretation of grief, seeking it not so much in grand gestures, such as the abandonment of work or the transcription of long mournful testimony, but, rather, in small symbolic deeds. In particular, I aim to demonstrate that whilst notions of gender, emotion and domesticity were far from fixed within working-class culture, representations of love and loss were often shaped by perceptions of manliness which were rooted in the role of provider. Indeed, far from being aloof from their children or other men, the bereaved adult male could articulate feeling through a variety of non-verbal expressions.

II

Crude stereotypes of the working-class father in late Victorian Britain fell into two broad categories: the good man who was a breadwinner and bastion of moral authority; and the idle wastrel dependent on charity, intemperate and a general brute.[18] Histories of the working-class family have tended to concentrate on the good man, casting fathers primarily in an absentee role of wage earner and 'provider' whilst wives and mothers have 'constituted the main actors' in domestic and familial life.[19] Works by Elizabeth Roberts, Ittman and Diane Gittins emphasize the perception of the good husband and father as a man who was not brutal and who 'tipped up' his wages every week.[20] Within a culture of death, therefore, it is not surprising that fathers have tended to be perceived in terms of their role as financier of the funeral. If contemporaries and historians have read the provision of the respectable funeral in terms of social and consumer status, it was also the most tangible and public expression of loss a father or spouse could make: providing was cathartic.[21] Of course, the antithesis of the respectable funeral, the pauper burial, carried associations of the workhouse, charity and idleness: the very negation of breadwinner and masculine ideals. Those who neglected to make provision for respectable interment in a family grave were expected to express shame and frustration not only in relation to the social stigma of the pauper burial but also in terms of their failure to meet a masculine ideal.

Notably, for some of the fathers who committed their children to a pauper grave, the burial provoked bitter self-recrimination for having failed one's family. Such was the remorse of some fathers that they sought to exhume their children from the pauper grave for reinterment in a family grave at a later date. Reinterment was an expensive and drawn-out affair, conducted away from the public gaze in the dead of night to avoid morbid onlookers. This also prohibited families from participating in the reburial, and relatives had to depend upon the reassurances of cemetery officials that the exchange of graves had taken place. It is unlikely, therefore, that such ceremonies could be reconciled with crude notions of working-class respectability which depended on an audience for validation.[22] Rather, such acts indicate that fathers were attempting to reclaim ownership of their deceased offspring from the parochial authorities; to reinstate their patriarchal role; and possibly to reaffirm in a personal and familial context that their offspring meant something to them.

III

Save for the role of financier, however, men appear fleetingly in historical narratives of mourning, often as peripheral figures who carry a coffin or indulge excessively in 'wakes' tributes to the deceased. Yet men could also draw emotional comfort and support from the symbolic rites associated with bereavement. Late Victorian and Edwardian working-class cultures of death were typified by a series of rituals (such as the laying out and visiting of the corpse, neighbourhood participation in the cortège, and wakes teas) that served to position personal loss within a public context. Such customs enabled the bereaved to express their grief, and friends and relatives to communicate sympathy, without necessitating a great deal of verbal articulacy. Indeed, much could rest on facial expression, intonation, touch and small acts of kindness.[23] Whilst many of these customs have been associated with a feminine culture of attending to stages in the life cycle, some networks of support were male-oriented and hinged upon work or trade-union identities, or friendships and acquaintances forged in the public house.[24]

Such customs permitted the symbolic expression of condolences to the bereaved whilst allowing the mourner to articulate a sense of loss. In his autobiography *A Hoxton Childhood*, Albert Jasper (born 1905) recalled accompanying his father to donate a collection of money to a workmate whose infant had died. Jasper's narrative details little verbal exchange between the adult men except that relating to an invitation to view the corpse and the awkward presentation of the gift. To a point, conversation was not necessary. The bereaved father opened the door to the Jaspers with his 'eyes swollen red', an indication of sleeplessness and sorrow. In presenting the workplace donation, Jasper's father enacted the sympathy of workmates, whilst the offering, given as a sign of respect for the deceased, avoided any suggestion of charity. Moreover, donations made from wage earnings could be read as an expression of solidarity among workers and breadwinner fathers. Accepting the gift from Jasper senior, the bereft colleague invited him to look upon the corpse. As he drew back the lid of the coffin, he asked Jasper's father what he thought of the child, possibly seeking some confirmation of the beauty of the corpse and, consequently, the extent of his loss. Furthermore, young Albert's presence on the expedition suggests that his father was anxious to articulate to the bereaved man a shared identity of fatherhood and an implicit expression of particular sympathy for the loss of a child.[25]

Jasper's memoir highlights several things. First, it reminds us that men shared in a culture of grief and condolence expressed through mutual aid; collections which were organized through the pub or trade union served a similar function. It also casts doubt on contemporary fears concerning working-class parents' indifference to the deaths of small infants. Importantly, the example illustrates how verbal articulacy was not necessary, or even desirable, for the expression of loss and sympathy: all could rest on gesture. Finally, it illustrates the ways in which such expressions could be articulated through specifically masculine identities rooted in work and paternity.

In his fictionalized autobiography *Cwmardy*, set in an Edwardian mining village in South Wales, Lewis Jones (born 1897) also explored how expressions of loss and sympathy rested on symbolic gesture and the gendering of emotion. The novel is peppered with scenes of death and disaster. One of the most poignant scenes in the book, however, is the death of the protagonist's sister, Jane, in childbirth. That her child is illegitimate and its father is not present to mourn the passing of Jane and her baby reminds us that fatherhood was not always welcome; in this case at least, the father of Jane's baby, the son of a mining official, vehemently rejected Jane and her claims upon him. Yet the abandonment of Jane by her erstwhile lover also serves to amplify the bonds between her and her parents, who fervently support their daughter in her shame. Devastated by her death, neither of Jane's parents can articulate verbally the depth of their loss. Shane, her mother, wails and sobs, rocks and moans. Later, at the funeral, tears 'overflowed and streamed down her face'. Jane's father Jim, meanwhile, is 'speechless with grief'. At the funeral, he hides his face while the other men present swallow hard, look awkward, and generally try 'to appear unconcerned'. Immediately after the burial, Jim resumes 'the usual routine of his life'. Months later, he has cause to wear his suit, prompting Shane to recall that the last time he wore the clothes was at Jane's funeral. Jim's response, 'it be no good worrying 'bout it now', sounds almost dismissive. However, at no point does Jones suggest that Jim does not share the grief or memories of Shane. Rather, Jim's grief is 'resigned'; it is quiet and solitary in comparison to Shane's tearfulness.[26]

Resignation in this account suggests the inarticulacy of grief, less from a specific wish to contain or repress feeling than from a tacit adherence to gendered cultures of emotional expression. Repeatedly, Jones emphasises the cultural distinctions between the miners and their wives and the differing social, political and occupational worlds they inhabit. Both are attributed with characteristics of fortitude and resilience, yet those traits are manifested in different ways: the miners cling to a stereotype of masculine emotional strength, whilst their wives are permitted to sob and wail in accordance with notions of feminine vulnerability. Similarly, Jones repeatedly reminds his readers of the physical immensity and power of miners' bodies, a compelling metaphor for their psychological courage and endurance.

IV

As Stephen Garton has noted in his microhistory of a Victorian middle-class widower, the public face of masculine emotional buoyancy did not operate in neat juxtaposition with private manifestations of loss; for many men, public and private experiences of loss overlapped. Crucially, public displays of restitution could not be equated with the speedy recovery from personal loss.[27] Rather, masculine performances of emotion were mediated through a series of complex needs and contexts, none of which were necessarily fixed or nicely juxtaposed.

Such multifaceted understandings of masculinity and emotion need not be confined to an analysis of the articulate bourgeois diary. In his memoir of a working-class Glasgow childhood, David Kirkwood (born 1872) observed that labouring men perceived their primary role in life as one of waging war on poverty for their families. Integral to this conception of masculine duty were characteristics of strength, endurance and fortitude. Against such qualities, it was considered shameful, weak and 'unmanly' to permit displays of sentiment and affection; such was the woman's domain. Yet, Kirkwood argues, notions of paternal duty must not be confused with indifferent attachments to one's children. Neither did the responsibilities of labouring fatherhood preclude the expression of feeling. Rather, they shaped the forms such expressions took. For instance, Kirkwood's father demonstrated his powerful emotions through awkward, inarticulate gestures of parental responsibility. Notably, the day his daughter left home to enter domestic service, Kirkwood's father was at pains to reassure her that wherever she was, if she ever had need of him, he would go to her aid immediately.[28] In this sense, the paternal identity that was rooted in providing for and protecting one's children could be invested with metaphorical and emotional significance.

When men did show unfettered emotion, it was often represented as shocking and exceptional behaviour. Patrick Macgill (born 1890) recalled that neither of his parents was particularly demonstrative. When his infant brother died, his mother turned her face away from the family and wept. To a point, this was expected because tears were a feminine characteristic. What was shocking to Macgill and his siblings was the sight of their stolid father breaking down into heart-rending sobs.[29] Elizabeth Flint described the scene of her father's reaction to the news that his youngest son had been killed in the First World War: 'great sobs shook his body. His arms were folded on the table before him, and his head was cradled on his arms. His breath came in great gulps, and the whole of him shook.' Perceived to be a strong and resilient man, the sight of him crying was a 'dreadful never to be forgotten' event.[30]

That these scenes took place within a domestic interior suggests, however, that home signified intimacy and, perhaps, a more feminized space where the exhibition of raw, if unexpected, emotion could occur without compromising a public conception of masculine status. Indeed, Margaret Loane, district nurse and self-proclaimed friend of the poor, claimed in 1910 that many poorer men were openly affectionate with small children within the private space of the home. Loane reflected that the sight of working-class fathers picking up their 'grimy, howling' children never ceased to challenge her perceptions of gruff, labouring masculinity: men would walk about with the child in their arms, 'pressing kisses in its cheeks, and crooning lovingly'. As children grew up, however, both parties became more self-conscious, especially where the burgeoning masculinity, and potential rivalry, of adolescent sons was concerned. For Loane, the deathbed was, perhaps, the only circumstance in which both parties could regress to a more intimate relationship unfettered by anxieties about their manliness. In particular, the death of a juvenile child could prompt a return of the playfulness of childhood:

> An artificer was sitting up at night with his dying son, a manly, intelligent lad of fifteen, suddenly struck down by a mortal disease. As death approached, the relations between the two insensibly slipped back some seven or eight years. Almost the last words uttered by the boy were a refusal to take his medicine: '*You* drink it, dad! Mother won't know the difference'. Twice the father drank it in a fond attempt at coaxing, and at day break the lad died.[31]

In this account, the dying son slipped into a former role of dependency and was, probably, afraid of what lay ahead. In adopting the role of nurse and overseer, his father redefined the role of patriarch to facilitate an intimate and nurturing framework to tend to his boy's final needs. More importantly, perhaps, in coaxing the boy to take his medicine, the father was articulating a powerful desire for his son not to die. Likewise, in teasing an absent mother, father and son can be seen as expressing and reaffirming a bond with each other, even if this was not verbalized in a sentimental way.

On the other hand, dying fathers were often keen to distribute their favourite possessions among offspring. Recollecting the death of his father, Joseph Barlow Brooks (born 1874) speculated that the sick man derived satisfaction from sorting and distributing favourite possessions to his young children (although these were pawned the day after his funeral).[32] Such small acts of generosity might well be sentimentally charged, prompting reminiscence and reflection. Moreover, the gift of an object imbued with a personal history acquired layers of symbolic meaning: it ensured the perpetuation of an item's significance; promoted the association between a known personality and the material gift; and, where objects had particularly intimate connotations (such as a wedding ring), indicated emotional esteem and affection for the recipient.

V

If death facilitated the expression of sentimental attachments, it also prompted the bereaved to renegotiate their relationships in much more pragmatic ways. This is perhaps most evident in the attempts of widowers to maintain family cohesion in the aftermath of a spouse's death. As noted above, the death of a male breadwinner usually precipitated the financial collapse of the working-class family economy. None the less, the death of a breadwinner was not automatically associated with the breakdown of the family unit. Rather, contemporaries expected the Poor Law or charitable organizations to step into the role of provider. Women were also able to call upon local networks of support to assist with child care, whilst many widows took employment that enabled them to work from home.[33] In this sense, fathers were seen as replaceable. In contrast, the death of a wife and mother was thought to precipitate the disintegration of domestic economy and the splintering of the nuclear unit. As Carl Chinn has noted, 'a family might survive without its father; it was rarer it did so without its mother'.[34] Hence, unless the widower remarried to provide a new mother, children were likely to be dispersed among relations or neighbours to permit the father to continue his primary duty of earning a living.

Again, this reinforces a perception that fathers were peripheral to the interpersonal dynamics of family life. Undoubtedly, some widowers with young families had little choice but to send children to live with neighbours or extended family. When Edna Thorpe's mother died in about 1900, her father (a packer in a Manchester factory) placed one infant daughter with his sister whilst he and five other children stayed in the family home. Edna, the eldest daughter, aged nine, took two half-days off school every week to attend to housework and the four remaining siblings whilst their father was at work. When it became clear that she could not cope with school, housewifery and child care, Edna and another sibling moved in with the aunt whilst their father and three brothers took lodgings. Despite this ostensible disintegration of the home, her father visited his daughters regularly, contriving to maintain a loose sense of the nuclear family.[35] Such visits may have entailed a sense of duty and a desire to retain paternal authority over one's offspring. Yet they may also indicate that some fathers simply took pleasure in their children's company and that familial ties could go beyond those of an economic contract. Moreover, children were often a living memorial to their deceased mother. Elise Pettigrew (born in about 1910) recalled that when the last of her father's offspring from a previous marriage expired, it dealt him a 'hard blow': not only had all the children from his first marriage died, whilst alive they had embodied the memory of his dead wife.[36]

The abrupt changes in lifestyle and environment at the death of a wife and mother exacerbated the shock of bereavement. Yet some fathers strove to maintain home and family in a bid to limit the upheavals occasioned by death. When Winifred Jay's mother died in 1910, the family 'just had to make the best of it': Winifred's father assumed responsibility for cooking meals after work, whilst Winifred attended school irregularly in order to do the laundry and pay the rent and club money.[37] This was far from ideal. None the less, Jay's account of struggle and compromise serves to heighten the significance her father attached to maintaining a family unit. Jim Walsh's mother died in 1908 when he was eight years old. One sister was already 'skivvying' in domestic service, whilst the eldest brother lived with an uncle. For the four children who remained at home, Jim's father 'struggled along' to provide 'the best he could'. A labourer, his father worked during the week and spent his weekends attending to domestic chores: washing on Saturday afternoons and baking bread and broth for the week ahead on Sundays. Jim's overriding recollection of his father was that 'life was really hard for him'. Indeed, one year following the death of their mother, his father 'must have got to the bottom of his patience' and escorted the family to the workhouse. When they arrived at the gates, however, 'he thought better of it' and returned home accompanied by his children. This is not to suggest that his father was a model of virtue and fortitude; every so often, he 'went on the [drinking] spree'. Yet this account of 'hard times' and the father's sense of conflict implied by the excursion to the workhouse suggests a quiet determination to preserve a home and family.[38]

Stories of widowed men striving to maintain a cohesive family unit alert us to the multiple tragedies occasioned by death, whilst providing a rare insight into domestic and emotional aspects of masculinity. The impetus to sustain a home for one's children highlights the importance attached to filial relationships, whilst illustrating how seemingly pragmatic priorities could be imbued with personal significance. Moreover, such examples demonstrate that fathers were rarely simply either good or bad, but, rather, very human. Indeed, to return to Eleanor Rathbone's observation, most fathers simply tried to do the best they could in difficult and trying circumstances.[39]

VI

This chapter has sought to reclaim working-class fathers from an historical silence where the performance of a breadwinner role has left men standing on the threshold of the interpersonal dynamics of family life. Rather, it is argued that the act of providing for one's family could, in itself, be interpreted as an expression of love and affection. Given the gravity accorded to the role of providing, the emotional consequence of being a 'good man' cannot be underestimated. Furthermore, the negotiation of a breadwinner identity created opportunities to express sentiment, attachment and empathy with other men. As a period of particular emotional stress, bereavement throws the complexity of masculine sensibility into relief: mediated through the role of breadwinner and often articulated in the public context of the funeral and mourning custom, masculine emotional life was no less potent for seeming obscured by gendered understandings of appropriate behaviour and the apparent absence of an eloquent vocabulary.

Notes

1. Ellen Ross's outstanding book, *Love and Toil*, epitomizes this trend. For classic studies of working-class families in this period, see: J. Bourke, *Working-Class Cultures In Britain 1890–1960: Gender, Class, and Ethnicity* (Routledge: London, 1994); E. Roberts, *A Woman's Place: An Oral History Of Working-Class Women, 1890–1940* (Blackwell: Oxford, 1984).
2. Ittman, *Work, Gender and Family In Victorian England*, pp. 142–223.
3. Woods and Shelton, *An Atlas Of Victorian Mortality*.
4. J. Martin, *The Life Story Of A Working Man* (Bolton: Stephenson, 1973), p. 15; A. Foley, *A Bolton Childhood* (Bolton: Manchester University Press, [1973] 1990), p. 3, p. 8; P. O'Mara, *Autobiography Of A Liverpool [Irish] Slummy* (Liverpool: Bluecoat Press, 1994; orig. pub. 1934) p. 42; G. Acorn, *One Of The Multitude* (London: William Heinemann, 1911).
5. See H. M. Burton, *There Was A Young Man* (London: Geoffrey Bles, 1958), pp. 35–6.
6. E. Rathbone, *Report On The Condition Of Widows Under The Poor Law In Liverpool: Presented To The Annual Meeting Of The Liverpool Women's Industrial Council* (Liverpool, 1913), p. 24.
7. See D. Cannadine, 'War and Death, Grief and Mourning in Modern Britain', in J. Whaley (ed.), *Mirrors Of Mortality: Studies In The Social History Of Death* (London: Europa, 1981), P. 241, pp. 187–242; Strange, 'Death and Dying: Old Themes and New Directions', *Journal Of Contemporary History*, 35:3 (2000), pp. 491–9.
8. P. Jalland, *Death In The Victorian Family* (Oxford: Oxford University Press, 1996).
9. See I. Blan, 'The History of Widowhood: A Bibliographical Overview' *Journal Of Family History* 16 (1991). See also a special issue of *The History Of The Family*, 7 (2000) dedicated to the history of widowhood.
10. J. London, *People Of The Abyss* (London: T. Nelson & Sons, 1903), pp. 251–2.
11. C. Booth, *Labour And Life*, Vol. II (London: Williams & Norgate, 1891), pp. 94ff, 69, 49, 178, 179, B. S. Rowntree, *Poverty: A Study Of Town Life* (London: Longmans, Green & Co., 1922, orig. pub. 1901), 69–73, 154, C. V. Butler, *Social Conditions in Oxford* (London: Sidgwick & Jackson, 1912), pp. 73–5; Rathbone, *Report On The Condition Of Widows*.
12. L. Rose, *The Massacre Of The Innocents* (London: Routledge and Kegan Paul, 1986).
13. Cooter, *In The Name Of The Child*; A. Hardy, 'Rickets and the Rest: Child-Care, Diet and the Infectious Children's Diseases, 1850–1914', *Social History Of Medicine*, 5, 3 (1992), pp. 389–412; I. Loudon, 'On Maternal and Infant Mortality, 1900-1960', *Social History Of Medicine*, 4, 1 (1991), pp. 29–73; N. Williams, 'Death in its Season: Class, Environment and the Mortality of Infants in Nineteenth-Century Sheffield', *Social History Of Medicine*, 5, 1 (1992), pp. 71–94.
14. Jalland, *Death In The Victorian Family*, pp. 251–64.

15. Chinn, *Poverty Amidst Prosperity*, p. 104; F. M. L. Thompson, *The Rise Of Respectable Society: A Social History Of Victorian Britain, 1830–1900* (London: Fontana, 1988), p. 200.
16. T. Laqueur, 'Bodies, Death and Pauper Funerals', *Representations*, 1, 1 (1983), pp. 109–31.
17. D. Vincent, 'Love and Death and the Nineteenth-Century Working Class', *Social History*, 5 (1980), pp. 223–47 repr. in Vincent, *Bread, Knowledge And Freedom*, pp. 39–61.
18. W. Grisewood (ed.), *The Poor of Liverpool and What Is To Be Done for Them* (Liverpool: Egerton Smith, 1899), p. 6.
19. Ittman, *Work, Gender And Family in Victorian England*, p. 223.
20. Roberts, *A Woman's Place*; Ittman, *Work, Gender And Family in Victorian England*; Gittins, *The Family In Question*.
21. On respectable funerals, see P. Johnson, 'Conspicuous Consumption and Working-Class Culture in Late Victorian and Edwardian Britain', *Transactions of the Royal Historical Society*, 38 (1988), pp. 27–42; and E. Ross, ' "Not the Sort that Would Sit on the Doorstep": Respectability in Pre-World War One London Neighbourhoods', *International Labour And Working Class History*, 27 (1985), pp. 39–59.
22. J-M. Strange, 'Only a Pauper whom Nobody Owns: Re-assessing the Pauper Grave, c. 1880–1914', *Past And Present*, 178, 1 (2003), pp. 148–75.
23. J-M. Strange, *Death, Grief And Poverty In Britain 1870–1914* (Cambridge: Cambridge University Press, 2005), pp. 194–229.
24. M. Chamberlain and R. Richardson, 'Life and Death', *Oral History*, 11, 1 (1988), pp. 31–43.
25. Albert Jasper, *A Hoxton Childhood* (London: Centerprise, 1969), p. 14.
26. Lewis Jones, *Cwmardy* (London: Lawrence and Wishart, 1937), pp. 64–8, 92.
27. S. Garton, 'The Scales of Suffering: Love, Death and Victorian Masculinity' *Social History* 27 (2002), 40–58.
28. D. Kirkwood, *My Life Of Revolt* (London: Harrap, 1935), pp. 1–2.
29. P. MacGill, *Children of the Dead End: The Autobiography of a Navvy* (London: H. Jenkins, 1914), p. 21.
30. E. Flint, *Hot Bread And Chips* (London: Museum Press, 1963), p. 101.
31. M. Loane, *The Queen's Poor: Life as they Find it in Town and Country* (London: Arnold, 1910), p. 22.
32. J. Brooks, *Lancashire Bred: An Autobiography* (Oxford: pub. by the author, 1950), p. 13.
33. E. Ross, 'Survival Networks: Women's Neighbourhood Sharing in London before World War One', *History Workshop Journal*, 15 (1983), pp. 4–27; Strange, *Death, Grief And Poverty*, pp. 196–200.
34. Chinn, *They Worked All Their Lives*, p. 17.
35. Manchester Studies Oral History Collection (MSOH), Tameside Archive and Local Studies, Edna Thorpe, transcript of tape 81.
36. E. Pettigrew, *Time to Remember: Growing up in Liverpool from 1912 Onwards* (Liverpool: Toulouse, 1989), p. 16.
37. MSOH, Winifred Jay, transcript of tape 43.
38. MSOH, Jim Walsh, transcript of tape 458.
39. Rathbone, *Report On The Condition Of Widows*, p. 24.

Part 4
Frontiers of Fatherhood

10
Missionary 'Fathers' and Wayward 'Sons' in the South Pacific, 1797–1825

Alison Twells

Fatherhood was central to nineteenth-century evangelical theology and social theory.[1] As Leonore Davidoff and Catherine Hall have shown, the family on earth was to emulate the heavenly family. Women's role was to 'guide the house' and bring up children, extending their maternal skills to the care of the local community and, more contestedly, to the regeneration of the nation. Sermons and conduct books disseminated knowledge of biblical fathers such as Jacob, Abraham and Joseph, and of God the Father, at once mysterious and known, benevolent and punishing, while implicitly prescribing good fatherly conduct. Men, as husbands and fathers, were placed at the head of the family, providing authority, protection and kindness, and operating as a role model to sons and others entrusted to their care.[2] Fatherhood was also a metaphor for the wider influence or 'empire' of men, as notions of paternal authority contributed to emerging middle-class and, later, national cultures and identities.[3] Good Christian men, as members of a missionary movement for global change, were expected to manage, guide, discipline and nurture 'other' males identified by missionary philanthropic discourses as objects of reform and in need of a careful steering from 'heathen' childhoods to Christian maturity.

This chapter explores paternal relationships in the context of the popular missionary movement in Britain during the early 1800s. The 1790s had seen the formation of the Baptist, London (largely Congregational) and Church Missionary Societies. The Wesleyans, without a formal organization until 1813, were already sending missionaries to America and the Caribbean. The first missionaries – all men, though many with accompanying wives, who were increasingly important in their husbands' selection[4] – were despatched by the societies to India (1792), Tahiti, Tonga and the Marquesa Islands (1796) and West Africa (1804).[5] These men were to take the Bible to heathen populations, and to 'civilize' savage and barbarian cultures through the encouragement of settled agriculture, the development of artisan skills, the construction of village settlements, and the observance of appropriate gender roles. As representatives of God the Father, their purpose was to confer His love on a heathen populace and make Christian communities according to a scriptural blueprint. Their commitment to re-educating the heathen male subject included guiding him as a father would his son, teaching him how to fulfil his 'natural' role as the economic provider for his family, encouraging an affectionate relationship with his wife and children, and steering him to an expression of his familial authority that was considered, restrained and legal.[6] Missionary fashioning of a new Christian subject also extended to more high-standing indigenous men, even royalty, through whom missionaries sought to shape the nation.

Missionary relationships were far more complex, though, than that suggested by a simple model of the transmission of biblical knowledge from one party to another. Missions elicited a range of responses from potential subjects: while some embraced the Christian message and others rejected it outright, there were also partial acceptances and appropriations. Even those 'heathen' who welcomed Christian intervention did so for a range of reasons not always associated with spiritual conversion.[7] Missionary relationships were also complicated by the differential status of the missionaries and society directors. The latter, the 'fathers and founders' of the movement,[8] tended not to venture overseas but to expend their philanthropic energies within the missionary movement at home.[9] By contrast, overseas missionaries between the 1790s and 1840s were predominantly from the artisan and lower middle classes.[10] Though they often had experience of lay preaching or Sunday school teaching, many came from working-class communities also designated as 'heathen' by the missionary society directors. Indeed, this status was reinforced by their treatment in the mission field by the directors, who underestimated the support required for comfort and survival, who were reluctant to accord the missionaries any degree of equality or responsibility within the enterprise, and who appeared to believe that missionaries too were to be improved through their Christian labours and supervision by their paternalistic superiors in England. To that extent they occupied a shared moral space with the 'heathen' overseas.

Given the discussion within women's history of the significance of 'maternalism' in carving out an authoritative role for female missionaries in the nineteenth century,[11] it is surprising that missionary fatherhood has been so little studied. A variety of subject positions were available to missionary men, however, and their deployment of languages of fatherhood, paternalism and patriarchalism was inconsistent and complex. Furthermore, missionary subjects frequently refused their designated role, and missionaries too could disappoint. While explicitly positioning themselves as brethren to each other, missionaries not only appreciated the paternal care provided by older men in the field, but sometimes extended this parental role to 'heathen' dignitaries. Each of these possibilities had profound significance for the shape of the civilizing mission in the nineteenth century.

I

George Vason (*c.* 1772–1838), a 24-year-old brick-layer from Nottingham, seemed to desire paternal discipline and care from the outset of his missionary adventure in 1796. In his reflections upon the voyage to the South Seas in the *Duff*, he expressed his appreciation of the 'paternal conduct' demonstrated by London Missionary Society (LMS) director Thomas Haweis, just prior to departure from Portsmouth. 'He visited us to the last', he wrote, 'and shed many tears of cordial friendship and tender anxiety for us, at parting, and did not leave us, until, like St Paul, at his farewell, he had accompanied us to the ship, and kneeled down and prayed with us all'.[12] On the journey out, the fatherly role was fulfilled by Captain Wilson, the godly captain of the *Duff*, whose son was to rescue Vason five years later.[13]

The South Seas mission had resulted from a series of meetings which had seen the formal constitution of the LMS in the autumn of 1795. Its founders took inspiration from letters from William Carey, the first Baptist missionary who had travelled to Serampore, in the north of India, in 1792.[14] Haweis, a founder of the LMS, had been impressed by the image of the South Pacific popularized by Cook's writing of the 1770s. The people were of an affable disposition and untouched by slavery; their religious beliefs did not amount to the systems of Islam and Hinduism; the climate was hospitable and the language supposedly easy to acquire. 'No region of the world', Haweis concluded, 'affords us happier prospects in our auspicious career of sending the Gospel to the Heathen lands.'[15]

Vason was one of ten missionaries sent to settle as a community of brethren in Tongatabu in 1797. Aged between 23 and 49, all were single men, none of them ordained, having been employed in artisan occupations. They were 'godly mechanics': uneducated men, with a useful trade and accomplished in the means of grace. They represented the lowly origins of the missionary movement, reflecting in part the biblical emphasis on labour; the Enlightenment association of artisan skills with civilization; and, more pressingly, the lack of educated and ordained men coming forward for the cause. Their selection for Tahiti and the islands reflected the directors' belief that the South Pacific was a comparatively receptive missionary field, and that better educated missionaries could be saved for more testing fields.[16] The missionaries were soon forced to revise their initial feelings of gratitude at being sent to an island where war and brutality were less frequent. Their arrival coincided with a political crisis, and from the outset they required the protection of chiefs, initially Tuku'aho, the most powerful man on the island and the Tu'i Kanokupolu, the head of the ruling family line. Soon the men were living in pairs or larger groups close to other protective chiefs. Vason separated from the rest of the brethren and went alone to live with Mulikiha'amea, a high-standing member of the former ruling line.[17]

Vason began almost immediately to slip away from the missionary project. He welcomed Mulikiha'amea's 'parental affection' and was 'delighted' by his household of wives, children and attendants. The 'patriarchal mode of life', whereby younger and inferior males lived in close relationship with the chief, impressed him greatly: it was an arrangement 'calculated much to refine and improve their mental faculties, and to polish their language and behaviour'. He especially enjoyed the 'nocturnal confabulations' initiated by the chief as all lay down to sleep. Sometimes the subject of conversation and interrogation, Vason felt 'surprised and improved, by the shrewdness of their observations, and the good sense of their reasonings'. Before long, he abandoned Western clothes and participated in native pastimes: swimming in the sea, playing music and dancing, drinking kava and shooting rats.[18] The life of a Tongan chief was pleasurable, and Vason soon aspired to such status.

Vason's descent into 'heathenism' began as he disencumbered himself of evangelical morality and was complete by the time he was persuaded by Mulikiha'amea to take a wife. Though she was 'a heathen, and perfectly destitute of every mental, as well as religious endowment who would most probably lead [him] still farther from the right way', he knew marriage would 'strengthen [his] interests with the rest of the natives', and, besides, 'she was a handsome girl of the age of eighteen'. With marriage, Vason's missionary work ended and he became barely distinguishable from his companions: 'I lament to say, that I now entered, with the utmost eagerness, into every pleasure and entertainment of the natives; and endeavoured to forget that I was once called a Christian, and had left a Christian land to evangelize the heathen.' Vason acquired land close to the residence of the chief and built a luxurious, Edenic plantation, an *api*, with smooth lawns, a lagoon, coconut, plantain and breadfruit trees, and sugar canes. With increased prosperity came more wives, a small canoe, and further indulgence, suggestive of sexual promiscuity. Vason even had his body tattooed. He had acquired 'Power and dignity', became one of the chiefs and participated in a brutal war which he later described with relish, despite the death of his protector.[19]

Although Vason's account is part redemption narrative and part attempt to protect other missionaries from erring, his lapses into a detailed cultural account betray his enjoyment of his early days on the island.[20] His descriptions of his 'amusements' are presented in an ethnographic style in which even early-morning Kava consumption is not moralized. His use of the term 'luxurious indolence', while reminiscent of the missionary register, is not condemnatory, but is followed in the text by lengthy descriptions of nights of dancing and singing and '[y]oung women of the most graceful figure and comely features' and 'ease, pleasure, grace and activity'. But Vason also had an ambivalent relationship to Tongan masculinity. While he appreciated Mulikiha'amea's domestic lifestyle, he was appalled by incidents of 'barbarity', as at the funeral of a chief – a 'palaestra for savage gladiators' – whose two widows were strangled and attendants murdered. In dynastic conflicts, Vason witnessed cannibalism, murder, mutilations and the annihilation of villages – scenes which disturbed him for the rest of his life.[21]

As he tried to signal to sailors aboard the *Royal Admiral* in 1801, Vason showed the true impact of his new life. He had momentarily settled under the protection of Chief Finau Ulukalala, but renewed political upheavals, food shortages, the realization that his missionary colleagues had been rescued by the *Betsy*, and the acknowledgement of his own mortal danger saw Vason desperate to find a passage home. He found himself calling to the sailors in sentences of mixed English and Tongan. His acculturation was so complete that he was unable to make himself clear; he no longer knew who he was.[22]

If his 'savage' self was to be kept in check, Vason had learned that his

Christian practice required the support of a strong Christian culture. With its discipline and prohibitions, Christianity, acquired within the context of his home culture, lost its significance in Tonga. He explained his aberration in terms of his own natural depravity and the temptation surrounding him, and as the result of the absence of a missionary community. Missionaries not only needed allies on the island but also some form of discipline, which could be provided by the brethren, especially those of mature years and experience, and also by marriage. His *Authentic Narrative of Four Years' Residence in Tongataboo* (1810) criticized the LMS for sending young, single men to the South Seas mission. 'What could be expected from young untried men, sent to such a place, – a place where temptation allured in every shape, and on every hand?' Vason asked with incredulity, 'No authentic record remains that even the Apostles went into a situation like that of these islands.'[23] Novices should only be sent to places where law and order was well established. As Rod Edmond wryly observes, while in England it was women who risked becoming 'fallen', in the South Seas it was missionaries who fell.[24] The LMS, and other societies, noted the point: missionary couples were becoming the norm when the next generation was sent out in 1816, and all had been given a more substantial training and alerted to the dangers of sexual temptation and moral backsliding.[25]

In addition to a wife, the men needed missionary protectors, 'tried veterans', who could support their endeavours at self-discipline.[26] While Vason blamed himself for his early lapse, the reader is left in no doubt that his 'steps out of the path of duty' might have been checked by the brethren. Indeed, describing an early visit to the brethren, he said, '[it] was of considerable use to revive and strengthen my religious principles, and to fortify me against those temptations with which I was daily surrounded and enticed. It would have been well', he added forebodingly, 'had I more frequently assembled with them.' In the absence of a strong paternalist Christian culture, Vason's 'evil inclinations' and the 'allurements' of the new culture combined to persuade him to 'listen to the voice of appetite, and to venture on indulgence'.[27] Let down by his evangelical fathers, he opted for the more spectacular patriarchal masculinity embodied by the Tongan chiefs.

Vason had travelled to the South Pacific in a supervisory capacity, with the intention of guiding heathen men and women towards Christianity and civilization. But, in abandoning the mission and adopting heathen manliness, he became more akin to his Tongan hosts than his missionary brethren. Choosing a different style of masculinity, in which he was one of a number of younger men in the household of Mulikiha'amea, Vason appreciated the latter's paternal care and the fraternal company of his new brethren. Even when he set up his own *api*, living with his Tongan wives, his independence and maturity did not preclude enjoyment of continued patronage from the chiefs. Vason left Tonga only when it became too dangerous for him to continue living on his island. He returned to England and evangelicalism. After a second conversion he became a member of Park Street (Friar Lane) Chapel in Nottingham. He was, however, never able to make a 'public profession' of his faith, and seemed to suffer from poor mental health until his death in 1838.[28] He married and worked as keeper at St Mary's workhouse in Nottingham and then for 18 years as the town's gaoler. Both occupations placed him in a disciplinary and supervisory relationship to other men. It is possible that his experiences in the South Seas meant that he could no longer rely on internal feeling, but required structured systems in which relationships were patriarchal, hierarchal and known.

II

The years following George Vason's departure saw the missionary language of brethrenship placed under stress in the South Seas, with patriarchal relationships between directors and missionaries, and missionaries and native men, made more explicit. These were difficult times: despite sanitized accounts in the *Evangelical Magazine*,[29] only one third of the original 30 men stayed with the mission. The group had been ill-prepared, few had linguistic skills, and there was scant appreciation of indigenous customs beyond a biblical expectation of gross immorality and the charms of native women.[30]

Despite the sternness of the LMS directors when selecting missionaries for the expedition, the board seemed to abdicate responsibility for the men during the early years of the mission.[31] At different times, missionaries sought guidance and care from the directors but their requests concerning salary, provisions, responsibility and furlough were unheeded or overruled. Correspondence from the board was infrequent: John Davies, a successful teacher, was in Tahiti for six years before receiving communication from London. Henry Bicknell, destitute on his return to England, had not worn shoes for eight years. Henry Nott, a bricklayer and Congregationalist, who was mid-way through a 30-year commitment to translating the Scriptures into Tahitian, was disappointed that when the LMS agreed to his return home for treatment for elephantiasis, he was instructed to pay for his passage. Missionaries repeatedly expressed their unhappiness at their treatment by the LMS, who kept them short of salaries and supplies, and criticized their 'commercial ventures' – petty trading – that supplemented their meagre salaries.[32]

The missionaries arriving in Tahiti in 1817 were horrified to discover their older brethren in a state of dishevelment and neglect, in homes that resembled 'bird cages'.[33] Exhibiting profound culture shock,[34] the new arrivals were damning of accommodations to native culture and especially of Davies's alleged 'gross immorality' with Tahitian women.[35] They were disturbed by the scarcity of conversions and the questionable integrity of those converted Tahitians who expressed their new faith in terms not easily recognizable to the missionaries. They called for an investigation, before removing to the Windward Islands where, in a 'spirit of independence and sufficiency', they set about procuring a true (and characteristically domestic) Christian revolution.[36]

If the missionaries appeared to their newly arrived brethren as errant youth, even more perplexing and distressing for them was the behaviour of the Tahitian island élites. The missionaries had from their arrival associated with the Pomare family, whom, following Cook, they believed to be Tahitian royalty.[37] Even when it became clear that this was not the case, they continued to support the family, especially the flamboyant Pomare II, on account of his considerable influence. Pomare II's power was frequently ill-used, however: during the early 1800s he ordered many human sacrifices. Despite his statement of conversion to Christianity in 1812, missionaries resisted baptizing Pomare until 1819. In 1815 he had returned from exile in Eimeo to fight the battle of Fei Pi in the name of Jehovah and had put into practice his commitment to abolish idolatry, holding visually spectacular bonfires of idols and making symbolic donations of family idols to British museums.[38] His promise to provide a Christian education for his infant son, born in 1820, further confirmed his Christian potential.

Pomare is represented in public LMS accounts as fulfilling the missionary reconstruction of the heathen subject.[39] The remoulding of heathen masculinity focused on persuading men to see the virtue of industrious labour, to become better husbands and fathers and to reject dissipated pastimes. The six-foot-tall king, despite his tattooed hands, beard and pony-tailed long hair, and remaining 'debasing habits', missionaries believed, had 'more of a personal dignity than could be expected from one who had been so lately a rude and fierce barbarian'. They learned from Nott that he spent his evenings teaching his attendants to read the Scriptures and that he was involved in translation work; noted for his cruelty in the past, he was now subduing warring groups. George Bennet and Daniel Tyerman, who formed the deputation sent to investigate conflict between missionaries in the islands, had been impressed by the well-dressed gathering of Christians – Pomare's wife, Queen Taaroa Vahine, their baby son Teariitaria, his ten-year-old daughter by a former spouse, Aimata, and Taaroamaiturai, the Queen's sister – who listened attentively as the King overcame the pain of his illness to converse with them on the subject of Christian progress. Like George III, whose influence on the public education system at home the missionaries relayed to Pomare, it was believed that the Tahitian royal could nurture his nation's progress. People everywhere followed their example: 'the mighty moral change', Bennet wrote, 'commenced from the King himself'.[40] Pomare's conduct as a benign, nurturing, Christian patriarch, along with the groundswell of Christian conversions in Tahiti and Eimeo, and missionary extension to the islands of Huahine, Raiatea and Borabora, all supported the interpretation of the South Seas mission, for a brief moment in the 1820s at least, as an unqualified story of success.

Bennet and Tyerman's public account of Pomare was very different from representations of him provided by other missionaries, and also from that hinted at by the visitors themselves in their personal correspondence with the directors. Some among the missionaries were distressed by the King's apparent reluctance to break free from 'sinful habits' and consequently doubted his true commitment to Christianity. Indeed, some such sinful habits could not even be talked about, including his having living with him a *mahu*, a man dressed as a female.[41] Other sources confirm such beliefs: Russian navigator Baron von Bellinghausen, for example, witnessed Pomare sending secret notes to passing whalers, requesting rum and wine, and Vahine asking for a bottle of rum for herself, complaining that her husband had consumed a whole bottle.[42] Pomare, argued LMS historian Lovett in 1893, was more similar to his father, Pomare I, described both as 'majestic' and 'a poor untaught heathen, under the dominion of a reprobate mind', than to civilized man. His mother, the Queen, died in 1806, apparently trying to bring on an abortion. She was known to have already killed numerous children, all conceived by 'common men' of lower rank.[43] Questioning the King's motivation for turning to Christianity, Lovett suggested that the combination of a general decline in idolatry, the role of missionaries and bounty hunters in assisting him to extend his rule, and the relative wealth of the missionaries, increasingly accompanied by gifts and other goods to barter, were of greater significance than spiritual motives. At his death in 1822, Pomare's friend, William Pasco Crook, wept with grief while also feeling that it might be 'a public benefit': 'the King's conduct', he wrote, 'has been the greatest check to the civilization of the people'.[44]

Christian prescriptions for desirable masculine practices were met with considerable resistance in the islands. Tyerman, writing from Huahine to reassure Samuel Marsden in New South Wales that 'Religion and Civilization' were 'going hand in hand', in the same letter reported on the thirty to forty 'profligate young men' on each island who breached law and order, sold liquor and were antagonistic to the missionaries.[45] Bennet and Tyerman noted in 1823 that while there had been fewer excommunications than they had expected, some had recently taken place in Haweis Town for tattooing. Generally undertaken by 'headstrong young men', tattooing – 'this barbarous species of embroidery' – was recognized by Bennet and Tyerman as 'a symbol of their [the men's] disaffection with the better order of things, and a signal for revolt against the existing government'.[46] Other instances of antagonism included the wearing of Western dress in an inappropriate style; the collective refusal of women to uphold missionary John Williams's moral objection to their preparation of food for the wife of a chief about to give birth to a child by another man; or the baring of bottoms in an expression of resistance.[47]

After the death of Pomare II, hopes were pinned on his little son who, as the four-year-old Pomare III, became the first king to experience a Christian coronation. Whilst a student at the missionary school at Eimeo, however, the young king died, and the throne then passed to Aimata, his half-sister. Richard Lovett, writing his history of the LMS in the harsher racial climate of the 1890s, emphasized the hereditary nature of moral failure. Lovett's does not seem to have been a strictly racial analysis; Tahitian Christians, he believed, were 'the merest babes in Christ'. Aimata, however, was influenced by the 'evil lives' of her mother and aunts and soon began 'to manifest many of the worst qualities of the vicious ancestry from which she sprang'.[48]

For early nineteenth-century missionaries, such a biological approach to Tahitian capacities held no appeal. Polynesians, like themselves, were God's children and members of the same human family. But they were beginning to question the length of time within which the mission might be expected to yield success. Henry, writing in February 1825, claimed, 'The best native teachers that any of these Windward or Leeward Islands can as yet produce are very defective, and little more than fit to clear away the rubbish in the places to which they are sent, and prepare the way for more effective labourers.' Orsmond, the most bitter and caustic of the 1816 group, put it more bluntly: 'Tahiti is the vortex of iniquity, the Sodom of the Pacific and gazing stock to the world, a thorn in the eyes of the just.'[49] From Huahine, Bennet and

Tyerman noted rather more generously that while progress was good, a 'greater care and circumspection are probably necessary here in the admission of persons to the Lord's table, than in England'.[50] Believers were 'often imperfect in either knowledge or practice. They are children of a larger growth.'[51]

Pomare II was believed by the missionaries, despite his physical stature and personal power, to be one such child, to be reconstructed by paternal missionaries in both his stately and familial roles. His conversion to Christianity in 1812 and his commitment in 1820 to provide a Christian education for his little son saw him established as a symbol of hope and a vindication of missionary assumptions about the possibility and desirability of a global Christian mission. Pomare's many failings, however, were a source of great disillusionment. For missionaries, unable to contemplate a rational basis for a refusal of Christian teachings, their encounter with Pomare unexpectedly gave challenge to the missionary philanthropic paradigm, providing an opening for a more essentialist racism to enter the culture from the 1840s.[52]

III

Middle-class evangelical men of the late eighteenth- and early nineteenth-centuries saw missionary paternalism established as a form of masculine practice and identity which fed into both emerging middle-class and, later, national cultures and identities. Directors at home and missionary men and women in the field were variously fathers, brothers, mothers and sisters to the heathen, sent to constitute new Christian families and communities. Through their cultural interventions, they were to counter savage depravity, both seeing the production of individual 'babes in Christ' and hastening the progress of 'infant' cultures in the transition to civilization. But, as this chapter has illustrated, there were numerous tensions between ideologies of paternalism at an institutional level and the actual working-out of both filial and fraternal relationships between men of different classes and cultures. As these case studies suggest, the responses of men on the receiving end of the mission reveal the complexities of the missionary enterprise and the challenges to the familial 'empire' of the middle-class missionary fathers at home.

Both Pomare's resistance and Vason's accommodations to native culture emphasize the extent to which the reception of the missionary message was shaped by the indigenous cultural context in ways utterly unanticipated by evangelicals. The case of Pomare II shows that while missionaries were successful in infusing cultures with new signs and commodities, they had little control over the interpretation of their message.[53] Tahitians received the gift of Christianity in a variety of ways not intended by the missionaries; like many missionary subjects, they did not fully embrace Christian belief and practice, but adopted aspects of it, and for reasons which may not have been spiritual and may not have involved a total rejection of indigenous cultural patterns, including those of patriarchalism. George Vason's (temporary) revolt against evangelical mores saw him embracing an alternative form of paternalism which was more patriarchal than the manly domesticity of the evangelical Christian. Vason demonstrates that it was not only the objects of Christian evangelicalism who exhibited independence. He was one of many missionaries who diverged from the hopes and wishes of both brethren and directors in their understanding and interpretation of the Scriptures, the extent of their independence, the respect they accorded the directors back home, and their style of relating to the indigenous culture. Discourses of paternalism, less pervasive and consistent than in 'woman's mission' because of the wider range of subject positions available to public men, played a significant part in the production of the complex visions and actual relationships between the 'men, brethren and fathers' of the missionary encounter.

Notes

I should like to thank the editors for their comments on this chapter at various stages of completion.
1. See Introduction.
2. Davidoff and Hall, *Family Fortunes*; Tosh, *A Man's Place*.
3. For colonies as children, see Catherine Hall, *Civilizing Subjects: Metropole and Colony in the English Imagination 1830–1867* (Oxford: Polity, 2002), pp. 9–10.
4. A. Twells, *The Civilizing Mission and the English Middle Class, 1780–1850: The Heathen at Home and Overseas* (Basingstoke: Palgrave, forthcoming).
5. For the early missionary movement, see E. Stock, *The History of the Church Missionary Society*, Vol. 1 (London: Church Missionary Society, 1899); R. Lovett, *A History of the London Missionary Society 1795–1895*, Vol. 1 (London: Henry Froude, 1899); J. Morrison, *The Fathers and Founders of the London Missionary Society* (London: Fisher and Son, 1844); B. Stanley, *The History of the Baptist Missionary Society, 1792–1992* (Edinburgh: T. T. Clark, 1992).
6. For missionary families, the 'family of Man' and the remaking of the 'heathen', see Hall, *Civilising Subjects*, pp. 86–98, 115–39; also Twells, *The Civilizing Mission*.
7. J. and J. Comaroff, *Of Revelation and Revolution: Christianity, Colonialism and Consciousness in South Africa* (London: University of Chicago Press, 1991).
8. J. Angell James, 'A Tribute of Affectionate Respect to the Memory of the Fathers and Founders of the London Missionary Society. A Sermon' (London, 1849).
9. S. Thorne, *Congregational Missions and the Making of an Imperial Culture in Nineteenth-Century England* (Stanford, CA: Stanford University Press, 1999).
10. S. C. Potter, 'The Making of Missionaries in the Nineteenth Century: Conversion and Convention', *A Sociological Yearbook of Religion*, 1975, pp. 103–24.
11. B. Ramusack, 'Cultural Missionaries, Maternal Imperialists, Feminist Allies: British Women Activists in India, 1865-1945', in N. Chaudhuri and M. Strobel (eds), *Western Women and Imperialism: Complicity and Resistance* (Bloomington, IN: Indiana University Press, 1992) pp. 118–36; J. Haggis, 'Gendering Colonialism or Colonising Gender? Recent "Women's Studies" Approaches to White Women and the Historical Sociology of British Colonialism', *Women's Studies International Forum*, Vol. 13, No. 1 (1990), pp. 105–15; Twells, *The Civilizing Mission*.
12. *Life of the late George Vason of Nottingham. One of the Troop of Missionaries first sent to the South Sea Islands by the London Missionary Society in the Ship Duff, Captain Wilson, 1796* (London: John Snow, 1840), p. 64.
13. Ibid., p. 116
14. A. Porter, *Religion Versus Empire? British Protestant Missionaries and Overseas Expansion, 1700–1914* (Manchester: Manchester University Press, 2004), pp. 40–1.

15. T. Haweis, *Sermons Before the Missionary Society. Sermon 1. The Apostolic Commission, preached at the Spa Fields Chapel, September 22 1795* (London: T. Chapman, 1795).
16. See N. Gunson, *Messengers of Grace: Evangelical Missionaries in the South Seas, 1797–1860* (Melbourne: Oxford University Press, 1978); and chapters on Tonga and Tahiti in M. Cathcart, T. Griffiths, L. Watts, V. Anceschi. G. Houghton and D. Goodman (eds), *Mission to the South Seas: The Voyage of the Duff, 1796–1799* (Melbourne: University of Melbourne, 1990), pp. 55–75; 81–100.
17. I. C. Campbell, *Island Kingdom. Tonga Ancient and Modern* (Christchurch: Canterbury University Press, 1992), pp. 37–50; S. Latukefu, *Church and State in Tonga: The Wesleyan Methodist Missionaries and Political Development 1822–1875* (Canberra: Australian National University Press, 1974), pp. 1–27.
18. *Life of the Late George Vason of Nottingham*, pp. 132, 122, 121, 130.
19. Ibid., pp. 132–3, 139–40, 151–5, 179–80, 144, 146–7 and chs 14–16. Vason witnessed the deaths of three missionaries; see p. 173. He consented to a Christian marriage performed by the brethren, but on discovery that only death could release her from the bond of faithfulness to her husband, his wife declined; see p. 136. For women in Tongan society, see Campbell, *Island Kingdom*, p. 28.
20. On his return to Nottingham and evangelicalism, Vason's story was written down by a clergyman: S. Piggott (ed.), *An Authentic Narrative of Four Years' Residence at Tongataboo, One of the Friendly Islands, in the South Seas, by ——, who went thither in the Duff, under Captain Wilson, in 1796* (London: Longman, Hurst, Rees, Orme, 1810).
21. *Life of the Late George Vason of Nottingham*, pp. 123–4, 126–7, 108–9. For these conflicts, see Campbell, *Island Kingdom*, pp. 44–50.
22. *Life of the Late George Vason of Nottingham*, pp. 193–6.
23. Piggott (ed.), *Authentic Narrative*, pp. 114–15, 117.
24. R. Edmond, *Representing the South Pacific. Colonial Discourse from Cook to Gauguin* (Cambridge: Cambridge University Press, 1998), p. 99.
25. Gunson, *Messengers of Grace*, pp. 64–70, 147–59.
26. Piggott (ed.), *Authentic Narrative*, pp. 118–19.
27. *Life of the Late George Vason of Nottingham*, pp. 111–12, 129–30, 156, 119, 130, 142.
28. His autobiography suggests that he suffered from anxiety throughout his life, and from mental illness prior to his death in 1838. *Life of the Late George Vason of Nottingham*, pp. 212–19.
29. *Evangelical Magazine*, January 1800, pp. 3–14, 33–5; July 1800, pp. 28, 95–6; May 1801, pp. 188–9; July 1802, p. 286; May 1803, pp. 214–20; February 1804, pp. 231, 278, 378; March 1804, pp. 231, 278, 378; March 1808, pp. 137–8; August 1808, p. 354; January 1810, p. 34; December 1813, pp. 473–7; February 1814, p. 174; April 1814, pp. 157–9; July 1814, p. 294; December 1814, p. 499; October 1816, pp. 36, 284, 321; 403, 408, 450; January 1817, pp. 75–6; Jan 1818, pp. 81–5; April 1818, pp. 173–4; December 1818, pp. 572–3; 1818 Supplement; 1819, pp. 40, 119, 349, 522; August 1821, pp. 349–52.
30. See Cathcart et al., *Mission to the South Seas*, pp. 55–69, 76–8.
31. Gunson, *Messengers of Grace*, p. 64.
32. D. Tyerman to S. Marsden, 26 October 1822 and 13 November 1822, SOAS Library, LMS Archive, Box 10; N. Gunson, *Messengers of Grace*, pp. 40, 114–19, 239–41.
33. N. Gunson, 'John Williams and his Ship: The Bourgeois Aspirations of a Missionary Family', in D. P. Crook (ed.), *Questioning the Past: A Selection of Papers in History and Government* (Brisbane: University of Queensland Press, 1972), pp. 73–95.

34. Edmond, *Representing the South Pacific*, pp. 101–2.
35. Gunson, *Messengers of Grace*, pp. 119–21 and 155–7; Bennet to Orsmond, 15 March 1824, SOAS, LMS Archive, Box 10 (1C).
36. Gunson, *Messengers of Grace*, pp. 123–4.
37. Cathcart et al., *Mission to the South Seas*, p. 57.
38. K. Howe, *Where the Waves Fall: A New South Sea Islands History from First Settlement to Colonial Rule* (Honolulu: University of Hawaii Press, 1984), pp. 125–51.
39. Hall, *Civilising Subjects*, pp. 115–19.
40. J. Montgomery (ed.), *Journal of Voyages and Travels by the Reverend Daniel Tyerman and George Bennet, Esquire, Deputed from the London Missionary Society to Visit their Various Stations in the South Seas, China, India etc, between the Years 1821 and 1829* (London: Frederick Westley and A. H. Davis, 1831), Vol. 1, pp. 102, 66, 75, 79, 81, 102, 61–3, 85.
41. D. Tyerman and G. Bennet, Haweis Town, Papara, Tahiti, 3 November 1823, SOAS Library, LMS Archive, Box 10; Montgomery (ed.), *Voyages and Travels*, Vol. 1, p. 102.
42. Quoted in A. Morehead, *The Fatal Impact: An Account of the Invasion of the South Pacific 1767–1840* (London: Penguin, 1966), p. 85.
43. *Sheffield Iris*, 10 May 1826; Montgomery (ed), *Voyages and Travels*, Vol. 1, pp. 71–2, 196.
44. Lovett, *History of the London Missionary Society*, Vol. 1, pp. 181, 186, 181, 228–30.
45. D. Tyerman to S. Marsden, Huahine, 26/10/1822, SOAS, LMS Archive, Box 10 (1).
46. D. Tyerman, Report, Oct 1823, SOAS, LMS Archive, Box 10; Montgomery (ed.), *Voyages and Travels*, Vol. 1, pp. 219, 239.
47. Edmond, *Representing the South Pacific*, pp. 124–6.
48. Lovett, *History of the London Missionary Society*, Vol. 1, pp. 291–2.
49. Edmond, *Representing the South Pacific*, p. 121, note 54.
50. Daniel Tyerman, Report from Huahine, 1822, SOAS, LMS Archive, Box 10 (3).
51. G. Bennet and D. Tyerman, Report from Eimeo, 1821–22, Aug 1821, SOAS, LMS Archive, Box 10 (3).
52. See Richard Price, 'Bad Education: How British Humanitarians Learnt Racism in the Empire, 1840–1860' (unpub. paper, March 2005).
53. Comaroff, *Of Revelation and Revolution*.

11
A Wealth of Fatherhood: Paternity in American Adoption Narratives

Claudia Nelson

If early nineteenth-century American commentators believed that the orphaned, abandoned or deprived children of the poor needed employment to save them from their parents' criminality or fecklessness, their early twentieth-century heirs increasingly contended that such children needed families. Although multiple methods of dealing with displaced children existed, including institutionalization, state-subsidized foster care, and forms of quasi-apprenticeship in which the child exchanged labour for room and board, eventually most social theorists and many lay persons agreed that adoption was the ideal. Between 1851 and 1929 every existing state enacted public adoption laws so that needy children might find homes.

But in the context of the Victorian cult of domesticity, which privileged emotions and ethics that the era associated with bourgeois femininity, 'home' often meant the mother. Accordingly, much turn-of-the-century journalism, social workers' commentary, and children's and adult fiction, all forms that both responded to and sought to influence public policy, implied, and sometimes asserted, that the father was replaceable while the mother was not. For instance, Adolph Lewisohn, president of New York City's Hebrew Sheltering Guardian Society, argued in 1909 that the state should fund pensions for widowed mothers in order to reduce the need for adoption and foster care. Children, he contended, belong 'with their own mothers, who can give them the parental love and the parental attention . . . which can not be obtained in any other way'. That 'any other way' includes the father is evident in Lewisohn's next paragraph, which cites 'the sheer inability on the part of the [widowed] father to give his children the home attention which they require'.[1] Here fathers appear exclusively as economic providers, a role that may, when necessary, be filled by the state; in contrast, mothers offer a nurture that depends on irreplaceable emotional bonds. Or, as Lewisohn's colleague Simon Wolf, founder of Atlanta's Hebrew Orphan's Home, put it, the mother's job was to ensure 'the safety and importance of the home' by bestowing 'the affection and love which emanates from the mother to the child'.² Home is love, and love is mother; the father's contributions are either non-existent or unimportant. Within the sentimental paradigm shared by Wolf, Lewisohn and many of their contemporaries, mothers loom so large that fathers may disappear, or at best hover in the background.³

But we cannot assume too readily that, even during the heyday of the cult of domesticity, American fathers were always cast in supporting roles, whether as emotionally insignificant wage-earners or as auxiliary and inferior mothers. Following the lead of John Tosh, who finds in Victorian England four basic patterns for middle-class fatherhood, absence, distance, tyranny and intimacy,⁴ we might view American writings on adoption from 1850 through the First World War as identifying multiple paternal roles, from household divinity to playmate to reclaimable sinner. The range of subject-positions available for fathers in such texts both reflects a perception that fatherhood means different things to different men and illustrates for male and female readers the benefits of fatherhood – for children, but also, often, for adults. Simultaneously, these positions acquire a masculine slant through association with domesticity's economic dimension, then widely regarded as a male purview. Adoption narratives of all types note the father's part as provider (while remarking that not all fathers enact it), but the varied ways in which they approach this role acknowledge its emotional complexity. Lewisohn's perception of the father as little more than his pay cheque is merely one point on a continuum; other commentators view the paternal economy in different lights.

I

The rapid urbanization of the early nineteenth century effected dramatic changes in the American family, which in turn led to a boom in domestic advice manuals in the 1830s. As Nancy Cott observes, while these books assume that the mother dominated middle-class child care, they simultaneously envision an important role for the father as what one advice-giver, Samuel Goodrich, called the 'Deity of Childhood': authority figure, intellectual guide, and ruler of the child's conscience.⁵ The contemporaneous strength of evangelical Christianity likewise created a climate that emphasized patriarchy alongside child-rearing. While some historians suggest that the 'father-as-Deity' model was more an ideal than a widespread practice, and that it reflected anxiety about the father's dwindling domestic involvement,⁶ the model's appeal was none the less considerable before the Civil War. We find it, for instance, in Susan Warner's *The Wide, Wide World* (1850), which was widely read (especially by girls and women) in Britain and, indeed, was the first American novel to become an international best seller – a success that illustrates the extent to which Warner's take on domesticity suited her day.

Warner's protagonist, Ellen Montgomery, is a Christian Cinderella. Aged ten as the narrative begins, Ellen is shortly to be separated from her mother, since Ellen's father is insisting that his wife join him on a European business trip. Captain Montgomery has recently declared bankruptcy, and, as in many subsequent American narratives, his failure in business symbolizes his failure as a parent. The Captain's deficiencies create a vacuum in the family; consequently, the story is studded with father-substitutes. Some, including his viraginous half-sister, Fortune Emerson,[7] and his wife's worldly brother, Mr Lindsay, prove to be false authority figures, whose proprietorship of Ellen does not provide the moral benefit to the child that the novel implicitly identifies as crucial to the father's role. A worthier mentor, who brings Ellen's nascent Christianity to fruition, is Ellen's spiritual father and future husband, John Humphreys.

Ellen encounters John after her parents die, her mother of illness, her father in a shipwreck. She meets him through his sister, Alice, who befriends her. After Alice dies, a plot twist that underscores women's inability to stay the course as parents, Ellen is invited to join the Humphreys family in her stead. Ellen happily accepts, but at 14 she belatedly receives her parents' instruction that she live with the aristocratic Lindsays in Edinburgh. The Lindsays disapprove of Ellen's evangelicalism and American loyalties; they forbid her to mention her foster-brother/father until John arrives and reclaims her for his country, his faith and himself. In contrast to Mr Lindsay's genteel old-world idleness, John's status as a worker identifies him as a representative of American energy, despite his own British origins. More specifically, the fact that he is a clergyman establishes his ability to serve as the novel's ultimate parental figure, a seasoned guide who can be relied upon in both secular and sacred matters.

The novel inserts Ellen into a series of constructed families. In each, her entry into the family is effected through a female tie: her relationship with her half-aunt, her friendship with Alice, her role as her mother's daughter. Yet Warner also reiterates the emotional, physical and/or religious weakness of these ties. Ellen's unstated goal thus becomes that of identifying not a surrogate mother to supply love and tenderness but the right kind of masculine authority. This she finds not in her undomesticated and insolvent biological father; not in Fortune's eventual husband, the genial but uneducated Van Brunt; and not in the dictatorial Mr Lindsay, who insists, 'I will not have you call me 'uncle' – I am your father – you are my own little daughter and must do precisely what I tell you.'[8] Rather, it is Christ and John Humphreys who together offer the kind of guidance coupled with strength that Ellen needs. And it is orphanhood that gives her the breadth of experience necessary to distinguish the true father from the false, and hence to learn to prefer patriarchal to matriarchal authority.

Yet, significantly, John is patriarchal without being a patriarch, since his most striking quality is the extent to which he enacts multiple familial roles. His father, not he, is the official paterfamilias of the Humphreys home. But John accepts the responsibility that the era's child-rearing manuals assign to Ellen's father, namely her intellectual and spiritual education, and it is he, not Mr Humphreys, who travels to Scotland to retrieve Ellen for the family. He is also Ellen's foster brother (since he is the brother of her dead 'sister', Alice) and romantic object. In playing all these parts, he proves himself the most versatile character in the novel, embodying in one figure – like the vision of Christ with which Thomas Hughes ends his contemporaneous *Tom Brown's Schooldays* – feminine 'love and tenderness and purity', masculine 'strength and courage and wisdom'.[9]

In his potency and flexibility, John proves himself superior to Ellen's initial love object, her mother. The narrator's early comment that 'love to her mother was the strongest feeling [Ellen's] heart knew' typifies the era's tendency to hold up the Christian mother, selfless and devoted, for adoration – from both her offspring and the reader.[10] Still, Warner shows that Mrs Montgomery lacks John's wisdom. Not only has she erred in marrying against her family's wishes and in failing to bring husband and daughter to true Christianity, she also jeopardizes Ellen's hope of salvation by posthumously moving her from America to Edinburgh. Mrs Montgomery's helplessness is endemic among the novel's women; even such seemingly strong figures as Fortune and Alice must confront their limitations when they encounter men whose views differ from their own. If Ellen is to be saved, she needs a powerful Christian foster-father, not merely a devoted Christian mother.

The narrative's perception that even the most loving birth mother may prove inadequate gives Ellen's odyssey elements in common with those of the displaced working-class children who were the objects of the New York Children's Aid Society. As the Society's founder, Charles Loring Brace, envisioned it, in a conception shared with his British counterpart Dr Thomas Barnardo, the 'orphan trains' that carried these children from the slums to new lives in the country were lifting them not only in a worldly sense but also in a moral one. In Brace's formulation, the young emigrés' parents were failures in more than economic terms; it was their lack of industry and initiative that had brought their offspring to destitution. He highlights the failings of even the loving biological mother, who emerges as foolishly possessive, holding back her child by blocking his or her migration to the West. And, as Brace later wrote, his major reason for deciding in the 1850s to send slum children to farms, besides the farmer's perennial need for labourers, was that farm workers, as live-in help, must 'share in [farmers'] social tone'.[11] His project, in short, was to find not kindly mothers for these children (who might, he noted, like Ellen Montgomery, already have their own), but father-surrogates who could model solvency.

Geared toward protecting the nation from what Brace termed the 'dangerous classes' (those of low 'social tone'), the efforts of the Children's Aid Society were not chiefly directed toward creating emotional bonds between child and foster parent. Rather, the transaction was seen as simultaneously moral and commercial, and the pairing of these qualities suggests that ethical and financial dimensions were related. Early advertisements seeking foster families, as Marilyn Irvin Holt observes, touted the children as 'sturdy workers'.[12] But instead of suggesting that erstwhile residents of slum homes would move from private to public sphere, a direction that would contravene the ideals of the home-obsessed cult of domesticity, this marketing campaign framed the displaced youngsters as always already 'public children'. The emphasis was on how bootblacks, newsboys or vendors would move from a street-based work-life devoid of authority figures to one that would harness their energies productively. Thus an 1859 report on the society's achievements remarked that children formerly 'in the most extreme misery, we beheld sitting, clothed and clean, at hospitable tables, calling the employer "father", loved by the happy circle'.[13] Emphasized here is the children's emotional health and their newly civilized state. That the foster parent is an 'employer', and that the important foster parent is the father, is taken for granted. Today, Brace's words evoke less a devoted family in the sentimental tradition than a job performed for a benevolent boss. Yet this vision illuminates what was often expected of paternity. Anthony Rotundo observes of the nineteenth-century American family that mother and father typically controlled different ethical areas, with the father overseeing 'values governing work, achievement, and property ... [namely] perseverance and thrift ... diligence and punctuality ... industry and ambition'[14] – and it was these values, not feminine tenderness and purity, that Brace wanted his wards to learn.

Brace and his fellows agreed with Warner that the blood tie was not all-important. The tenement home was presumed to pose moral dangers: parents here were probably abusive, distanced from their children by drudgery or drunkenness, and incapable of providing Christian nurture. Move the child from the slums to a middle-class setting, and moral as well as social benefits would ensue. The new guardians could nurture the child better than its impoverished parents could – even when the original parents loved the child and the replacements did not – because the effect of destitution was to shatter the family's 'natural' defences against an evil world, to turn the private into the public. Such assumptions hint that although domestic rhetoric insisted that families, especially mothers, were the wellspring of virtue, a suspicion nevertheless existed that money and social class, which typically derived not from the mother but from the father, might be the true source of good. To save a child in the 1850s, one did not need to find it a new mother for emotional or sentimental reasons; what it required was the respectability associated with the successful paterfamilias.

II

Two decades after the orphan trains sponsored by the New York Children's Aid Society and by its inspiration and rival, the Boston Children's Mission, had begun to implement this philosophy, we can discern in the children's fiction of the era the practical patriarchalism articulated by Brace. A serial published in *Our Young Folks* in 1871 by the magazine's coeditor, J. T. Trowbridge, reads like a dramatization of Brace's assumptions about the displaced child's needs. The protagonist of *Jack Hazard and His Fortunes* enters the story as a petty thief and 'the most profane little driver on the canal', failings attributable to the influence of Jack's stepfather, his sole remaining parent: 'with such a man as Old Jack Berrick for a father ... how was it possible for him to be different?'[15] That Berrick is not Jack's blood kin underscores the illegitimacy of the working-class father's claims; a man who fails to provide protection, guidance and security for his family is no true father, as even Berrick's cronies suggest. Encouraged to flee by a passing gentleman, who promises to get Jack taught 'a trade, or to work on a farm' and to protect him against Berrick's legal claims, the boy begins to see that life with (step)father is not his only option.[16] Although he rejects the gentleman's help, Jack runs away from Berrick's canalboat and eventually joins the family of a respectable deacon-cum-farmer, where he manages to 'put off all [his] bad habits with [his] old clothes, and put on new behavior with this clean suit'.[17]

When decently clad, Jack not only 'look[s] as well as anybody's boy', but also finds it easier to follow the unknown gentleman's recipe for success: 'First, don't be afraid of hard work. Second, be honest and truthful, and decent in your speech and behavior. Third, help others.'[18] While Jack is assisted in his quest for 'decency' by the deacon's wife and the schoolmistress, the ideal toward which he strives is one of good business practice, instilled in him not by mother- or sister-figures but by a man. As with the early orphan-train riders, his new home is also his workplace; his informal acceptance as an apprentice to the economy and morals of the family farm is symbolized by the deacon's offer to buy him 'a decent suit for Sunday, that'll do for you to wear to school next winter'.[19] Readers understand that the arrangement has dimensions beyond the financial. If Jack is right to acknowledge that his 'board and [work] clothes are about all [he's] been worth', the deacon's proposal – which brings tears to Jack's eyes – is both a fair man's desire to reward a hard-working employee and a tacit invitation to join the family.[20]

Moreover, the denouement identifies the tale as a paternal melodrama in which Jack must negotiate the competing claims of multiple 'fathers'. First, he discovers that Berrick is in jail awaiting trial for having murdered him; the false accusation is metaphorically true, as Berrick's encouragement of qualities that made Jack 'an outcast in the dismal night' was a form of spiritual violence.[21] Berrick is penitent, however. Upon discovering that Jack is still alive, he proves his affection in a way that Brace would applaud, by signing a document relinquishing his rights to the boy and remarking, 'For my part, I'm glad as anybody that he has done better for himself; and I cheerfully give up my claim to him here and now.'[22] We learn, too, that a charcoal-burner, now 'drowned in six inches of water' after a drinking bout, but earlier a possible 'patron and example in life' to Jack, was Berrick's half-brother, gone to the bad after a boyish escapade led to tragedy; that the unknown gentleman without whose words Jack 'never could have begun life new' is the deacon's wife's cousin and Berrick's prison physician; and that Jack's dog's former owner, another alcohol-related fatality, was the ne'er-do-well son of the forbidding local squire, whose hardness and censoriousness presumably contributed to his son's downfall.[23] When the schoolmistress jokes that a proper ending would be 'for Squire Peternot to adopt [Jack] and Lion [the dog] in place of his son', the deacon asserts his paternal authority, promising 'to keep him, if he'll stay and be to us as our own son'.[24]

At this suggestion, which fulfils Jack's dearest hopes, tears again fill the boy's eyes. As in the episode of the Sunday suit, his response assures the reader that the business arrangement between child and deacon is more than an economic exchange; it is an emotional bond that represents Jack's best chance for a productive future life. Simultaneously, however, it remains a business arrangement. Such fiction makes a point important to the ethos of the contemporaneous society: if the cult of domesticity sometimes positioned work and home as mutually hostile, works such as those of Trowbridge (and of his colleague Horatio Alger) reassured readers by asserting that the work ethic *was* the sentimental ethic. Within this philosophy, fathers were free to retain their eighteenth-century position as the masters of the home and the dominant socializing agents for boys – a position whose erosion social commentators had been combating for decades.

That Trowbridge's novel measures the impoverished father's efforts to rehabilitate himself by his willingness to relinquish custody of his son similarly reflects contemporaneous social practice. In life and fiction alike, working-class families by the 1870s were presumed more fragile than their affluent counterparts, partly because making a living could be a desperate matter. In the United States as in Britain, the father thus loomed particularly large in discussions about the families of the poor, and was particularly likely to be seen as inadequate. Had he not already demonstrably failed, inasmuch as he was not supporting his family in middle-class style? Thus a stereotype of the father as wastrel operates not only in post-Civil War waif fictions such as *The Adventures of Huckleberry Finn* and in journalism on both sides of the Atlantic, but also, to some extent, in legal doctrine. In some states, common law held that a father's social standing affected his claims over his children; a rich man had a better chance than a poor man in a custody dispute, even if the latter was the biological parent and the former was not.[25] Men's insolvency was often thought to signal a corresponding poverty of character, an assumption that helps to explain Brace's belief that even when the families of the poor were intact, transferring the children to the care of middle-class caregivers/employers was best.

For if Brace was not much concerned with the feelings of orphan-train riders, he was heavily invested in their morals. His was not simply a slum-clearance project, under which New York City could rid itself of the excrescence represented by its poorest inhabitants. Rather, he proposed a reformation of his protégés that would embrace personal finance, livelihood, class, diet, hygiene, wardrobe – all the accoutrements of respectability, but in this list the markers of economic status (associated with the father) trump those of gentility (associated with the mother). Most importantly, he believed that as children's actual or potential economic status rose, their characters would change too. It was not maternal influence but suitable work that would reveal the virtue that lurked inside. Thus the Children's Aid Society measured its success by tabulating its male graduates' employment records, counting the governors, soldiers, lawyers, and landowners produced rather than, say, the churchgoers. That Brace encouraged the children to write to him from their new homes, addressing him as 'Dear Friend', suggests both his acceptance of responsibility for their welfare and his perception of the power of the right kind of masculine presence. In a sense, he offered himself as the ultimate replacement for their birth parents, a distant but kindly father who not only modelled accountability for his charges but also demanded it from them in return.[26]

III

By the early twentieth century, however, the father's economic success might be portrayed as trivial compared to his emotional success, which was sometimes divorced from his erstwhile role as authority figure. To be sure, we can point to ideal adoptive fathers such as Mr McLean in Gene Stratton-Porter's *Freckles* (1904), who follows Brace's lead in bestowing upon the protagonist not only a social identity (he gives him the name of his own idealized father) but also a job and an education. Upright and productive, McLean represents both the virtues and the power of democratic capitalism. Yet more typical is Frances Hodgson Burnett's 1905 novel *A Little Princess*, another text popular on both sides of the Atlantic. Here, motherless Sara Crewe has been placed in a London boarding school by her father, an Anglo-Indian whose fortune is invested in a friend's diamond mines. When the mines apparently prove worthless, Ralph Crewe dies of the shock, leaving his daughter destitute; fatherly weakness turns the one-time parlour-boarder into the school drudge. But Sara's perfect deportment and fluent Hindustani attract the interest of Tom Carrisford, a rich invalid with an Indian past of his own, who amuses himself by anonymously showering her with presents. When he discovers her identity – for he is, of course, Ralph Crewe's friend – he adopts her, and we learn that the mines, literal and paternal, are full of diamonds after all.

Certainly the financial status of her biological and adoptive fathers is crucial to Sara's physical comfort. Yet what seems most important to her happiness is that her worth be recognized and that no one seek to dominate her. In this regard, she is fortunate in both her fathers. Although Ralph Crewe is an army officer, he lacks the habit of command where his daughter is concerned; he and seven-year-old Sara are 'the dearest friends and lovers in the world'.[27] During her father's lifetime, Sara takes her dead mother's place as his 'comrade' and 'companion'; they plan that when she finishes her education, she will become his hostess and housekeeper. At their parting, she tells him, '"I know you by heart. You are inside my heart". And they put their arms round each other and kissed as if they would never let each other go'. This byplay has the same adult overtones that characterize the wardrobe he buys her, full of ostrich feathers and ermine.[28] But if in *The Wide, Wide World* the fact that the father is also the husband suggests the wife's need for masculine guidance, in *A Little Princess* Captain Crewe's loverlike demeanour toward Sara indicates *his* need to lean on *her* – a need that the novel endorses by transferring it to his successor, whom Sara must cure of the invalidism imposed by the Indian climate and by guilt at his friend's death.

If fathers need healing in this novel, they none the less have an edge on mothers, whose flaws generally seem here too grave to be cured. Thus Burnett details the sins of the school's preceptress, Miss Minchin, a cold phallic-mother type whose exalting of business over sentiment makes her, like Warner's Fortune Emerson, resemble the type of Victorian male critiqued through figures such as Charles Dickens's Mr Dombey more than any man in the novel. Miss Minchin's sister and business partner is ineffectual; the adult female servants do not nurture. With only one exception, biological mothers are snobs who have taught their daughters false morals, or they have become irretrievable by dying. In this context, the sins of the fathers of Sara's schoolmates Lottie Legh and Ermengarde St John seem venial.

Lottie is used to illustrate the father's disciplinary failings. After her mother's death, she 'had been sent to school by a rather flighty young papa who could not imagine what else to do with her ... As the child had been treated like a favorite doll or a very spoiled pet monkey or lap-dog ever since the first hour of her life, she was a very appalling little creature.'[29] Since Mr Legh's paternal tactics recall Captain Crewe's tendency to shower his daughter with luxuries and surround her with servants who '[give] her her own way in everything', Sara's virtues signal her incorruptibility rather than Crewe's fatherly virtues.[30] As Mr Legh has fled from child-rearing, it is up to Sara to take care of Lottie, just as she has earlier taken care of her own father; Captain Crewe's pet name for her, 'the little missus', acknowledges her status as the family's real adult. But that Sara *can* successfully nurture Lottie suggests that the father's errors are retrievable.

Unlike Mr Legh and Captain Crewe, Mr St John has grown up, but he too is no paternal paragon. A clever man, he finds his daughter Ermengarde's stupidity maddening, with the result that he has browbeaten her until she 'would do anything desperate to avoid being left alone in his society for ten minutes'.[31] In contrast, Sara 'always felt very tender of Ermengarde, and tried not to let her feel too strongly the difference between being able to learn anything at once, and not being able to learn anything at all'.[32] Sara's kindness to Ermengarde thus functions as a reproach of her friend's father, whose demeanour looks abusive by contrast. Yet in the earlier Burnett story upon which *A Little Princess* is based, Sara shares Mr St John's disdain for Ermengarde's slowness: ' "He will like it, I dare say, if you learn anything in any way," said Sara. "I should, if I were your father." '[33] In this rendition, Sara's attitude excuses Mr St John's, and her ability to drum facts into Ermengarde makes her his ally. The revision establishes her rather as his superior.

But Sara's greatest achievement is not her ability to stand in for absent or inadequate fathers, but her transformation of one of these men into the novel's male ideal. Thus the narrative, which so extensively criticizes families, also suggests that family, and specifically fatherhood, is the ultimate therapy. If the Select Seminary and its inmates show what can go wrong with domesticity and with the monied classes, the newly formed Carrisford family shows what affluent homes can accomplish. What really ails Carrisford is childlessness, and his adoption of Sara – his coopting of Ralph Crewe's domestic duties, which both men define as the unlimited indulgence of their 'little princess' – is the cure. In short, Burnett's point is not only that the dependent child deserves possessions and status even when cold-hearted worldliness (personified in Miss Minchin) denies her claim, but also that the child's happy ending is simultaneously that of the adoptive father, who finds in parenthood an outlet for both pent-up emotions and pent-up money. Stratton-Porter's McLean is a good father because, like Warner's John Humphreys, he is already stable and solvent; Burnett's Crewe and Carrisford must become fathers because they are wealthy without being strong. They both need and can afford the paternity that is to be their anchor.

The latter perception was again characteristic of the era. By 1900, Viviana Zelizer has argued, the middle-class child's familial role was more emotional and moral than practical.[34] It is 'children who do the saving', adoption advocate Lydia Kingsmill Commander wrote in 1907; 'To be responsible for a child

... whether he be your own by birth or by adoption, is the old, old way of purifying the dross out of human nature.' In Commander's view, the child's 'hardest task' is to deal with the dross of the *male* nature, 'To bind his restless, roving father to the home, and teach him the beauty of lifelong love between one man and one woman.'[35] While this perception criticizes men's domestic conduct, it simultaneously acknowledges that men may be reclaimed by paternity. And indeed, adoption was often described as therapy for men and women alike, as in a 1916 article by Dr Charles Gilmore Kerley, which mentions adoption's power to cure adult 'neurasthenia, despondency, and habitual grouch, particularly in men', or an adoptive father's comment in the *Woman's Home Companion* in 1913 that his son has transformed the psyches of both his wife and himself.[36]

Thus while at the turn of the century we find many fictions highlighting adoption's power to ennoble and fulfil women, others make the equivalent point about men. In François Coppée's 'Adoption', for example, reprinted in *The Chautauquan* in 1909, a hack writer shelters a destitute woman and her grandson to save the baby from institutionalization. In part he acts out of a sense that he 'has no talent, never has had', so that rescuing the child is a substitute 'for the book [he] ought to write'. But the adoption gives 'his [most recent] story, "The Orphan of Belleville", a certain something not to be found in the others', and 'the foremost novelist of his time' compliments him on the 'touches about children that are extremely fine, sincere, affecting'.[37] The implication, of course, is that men's domestic and professional lives need not be at odds. Fulfilment at home brings public success, and the man's fatherly impulse to protect the helpless child receives financial reward – enabling him, in turn, to be a better provider. Note, though, that emotion must precede money in this cycle.

IV

Historian Mark Carnes has written that 'the dilemma for boys in Victorian America was not simply that their fathers were absent, thereby depriving them of psychological guides to their core masculinity, but that adult gender roles were invariant and narrowly defined, and that boys were mostly taught the sensibilities and moral values associated with the adult female role'.[38] Richard Sennett goes further: not only did 'the roles of ... middle-class fathers narro[w] to providing the money necessary for the family to live', but, in addition, 'the father in the eyes of his offspring became a weakling who did not count, who failed to prepare the sons for their own tasks in the world'.[39] Over the last 35 years of American family historiography, we may find many such pronouncements. Yet one lesson taught by the literature of adoption – a literature that both critiques and exalts the family – is that what Carnes, Sennett and others see as '*the* dilemma' of the masculine gender role is merely *a* dilemma, one possibility among many.

The representations of American adoptive and biological fatherhood cited above share certain characteristics, particularly the perception that a man's economic behaviour is indispensable not only to his identity but also to his domestic role. Yet in other regards these representations diverge. Some participate in what Joe Dubbert terms 'the home-in-peril theme of countless books and magazine articles', others in what Margaret Marsh identifies as a 'model of masculine domesticity' reflecting ideals of companionate marriage, still others in a covert challenge to the cult of domesticity.[40] Some identify the good father as authoritarian, others as ready to learn from his child. In addition, some juxtapose their descriptions of good fathers with descriptions of men who are brutal, irresponsible and as impoverished emotionally as they are financially. Nevertheless, that good fathers exist in these texts is a commonplace, not a rarity. And if the texts stress the father's role as provider, economic provision often serves not as his only function but as a synecdoche for *all* his functions. His relationship to his adopted and biological offspring, then, is complex, varied and frequently productive, both socially and emotionally. In several senses, late nineteenth- and early twentieth-century visions of fatherhood constitute a rich lode for scholarly exploration.

Notes

Some material here recapitulates material in my book *Little Strangers: Portrayals of Adoption and Foster Care in America, 1850–1929* (Bloomington, IN: Indiana University Press, 2003). Fathers are not a major focus of that study, and I thank Trev Broughton and Helen Rogers for inspiring me to examine this research from a new angle.

1. *Proceedings of the Conference on the Care of Dependent Children Held at Washington, D.C. January 25, 26, 1909* (New York: Arno, 1971), p. 145.
2. Ibid., p. 149.
3. Such rhetoric continues well beyond the timespan of this chapter. Consider 'Train Brings 18 Babies to Nebraska: Trainload of Thirty-Five Arrive in Omaha for Distribution in Three States; Four Mothers Wait', Omaha *World-Herald*, 15 December 1921), repr. *Crossroads*, 14 (January 1991), p. 11, which reports the arrival of a group of adoptable children from the New York Foundling Hospital. The journalist records the adoptive mothers' public 'outpouring of such affection as only a mother can give'; the adoptive fathers watch, their faces 'reflect[ing] *a portion* of the joy radiating from the faces of their wives' (my emphasis). A contemporary version might be 'What Fathers Do Best', *Weekly Standard*, 10,38 (20 June 2005), pp. 17–18, whose author, Steven E. Rhoads, comments that hormonal differences ensure that mothers will be the important parents for young children where child care is concerned: 'Testosterone inhibits nurturing', although 'By faithfully working at often boring jobs to provide for their families, dads make . . . moms' nurturing of children possible.'
4. Tosh, *A Man's Place*, pp. 93–9.
5. N. F. Cott, 'Notes Toward an Interpretation of Antebellum Childrearing', *Psychohistory Review*, 6.4 (Spring 1978), pp. 4–20, 8.
6. See, for example, S. Curtis, 'The Son of Man and God the Father: The Social Gospel and Victorian Masculinity', in M. C. Carnes and C. Griffen, eds, *Meanings for Manhood: Constructions of Masculinity in Victorian America* (Chicago: University of Chicago Press, 1990), pp. 67–78, 69–70.
7. Despite her sex and her housewifery, Fortune functions as a surrogate father not only because, as a feme sole, she enjoys a freedom usually reserved for men, but also because of her personal attributes. Like many fictional Yankee males, she is

'sharp all over', 'very smart', and 'rich – she's [sic] one of the very best farms in the country'. So strong is her aversion to feminine sentiment that she forbids Ellen's grandmother to caress the child, 'avowing that it "made her sick"'. See S. Warner, *The Wide, Wide World* (New York: Feminist, 1987), pp. 111, 118, 119, 134.
8. Warner, *The Wide, Wide World*, p. 510.
9. T. Hughes, *Tom Brown's Schooldays* (New York: Puffin, 1971), p. 288.
10. Warner, *The Wide, Wide World*, p. 13.
11. C. L. Brace, *The Dangerous Classes of New York: And Twenty Years' Work Among Them* (Washington, DC: National Association of Social Workers, 1973), p. 225.
12. M. I. Holt, *The Orphan Trains: Placing Out in America* (Lincoln, NE: University of Nebraska Press, 1992), p. 138.
13. Brace, *The Dangerous Classes of New York*, p. 239.
14. E. A. Rotundo, *American Manhood: Transformations in Masculinity from the Revolution to the Modern Era* (New York: Basic, 1993), p. 27.
15. J. T. Trowbridge, 'Jack Hazard and His Fortunes', serialized *Our Young Folks* (January–December 1871), 2.
16. Trowbridge, 'Jack Hazard', p. 7.
17. Trowbridge, 'Jack Hazard', p. 259.
18. Trowbridge, 'Jack Hazard', p. 259, 7.
19. Trowbridge, 'Jack Hazard', p. 646. Apprentices and working foster children differed from conventional farmhands in that their employers typically provided not only room, board and perhaps wages, but also clothing and access to education.
20. Trowbridge, 'Jack Hazard', p. 646.
21. Trowbridge, 'Jack Hazard', p. 71.
22. Trowbridge, 'Jack Hazard', p. 710.
23. Trowbridge, 'Jack Hazard', p. 644–5, 709.
24. Trowbridge, 'Jack Hazard', p. 714.
25. P. J. Joachimsen, 'The Statute to Legalize the Adoption of Minor Children', *Albany Law Journal*, 8 (6 December 1873), pp. 353–7, 353–4.
26. Somewhat similarly, texts such as *Anne of Green Gables* (1908) use the term 'Barnardo boy' to denote a child sent from England to the colonies on a transoceanic version of the orphan train. The bestowing of the reformer's surname on his charges again implies that becoming one of these charges supersedes one's original family membership.
27. F. H. Burnett, *A Little Princess* (New York: Dell, 1979), p. 222.
28. Burnett, *A Little Princess*, pp. 16, 10, 17.
29. Burnett, *A Little Princess*, pp. 38–9.
30. Burnett, *A Little Princess*, p. 8.
31. Burnett, *A Little Princess*, p. 33.
32. Burnett, *A Little Princess*, p. 172.
33. F. H. Burnett, *Sara Crewe, or What Happened at Miss Minchin's* (New York: Putnam's, 1981), p. 27.
34. V. Zelizer, *Pricing the Priceless Child: The Changing Social Value of Children* (New York: Basic, 1985), p. 5.
35. L. K. Commander, 'The Home without a Child', *Delineator*, 70, 5 (November 1907), pp. 720–3ff., 830.
36. C. G. Kerley, 'The Adoption of Children', *Outlook*, 112 (12 January 1916), pp. 104–7, 105; 'The Making of a Father', *Woman's Home Companion*, 40, 2 (February 1913), p. 5.
37. F. Coppée, 'Adoption', *Chautauquan*, 53.2 (January 1909), pp. 249–55, 254, 255.

38. M. C. Carnes, 'Middle-Class Men and the Solace of Fraternal Ritual', in Carnes and Griffen (eds), *Meanings for Manhood*, pp. 37–52, 47–8.
39. R. Sennett, *Families Against the City: Middle Class Homes of Industrial Chicago 1872–1890* (Cambridge, MA: Harvard University Press, 1970), pp. 59, 217.
40. J. L. Dubbert, *A Man's Place: Masculinity in Transition* (Englewood Cliffs, NJ: Prentice-Hall, 1979), p. 102; M. Marsh, 'Suburban Men and Masculine Domesticity, 1870–1915', *American Quarterly*, 40, 2 (June 1988), pp. 165–86, 166.

12
Fatherhood Real, Imagined, Denied: British Men in Imperial India

Elizabeth Buettner

Looking back on her childhood during the First World War and the 1920s, the novelist M. M. Kaye recalled one of her father's rare trips to England in the course of his Indian Army career. For Kaye's mother, his return ended a separation that was, by the standards of British families linked to empire by virtue of the fathers' professions, a fairly brief one following her own earlier journey back from India. As was customary in officer-class families, however, his three children born in the subcontinent had long since been sent home for their schooling, his eldest son Bill at the age of six. Since the war postponed his next visit, by the time Cecil Kaye rejoined his family on leave it had been eight years since he had last seen his son. Kaye's rendition of their family reunion underscored the problematic relationship between father and son that was part of the 'price of empire' which such Raj families paid:

> When the day and the hour of his arrival finally came, all four of us were lined up waiting with our noses pressed to the window-panes of Mother's bedroom upstairs . . . when at last the taxi stopped in front of the gate and [he] got out, Bill, who had not seen his father for the best part of a decade and thought this must be a stranger, said: 'Who's that funny little man?' . . . Now that is real tragedy . . . Those five words . . . were Bill's instant reaction on seeing again the loved and admired parent to whom, as a bewildered and tearful little boy, he had waved goodbye so many long years ago . . . We never told [our father] what Bill had said. Their situation was difficult enough without that. And they had so little time in which to resolve it and get to know each other. That they never did succeed in closing the gap left by those lost years is not surprising: it yawned too wide and they had barely ten days in which to build a bridge that would span it.[1]

Family life as Kaye depicts it here was typical among many middle- and upper middle-class Britons connected with India during the late imperial era. Between the mid-nineteenth century and the Raj's collapse when India and Pakistan became independent in 1947, men whose professions took them to the empire were much more likely to have British wives and children living with them overseas than in the eighteenth or early nineteenth centuries. Males still far outnumbered females in the colonial community until the end of empire, but better transport facilities and colonial state support for white conjugality and domesticity worked together to bring more women to India. After the overland route through the Middle East replaced the need to travel around the Cape of Good Hope in the 1840s, journeys between Britain and India became much faster and cheaper, and once the Suez Canal opened in the 1860s they were reduced to three weeks. Colonial authorities favoured male colonizers' marriages to white women, and from the late 1700s onwards officials' once-prevalent (and tacitly accepted) sexual relationships and cohabitation with Indian women increasingly fell into disrepute.[2] Correspondingly, the sizeable Eurasian community that originated through European men's associations with Indian women progressively became marginalized throughout the nineteenth century.[3] British men were clearly the Eurasians' forefathers, but these 'children of colonialism' were largely disowned and stigmatized once white bourgeois domesticity became the morally acceptable public face of colonial culture.[4]

Racial distancing from Indians and Eurasians (later known as Anglo-Indians) grew after Crown rule replaced government by the East India Company in 1858 and steamship technology facilitated contacts with Britain. Yet colonial ideology and improved transport simultaneously encouraged and compromised British family life in India. More convenient and affordable journeys home coupled with ongoing concerns about the dangers that prolonged exposure to India's climate and indigenous culture entailed – especially for white children – caused the more affluent to prioritize periodic returns to Britain on leave and send children to school there at an early age. Children sent away from India avoided the 'tropics', contacts with 'natives' that many parents feared would jeopardize their British cultural affiliations, and being educated alongside Eurasians who were usually too poor to attend schools in the metropole. Leaving India, and remaining transient as opposed to settling, both symbolically and practically separated colonizers not only from the colonized but also from Eurasians, who were socially and economically difficult to distinguish from Europeans who had become 'domiciled' in the subcontinent. While remaining connected with Britain and distinct from those permanently settled in India was thus seen as essential, paradoxically these beliefs and practices effectively curtailed the very form of family life that had received official encouragement. Parents and children were often separated for years at a time once the latter began school. In some families women remained behind with their husbands in India and saw little of their children, while in others they largely lived with their children in Britain and left men alone in India.[5] In both cases, men's roles as either husbands or fathers, if not both, became disrupted and played out from a distance. As M. M. Kaye's account suggested, the emotional dimensions of fatherhood in particular were placed under considerable strain.

Lacking regular direct contact with their children once they returned to Britain, men none the less were understood – and understood themselves – as fathers and as father figures. This chapter juxtaposes divergent and contradictory meanings of fatherhood as it applied to middle-class British men in late imperial India, contrasting how it encompassed their history as progenitors of the Eurasian community, their experiences as the fathers of British children from whom they became geographically and often emotionally estranged, and their views of their role vis-à-vis Indian society. Fatherhood entailed, by turns, an actual, biological status that was compromised through lengthy and habitual family separations; a publicly repudiated history wherein those whose predecessors in India (if not also they themselves) had fathered a mixed-race community both disclaimed affiliation with it and were challenged by Eurasians/Anglo-Indians to recognize their responsibilities; and a means of idealizing their relations with Indians whom they depicted as 'childlike', immature and in need of paternal governance. By the later nineteenth century and after, these overlapping but conflicting patterns of real, imagined, and denied fatherhood reached their zenith at the same time as fractures developed which systematically undermined them.

I

Between the late eighteenth and early nineteenth centuries, persons having both European and Indian ancestry encountered a growing range of obstacles in their interactions with the British administration of the East India Company and colonial society. Some Eurasians had British fathers while others claimed a more distant European male ancestor, who may also have been Portuguese, French or Dutch. A group once accepted or at least tolerated became discredited as the Company expanded and consolidated its control over the subcontinent and sought to distance itself and its representatives from a group that attested to a history of sexual relationships with Indians increasingly condemned as immoral. As Christopher Hawes summarizes, 'Eurasian populations were the living evidence to colonial whites of the distressing frailty of their men. They undermined, in the most public manner possible, concepts of colonial rule which depended ultimately on maintaining the illusion of racial superiority of white European males.'[6] Men of the officer class who had fathered children with Indian women often sent them back to Britain for their education, thus separating them from the majority of Eurasians whose fathers or ancestors were rank-and-file soldiers.[7] In the eyes of colonial authorities, the Eurasian community was largely descended from the working classes and both a class and a race apart from élite colonizers who largely refused personal accountability.

Eurasians in India were marked as 'inferior' on both social and racial grounds, yet unless absorbed into Indian society they remained dependent on the British who repeatedly proved loath to fulfil their parental responsibilities on either an individual or a collective level. Throughout the colonial era British men often abandoned both Indian and Eurasian women along with their offspring from these unions, and colonial authorities consistently denied Eurasians equal opportunities with Europeans.[8] Defined as 'Natives of India' because of their maternal ancestry, from 1791 they were excluded from covenanted civil and military appointments. Successive legislation intensified restrictions on Eurasian men's occupational and social prospects. As Hawes notes, however, the colonial state grudgingly accepted a limited degree of 'parental and racial obligation, spurred on by the more mundane considerations of social order and British prestige'. It provided some support for orphanages and free schools, and attempted 'to find employment in later life suitable to the class of Eurasian children' attending them – a class far beneath that of the officers and their European families publicly recognized as 'legitimate'.[9]

Eurasians resisted British discrimination and condescension by proclaiming both their ancestral affiliations with and longstanding loyalty to the colonizers. In 1830–1 they sent a delegation to London to petition Parliament, asking for status as 'British Subjects' and not as 'Natives of India' – a wish that remained unfulfilled.[10] Britain's reluctance to give Eurasians what they considered their rightful inheritance owing to their paternal ancestry became deeply entrenched, but community spokesmen tirelessly invoked their faithful affiliations to Britain through the idiom of kinship. By the twentieth century, its leading voices had long reiterated unwavering support for 'the nation of their fathers', as Herbert Stark phrased it in his book *Hostages to India*.[11] Originally published in 1926, Stark's text appeared at a critical juncture when Anglo-Indians (as Eurasians had become known in official parlance since 1911) were confronted with new official employment policies allowing Indians to compete for many of the subordinate posts once reserved for them. Because of their traditional dependence on employment within the state sector, Eurasians/Anglo-Indians had long been seen as 'children of the Government', as one Victorian writer summarized it.[12] But when faced with strong Indian competition in the inter-war years, Anglo-Indians struggled to retain even the appointments inferior to those held by Britons recruited from 'Home' against which they had long protested.

In his defence of the community's jeopardized interests, Stark stressed its centrality to Britain's history of building and defending the empire. Its loyalty became particularly evident in moments of crisis such as the Indian 'Mutiny' of 1857–8, when 'these tawny sons of Britain helped to man the guns . . . ever at the side of their brave fathers where dangers were thickest and courage the highest'. Ever quick to obey 'the call of the blood' in battles against Indian 'malcontents and rebels', 'to a man they remained true to their fathers' people'. England was 'the land of our fathers', yet the 'paternal government' responded only with 'step-motherly treatment, denying Anglo-Indians fellowship with their kinsmen, socially as well as legally'. When Stark's book was reissued in 1936, anxieties about the community's future once Indians had achieved self-government were even more acute. Fearing for their future in an independent India, Stark concluded with the plea, 'O England! Who are these if not thy sons?'[13]

Anglo-Indians' 'childlike' dependence on the colonial state, then, jarred with Britain's reluctance to acknowledge parental obligations towards descendants of earlier generations of male colonizers seen as illegitimate and largely as a source of shame. Anglo-Indians long accused Britain of betrayal, condemning colonial attitudes and policies as unworthy of what a good father owed his children. 'Step-motherly' concisely summarized their reading of the contemptuous British attitude towards those dismissed as racial and social inferiors – those deemed unworthy of counting as equal, legitimate kinsmen by a paternal Raj.

By the later imperial era, British men's perceptions of fatherly responsibilities focused largely on the European children whom they acknowledged as their rightful progeny in biological and social terms, as well as on Indian society towards which they directed their ideals of paternalist rule.

II

Once it became more common for colonial officials and other middle-class men to marry and head a British family while in India, the children to whom they showed any dedication or public recognition were largely those born in the context of 'respectable' white conjugality. Yet while white children were accorded legitimacy, their health, morals and character became subjects of endless concerns voiced in family correspondence, medical writings and prescriptive literature about colonial housekeeping. As noted above, these concerns caused parents to send their children to Britain at a young age if they could afford to do so, thereby placing family members thousands of miles apart. Children's distance from their fathers, however, could well have begun before they left India. While many personal narratives of colonial childhood years foreground happy memories in contrast to the loneliness and family separations experienced once children returned to Britain, they also illustrate that children often spent less time with either parent than with the Indian servants who looked after them. Time with fathers almost invariably had been more limited than time with mothers or servants, and many wrote far more about missing the latter than about their fathers once long separations began. Mother–child separations were portrayed as considerably more difficult for children, illustrating the peripheral role of fathers in many domestic arenas from the start. As John Gillis's work argues, fathers were 'at the threshold of family life, never at its center', while Lynn Abrams stresses that 'a family without a mother was not deemed to be a family in any real sense'.[14]

None the less, during decades when ideals of bourgeois family intimacy achieved new prominence within Victorian British culture, colonial family breakup and its impact on relations between fathers and children as well as mothers and children – not to mention those between husbands and wives – was widely bemoaned by all concerned.[15] One writer outlining the conditions of a career in the Indian Civil Service in 1873 stressed that 'the cruellest disruption of domestic ties; always a life of expatriation, with all that that word includes of bitter partings and of sad memories' counted among the hardest aspects of Englishmen's lives in India.[16] But what were sad memories for fathers and mothers could, for children sent home at a young age, be offset if not overwhelmed by a gradual process of forgetting over the course of years apart. Rudyard Kipling's short story 'Baa Baa, Black Sheep' – a reworking of his own childhood miseries of the early 1870s published in 1888 – charted the experiences of a five-year-old boy left with abusive guardians in England. Over time, fond memories of his parents 'became wholly overlaid by the unpleasant task of writing them letters' until ultimately 'Papa and Mamma were clean forgotten'.[17]

Father–child separations were those most likely to produce estrangement, as fathers had fewer opportunities to visit children while on leave than mothers.

Letters exchanged between Adelbert Talbot over the course of his career in the Indian Political Service and his daughter Guendolen in the 1880s and 1890s repeatedly alluded to fears about the effects of prolonged geographical distance. Writing to ten-year-old Guendolen after a five-year absence, Adelbert expressed his fears: 'it is sad to me to think that I have been away from you now for half your life but I hope to see you some time this year'. 'You must have forgotten Papa quite by this time', he continued, 'and will not know me if I walk into the house some fine day not very many months hence I hope.'[18] By the time Guendolen was 17 she had only seen her father on several fleeting visits, with photographs and letters being their sole means of contact. Photographs, however, often provoked anxiety and disappointment, for they served as visual testament to the ageing process and forced each recipient to acknowledge the years and intimacy they had lost. Guendolen confessed her displeasure at a new photograph of her parents in which 'both of you look so awfully stern ... I think you have both altered a great deal' – a far cry from her idealized memories of a loving mother and father. Adelbert for his part was taken aback to see Guendolen and her sisters with their hair up and wearing long dresses – sure signs that they had irrevocably left their childhoods behind and become young women unobserved.[19]

Men working in India often lost the companionship of their wives as well as their children if mothers chose either protracted visits or permanent resettlement with the children in Britain. Sir George Trevelyan described this possibility in his 1864 book on the Indian Civil Service, *The Competition Wallah*:

> The drawbacks of Indian life begin to be severely felt when it becomes necessary to send the first-born home. From that period until his final retirement there is little domestic comfort for the father of the family. After two or three years have gone by, and two or three children have gone home, your wife's spirits are no longer what they were. She is uneasy for days after a letter has come in with the Brighton post-mark ... scrawled over in a large round hand, and smeared with tears and dirty fingers, which puts her beside herself.

From then on, Trevelyan explained, a man's wife spent increasing periods visiting the children until she finally left India 'with a tacit understanding that she [was] never to return'.[20] At which point, the Indian Civil Servant reverted to 'bachelor habits' in India while living family life from afar – returning, in effect, to an overwhelmingly male-oriented social circle that many historians highlight as a defining feature of the lifestyles of colonizers.[21]

Lacking direct access to their children if not their wives as well, British men found the emotional dimensions of fatherhood superseded by the practical, both in everyday matters and in the imagination. When painful separations were discussed within family correspondence, men's careers and the incomes they earned in India were enlisted to justify their absence to young children. In response to Guendolen's question 'Can't you come home this year?', Adelbert Talbot explained: 'I must follow my profession in order to get money to bring you up and all the others.'[22] Similar rationalizations recurred in late-Victorian Indian Civil Service family letters. When Annette Beveridge wrote to her children at an English boarding school and praised them for good reports about their studies, she said, 'you know that your father works very hard to get rupis to have you taught and taken care of and so when I see that you are all learning so much I am glad; I think "All dear Papa's hard work is being made use of by his children"'.[23] The breadwinner role of imperial men was thus promoted as the paramount element of fatherhood when sentimental and cultural aspects became challenged and sidelined.

Indeed, fathers working in India effectively devolved paternal responsibilities to others once prolonged separations from their children began. If mothers had gone to Britain for extended visits or returned permanently, they made many important child-rearing decisions on an everyday basis; if mothers remained in India, parental supervision became the long-term responsibility of guardians, relatives or boarding schoolmasters and schoolmistresses. A school for missionaries' children near London claimed in the 1920s that for decades its staff had acted as 'foster parents' to the 'grass orphans' long parted from their parents stationed overseas. As a result, teachers and the institution became 'Mother and Father and indeed home itself to their charges'.[24]

Fatherhood, then, involved surrogates acting *in loco parentis* between the time children were sent away from India and men's retirement. Trevelyan continued his depiction of the man bereft of wife and children alike by suggesting that family concerns led some men to end their careers prematurely: as the years go by, one day 'it strikes you that your clever idle son will be more likely to pass his competitive examination if you are on the spot to superintend his studies. So you resign your seat in Council, accept a farewell dinner from your friends' and go home to a pension. A man abandoning long-established acquaintances, an important position and satisfying work then experienced 'a severe trial, when settling down at Rugby or Harrow, seeing that his boys learn their repetitions and get up in time for morning school, [and] quarrelling with their tutor'.[25]

In Trevelyan's view, retired civilians might take solace in fatherhood and a return to nuclear family life as compensation for leaving their careers behind. Some men, Adelbert Talbot among them, yearned to reach the compulsory retirement age in order to rejoin their families in Britain permanently. While John Tosh's research convincingly argues that young men often found Indian careers attractive because they promised a 'flight from domesticity', imagined to be stifling, into a masculine imperial world, older men with wives and children displayed a range of responses. Some fathers undoubtedly dispatched their children to Britain with relief, although they may have suppressed socially unacceptable paternal attitudes in writing. Others, however, appeared to develop more of a longing for family life in Britain than for continued work and possible adventure in India.[26] Graham Dawson's analysis of Major-General Sir Henry Havelock, whose actions during the 1857–8 revolt elevated him high within the pantheon of British 'Mutiny' heroes, succinctly encapsulates the tensions between men's public and private imperial lives and desires during this era. Upon leaving his family behind to return to India alone after home leave several years before the uprising, Havelock conveyed his pain in letters to his wife and described himself as 'a sad houseless wanderer' – yet his financial concerns precluded forsaking the profession that necessitated his departure.

With Havelock, as Dawson suggests, 'the possibility of domestic composure has been renounced, but not the desire for it'; like many other narratives of imperial service, Havelock's story illustrates 'the underlying contradiction between work and family, public and private lives, the soldier and the domestic man'.[27] Active fatherhood and married life never ceased to clash with leading a satisfying professional life in the empire; as Trevelyan concluded, the pensioned father fondly 'look[ed] back to the days when he coerced refractory rajahs' and needed to 'console himself with . . . the consciousness of a good work well done, and a good name handed on unstained to the children who are growing up around him'.[28]

III

Trevelyan's rendition points, moreover, towards further understandings of paternal roles which, by turns, competed with and complemented one another. Fathers bereft of the company of their own children for extended periods could simultaneously see themselves as playing a parental role vis-à-vis Indians. This might take the form of strict patriarchy, as with Civil Servants who 'coerced refractory rajahs'. Just as commonly, however, British men in positions of authority could be held up as benevolent paternalists to Indians who reciprocated by respecting and honouring them as father figures. As David Omissi summarizes in his description of army officers' relations with Indian sepoys serving under them, 'British officers liked to imagine themselves as the strict but paternal guardians of the supposedly childlike ranks', who exhibited ' "enthusiastic courage and an almost boyish simplicity of character" '.[29] Crucially, however, in an era replete with efforts at racial distancing, Britons commonly used familial language to describe colonizer–colonized relations yet explicitly neglected to suggest blood ties while stressing their 'guardianship' or 'tutelage' of childlike natives.[30] Catherine Hall's discussion of colonizers' uses of familial discourse in other nineteenth-century contexts emphasizes how it denoted 'both kinship and a gap' between themselves and disempowered racial 'others'.[31] Indians could be depicted as analogous to children and Britons seen as parental – yet in a political and cultural as distinct from a biological sense.[32]

Such portrayals appear frequently in both colonial and post-colonial British writings, including those describing relationships with domestic servants and labourers. One woman's recollections of the Raj after decolonization described her family's servants as 'very faithful' and 'almost like our children', considering her and her husband 'as their parents and calling us "Ma", "Bap" (Mother and Father), bringing their troubles and trusting us implicitly'.[33] As this account illustrates, British women could include themselves within the parental 'Ma–Bap' metaphor, their membership within the upper echelons of colonial society enabling them to take on aspects of a structure of authority predominantly coded as 'masculine'. Portraying the colonized as 'childlike' was only one way in which Britons asserted their own superiority and the subordination of the Indians. Mrinalini Sinha's discussion of British constructions of the 'manly Englishman' and the 'effeminate Bengali' suggests that hierarchies along the lines of gender, race and age coexisted and could become mutually reinforcing.³⁴ Casting the British as manly, adult and independent rendered them – and the nation they represented – as capable of ruling themselves as well as others who remained their 'dependants', whereas Indians labelled effeminate and childlike (or perhaps adolescent) could be claimed politically immature and still in need of the 'friendly guiding hand' of the paternalist imperialist, or legitimate, well-meaning, fatherly authority.³⁵ This 'mythology of benevolent imperialism', as Benjamin Zachariah has phrased it, proved a durable one; indeed, its resilience gained in strength during and after decolonization.³⁶ British policymakers made 'myths as fast as they unmade colonies', John Darwin summarizes, portraying 'their demission of empire as the actions of an enlightened father, wisely conferring responsibility on his boisterous, but essentially good-natured, offspring'.³⁷

IV

Most Indians remained unconvinced of such British assessments of their relationship, decidedly refusing the role of grateful children bestowed upon them in British rhetoric and increasing their support for the nationalist movement. Writing his autobiography from a colonial prison cell in the 1930s, nationalist leader Jawaharlal Nehru ridiculed this pervasive mentality among men in the Indian Civil Service: 'In spite of their amusing assumption of being the trustees and guardians of the Indian masses, they knew little about them and even less about the new aggressive *bourgeoisie*,' he asserted. 'They judged Indians from the sycophants and office-seekers who surrounded them and dismissed others as agitators and knaves.'³⁸ British understandings of imperial fatherhood and guardianship, in the end, satisfied few. Indians rejected the 'childlike' status attributed to them and fought for the political independence which finally came in 1947; Anglo-Indians resented Britain's refusal to deem them legitimate 'children of colonialism' and consider them as equals in the imperial ruling family; and British offspring of white colonial families regretted the geographical and emotional distance from their fathers overseas while they grew up at home. Fatherhood imagined vis-à-vis the colonized and denied vis-à-vis those of mixed European and Indian ancestry provoked bitter responses, leaving the offspring with whom blood ties were acknowledged as the only children who, in the long run, demonstrated the style and degree of filial loyalty that the self-professed father figures of the colonizing community craved.

Despite the distance dividing British children from their fathers during school years in the metropole, they were by far the most likely to pay homage to these men both during and after empire. They did so in part by following in their parents' footsteps and returning to India after completing their education. Daughters commonly rejoined their parents and remained overseas after marrying men who resembled their fathers professionally, often having met their husbands through parents' social circles. Fathers were often crucial to sons' decisions to re-enter the colonial community, either helping them find private employment or (as was the case with Trevelyan's *Competition Wallah*) providing moral and financial support while they competed to enter the civil and military services.³⁹ Whatever their regrets about the obstacles which India threw in the way of British family contentment, many fathers actively facilitated their children's perpetuation of imperial family traditions. Of the families discussed above, all of Adelbert Talbot's children spent much of their adult lives in the subcontinent, his son entering the Indian Civil Service and his daughters marrying British administrators. Rudyard Kipling, meanwhile, spent his early adulthood in India and launched his writing career working for a newspaper after his father's networking secured him the job.

M. M. Kaye's family story, introduced at the outset, succinctly illustrates how children commonly honoured their fathers' imperial legacy across the colonial and the post-colonial era. Regardless of the emotional gulf dividing them following years of separation throughout his childhood, her brother Bill paid tribute by entering his father's branch of service and becoming an Indian Army officer. Kaye herself returned to India and married another army officer, but she demonstrated her support for her father's Indian work most prominently through her writing after the end of empire. Her memoir published in 1990 foregrounds the value of her father's contributions and commitment to the Raj as much as it recalls her own youth, beginning with her dedication of the book to his memory. She repeatedly asserts that Indians who knew her father shared her feelings: subalterns working under him 'worshipped' him and 'loved and revered him and would be forever grateful for the encouragement he had given them'. He was typical of countless British men who selflessly committed their lives to India: 'men of my race who spent their lives in Indian service were not overpaid and pampered "Burra-Sahibs" lording it over "the natives"', she insists, 'but were really people like [my father] who worked themselves to the bone to serve, to the best of their ability, a country and a people whom they had come to love so much'.[40]

While Indians' affection for and appreciation of her father are impossible to substantiate, Kaye's defensive tone and emphasis on British family sacrifices – hard work and father–child separations chief among these – suggests her familiarity with opposing views long expressed by figures such as Nehru. Like other British children who later wrote in praise of their fathers' endeavours in India, however, Kaye made attitudes which Indians commonly failed to exhibit part of Raj history as recorded after its demise. Colonizers' post-colonial eulogies were largely penned by their British descendants, not by Indians long envisioned as grateful children or Anglo-Indians who felt betrayed by descendants of the forefathers seen to have shunned the responsibilities of paternity.

Notes

1. M. M. Kaye, *The Sun in the Morning: My Early Years in India and England* (New York: St Martin's Press, 1990), pp. 77, 367–8.
2. Key studies on European sexuality, respectability, and domesticity in the colonies include A. L. Stoler's comparative analyses, especially *Race and the Education of Desire: Foucault's History of Sexuality and the Colonial Order of Things* (Durham, NC: Duke University Press, 1995) and *Carnal Knowledge and Imperial Power: Race and the Intimate in Colonial Rule* (Berkeley, CA: University of California Press, 2002). Works specifically concerned with India include K. Ballhatchet, *Race, Sex and Class under the Raj: Imperial Attitudes and Policies and their Critics,*

1793–1905 (New York: St Martin's Press, 1980); M. A. Procida, *Married to the Empire: Gender, Politics, and Imperialism in India, 1883–1947* (Manchester: Manchester University Press, 2002); D. Kennedy, *The Magic Mountains: Hill Stations and the British Raj* (Berkeley, CA: University of California Press, 1996); E. M. Collingham, *Imperial Bodies: The Physical Experience of the Raj, c. 1800–1947* (Cambridge: Polity, 2001); M. MacMillan, *Women of the Raj* (London: Thames and Hudson, 1988); A. Blunt, 'Imperial Geographies of Home: British Domesticity in India, 1886–1925', *Transactions of the Institute of British Geographers*, NS 24 (1999), pp. 421–40.

3. D. Ghosh, 'Colonial Companions: *Bibis, Begums,* and Concubines of the British in North India, 1760–1830' (Ph.D. dissertation, University of California, Berkeley, 2000); W. Dalrymple, *White Mughals: Love and Betrayal in Eighteenth-Century India* (London: Flamingo, 2003); S. Sen, *Distant Sovereignty: National Imperialism and the Origins of British India* (New York: Routledge, 2002), chs 4 and 5.
4. C. Hawes, *Poor Relations: The Making of a Eurasian Community in British India, 1773–1833* (Richmond: Curzon Press, 1996); L. Caplan, *Children of Colonialism: Anglo-Indians in a Postcolonial World* (Oxford: Berg, 2001).
5. E. Buettner, *Empire Families: Britons and Late Imperial India* (Oxford: Oxford University Press, 2004).
6. Hawes, *Poor Relations*, p. 154.
7. Dalrymple, *White Mughals*, pp. 51, 67, 170, 316, 381–8; Ballhatchet, *Race, Sex, and Class*.
8. Caplan, *Children of Colonialism*, pp. 73–4, 178.
9. Hawes, *Poor Relations*, p. 156; see also p. 62. Much more extensive discussions of East India Company policies regarding children and orphans of its British personnel can be found in Ghosh, 'Colonial Companions', ch. 5; D. Ghosh, 'Making and Un-making Loyal Subjects: Pensioning Widows and Educating Orphans in Early Colonial India', *Journal of Imperial and Commonwealth History*, 31 (2003), pp. 1–28; D. Arnold, 'European Orphans and Vagrants in India in the Nineteenth Century', *Journal of Imperial and Commonwealth History*, 7 (1979), pp. 104–27.
10. Hawes, *Poor Relations*, p. 135.
11. H. A. Stark, *Hostages to India, or The Life Story of the Anglo-Indian Race*, 2nd edn (Calcutta: Star, 1936), p. 26.
12. T. G. Clarke, *The Fortunes of the Anglo-Indian Race* (Madras: Higginbotham, 1878), pp. 7–8.
13. Stark, *Hostages to India*, pp. 40, 82, 102, 136, 140, 143. Similar familial terminology was repeatedly deployed in statements by community leaders, for example by Sir Henry Gidney in 'The Future of the Anglo-Indian Community', *Asiatic Review* 30, 101 (1934), pp. 41–2. For an excellent analysis of related themes, see A. Blunt, '"Land of our Mothers": Home, Identity, and Nationality for Anglo-Indians in British India, 1919–1947', *History Workshop Journal* 54 (2002), 49–72.
14. Gillis, *A World of Their Own Making*, p. 179; L. Abrams, ' "There Was Nobody like my Daddy": Fathers, the Family, and the Marginalisation of Men in Modern Scotland', *Scottish Historical Review*, 79/2, 206 (1999), p. 237.
15. Davidoff and Hall, *Family Fortunes*; Gillis, *World of Their Own Making*.
16. 'The Indian Civil Service: Part I – What It Is', *Fraser's Magazine*, NS VIII, No. XLVI (Oct. 1873), p. 435.
17. R. Kipling, 'Baa Baa, Black Sheep', in T. Pinney (ed.), *Rudyard Kipling: Something of Myself and Other Autobiographical Writings* (Cambridge: Cambridge University Press, 1990), pp. 156, 159.

18. Oriental and India Office Collections, British Library, London (hereafter OIOC), MSS Eur E410/6, Adelbert Talbot to Guendolen Talbot, 20 Jan. 1883.
19. OIOC, MSS Eur E410/38, Guendolen Talbot to Adelbert Talbot, 28 Aug. 1890; E410/4, Adelbert Talbot to Guendolen Talbot, 21 Sept. 1890.
20. Sir G. Trevelyan, *The Competition Wallah* (1864; repr. London: Macmillan, 1907), pp. 127–8.
21. J. Tosh, 'Imperial Masculinity and the Flight from Domesticity in Britain, 1880–1914', in Timothy P. Foley et al. (eds), *Gender and Colonialism* (Galway: Galway University Press, 1995), pp. 72–85. For a controversial assessment of colonial homosociality, see R. Hyam, *Empire and Sexuality: The British Experience* (Manchester: Manchester University Press, 1990).
22. OIOC, MSS Eur E410/6, Adelbert Talbot to Guendolen Talbot, 17 Feb. 1884.
23. OIOC, MSS Eur C176/120, Annette Beveridge to 'My dear children', 9 Sept. 1885.
24. Walthamstow Hall School Archives, Sevenoaks, Kent, Newspaper Cuttings Book, 'Children of Our Missionaries', *Christian World* (6 Oct. 1921); 'Concerning Some "Grass Orphans"', *Outward Bound* (Jan. 1921).
25. Trevelyan, *Competition Wallah*, pp. 128–9.
26. Tosh, 'Imperial Masculinity'.
27. G. Dawson, *Soldier Heroes: British Adventure, Empire and the Imagining of Masculinities* (London and New York: Routledge, 1994), pp. 143–4; 138–9.
28. Trevelyan, *Competition Wallah*, pp. 128–30.
29. David Omissi, *The Sepoy and the Raj: The Indian Army, 1860–1940* (Basingstoke: Macmillan, 1994), p. 27.
30. As Lynn Hunt argues in *The Family Romance of the French Revolution* (Berkeley, CA: University of California Press, 1992), p. 8, narratives about the family have been integral to understandings of political authority in many historical contexts.
31. Hall, *Civilising Subjects*, p. 19.
32. Indeed, to the extent that Indians were imagined to require their 'tutelage', British conceptions of their role bore resemblance to 'the tasks of the schoolmaster' as well as those of the father. See T. R. Metcalf, *The New Cambridge History of India III, No. 4: Ideologies of the Raj* (Cambridge: Cambridge University Press, 1995), pp. 199–200; 228–30.
33. B. Macdonald, *India . . . Sunshine and Shadows* (London: BACSA, 1988), p. 135.
34. M. Sinha, *Colonial Masculinity: The 'Manly Englishman' and the 'Effeminate Bengali' in the Late Nineteenth Century* (Manchester: Manchester University Press, 1995).
35. B. Zachariah, 'Rewriting Imperial Mythologies: The Strange Case of Penderel Moon', *South Asia* XXI, 2 (2001), p. 71. Further discussions of 'Ma–Bap' as an ideology of paternalist British rule can be found in C. Dewey, *Anglo-Indian Attitudes: The Mind of the Indian Civil Service* (London: Hambledon Press, 1993), pp. 43, 46, 55–9; P. Chatterjee, *A Time for Tea: Women, Labor, and Post/colonial Politics on an Indian Plantation* (Durham, NC: Duke University Press, 2001), pp. 120–1.
36. Zachariah, 'Rewriting Imperial Mythologies', 58.
37. J. Darwin, 'British Decolonization since 1945: A Pattern or a Puzzle?', *Journal of Imperial and Commonwealth History* 12 (1984), pp. 188, 206.
38. J. Nehru, *An Autobiography* (1936; repr. New Delhi: Oxford University Press, 1982), p. 443.
39. For a detailed discussion of the next generation's return to India, see Buettner, *Empire Families*, pp. 175–87, 245–51.
40. Kaye, *Sun in the Morning*, pp. 383, 303.

Select Bibliography

Buettner, Elizabeth, *Empire Families: Britons and Late Imperial India* (Oxford: Oxford University Press, 2004).

Chinn, Carl, *They Worked All Their Lives: Women of the Urban Poor in England, 1880–1939* (Manchester: Manchester University Press, 1988).

—— *Poverty Amidst Prosperity* (Manchester: Manchester University Press, 1995).

Clark, Anna, *The Struggle for the Breeches: Gender and the Making of the British Working Class* (Berkeley: University of California Press, 1992).

Cooter, Roger (ed.), *In the Name of the Child: Health and Welfare, 1880–1940* (London: Routledge, 1992).

Danahay, Martin, 'Subjected Autonomy in Victorian Autobiography: John Stuart Mill and Edmund Gosse', in Danahay, *A Community of One: Masculine Autobiography and Autonomy in Nineteenth-Century Britain* (Albany: State University of New York Press, 1993), pp. 147–70.

—— *Gender at Work in Victorian Culture: Literature, Art and Masculinity* (Aldershot: Ashgate, 2005).

Davidoff, Leonore, Megan Doolittle, Janet Fink and Katherine Holden, 'Fathers and Fatherhood: Family Authority', in Davidoff et al., *The Family Story: Blood, Contract and Intimacy, 1830–1960* (London: Longman, 1998), pp. 135–57.

Davidoff, Leonore and Catherine Hall, *Family Fortunes: Men and Women of the English Middle Class 1780–1850* (London: Hutchinson, 1987).

Doolittle, Megan, 'Missing Fathers: Assembling a History of Fatherhood in Mid-Nineteenth-Century England', PhD thesis, University of Essex, 1996.

—— 'Sexuality, Parenthood and Population: Explaining Fertility Decline in Britain from the 1860s to the 1920s', in Jean Carabine (ed.), *Sexualities: Personal Lives and Social Policy* (Bristol: Policy Press, 2004), pp. 49–84.

Fletcher, Anthony, *Gender, Sex and Subordination in England, 1500–1800* (New Haven, CT: Yale University Press, 1996).

Francis, Martin, 'The Domestication of the Male? Recent Research on Nineteenth- and Twentieth-Century British Masculinity', *The Historical Journal*, 45:3 (2002), pp. 637–52.

Frank, Stephen M., *Life with Father: Parenthood and Masculinity in the Nineteenth-Century American North* (Baltimore, MD: Johns Hopkins University Press, 1998).

Gillis, John R., *A World of Their Own Making: Myth, Ritual and the Quest for Family Values* (Cambridge, MA: Harvard University Press, 1997).

Gittins, Diana, *The Family in Question: Changing Households and Familiar Ideologies* (London: Macmillan, 1985).

Gray, Robert, *The Factory Question and Industrial England, 1830–1860* (Cambridge: Cambridge University Press, 1996).

Griswold, Robert L., *Fatherhood in America: A History* (New York: Basic Books, 1993).

—— (ed.), Special Issue on Fatherhood, *Journal of Family History*, 24:3 (1999).

Hall, Catherine, *Civilising Subjects: Metropole and Colony in the English Imagination, 1830–1867* (Oxford: Polity, 2002).

Hall, Catherine, Keith McClelland and Jane Rendall, *Defining the Victorian Nation: Class, Race, Gender and the Reform Act of 1867* (Cambridge: Cambridge University Press, 2000).
Hammerton, A. J., *Cruelty and Companionship: Conflict in Nineteenth-Century Married Life* (London: Routledge, 1995).
Ittman, Karl, *Work, Gender and Family in Victorian England* (Basingstoke: Macmillan, 1995).
Johansen, Shawn, *Family Men: Middle-Class Fatherhood in Early Industrializing America* (London: Routledge, 2001).
Kestner, Joseph, *Masculinities in Victorian Painting* (Ashgate: Aldershot, 1995).
LaRossa, Ralph, *The Modernization of Fatherhood: A Social and Political History* (Chicago: University of Chicago Press, 1997).
Levene, Alysa, Samantha Williams and Thomas Nutt (eds), *Illegitimacy in Britain, 1700–1920* (Basingstoke: Palgrave Macmillan, 2005).
Lowe, Nick, 'The Legal Status of Fathers Past and Present', in Lorna McKee and Margaret O'Brien (eds), *The Father Figure* (London: Tavistock, 1982), pp. 26–42.
Lown, Judy, *Women and Industrialization: Gender and Work in Nineteenth-Century England* (Cambridge: Polity, 1990).
Lummis, Trevor, 'The Historical Dimension of Fatherhood: A Case Study 1890–1914', in Lorna McKee and Margaret O'Brien (eds), *The Father Figure* (London: Tavistock, 1982), pp. 43–56.
Maidment, Brian, 'Domestic Ideology and its Industrial Enemies: The Title Page of the Family Economist, 1848–1850', in Christopher Parker (ed.), *Gender Roles and Sexuality in Victorian Literature* (Aldershot: Scolar, 1995), pp. 25–56.
Mangan, J. A. and James Walvin (eds), *Manliness and Morality: Middle-Class Masculinity in Britain and America, 1800–1940* (New York: St Martin's Press, 1987).
McClelland, Keith, 'Masculinity and the "Representative Artisan" in Britain, 1850–80', in Michael Roper and John Tosh (eds), *Manful Assertions: Masculinities in Britain since 1810* (London: Routledge, 1991), pp. 74–91.
Nash, John, 'Historical and Social Changes in the Perception of the Role of the Father', in Michael E. Lamb (ed.), *The Role of the Father in Child Development* (New York: Wiley, 1976), pp. 62–88.
Nelson, Claudia, *Invisible Men: Fatherhood and Victorian Periodicals, 1850–1910* (Athens, GA and London: University of Georgia Press, 1994).
Pollock, Linda A., *Forgotten Children: Parent–Child Relations from 1500 to 1900* (Cambridge: Cambridge University Press, 1983).
Poovey, Mary, *Uneven Developments: The Ideological Work of Gender in Mid-Victorian Britain* (Chicago: Chicago University Press, 1988).
Roberts, David, 'The Paterfamilias of the Victorian Governing Classes', in Anthony Wohl (ed.), *The Victorian Family: Structures and Stresses* (London: Croom Helm, 1978), pp. 59–81.
—— *Paternalism in Early Victorian England* (London: Croom Helm, 1979).
Roper, Michael and John Tosh (eds), *Manful Assertions: Masculinities in Britain since 1800* (London: Routledge, 1991).
Rose, Sonya, *Limited Livelihoods: Gender and Class in Nineteenth-Century England* (Berkeley: University of California Press, 1992).
Ross, Ellen, *Love and Toil: Motherhood in Outcast London, 1870–1918* (Oxford: Oxford University Press, 1993).
Sadoff, Dianne F., *Monsters of Affection: Dickens, Eliot and Brontë on Fatherhood* (Baltimore, MD: Johns Hopkins University Press, 1982).

Seccombe, Wally, *Weathering the Storm: Working-Class Families from the Industrial Revolution to the Fertility Decline* (London: Verso, 1993).

Stone, Lawrence, *The Road to Divorce: England 1530–1987* (Oxford: Oxford University Press, 1990).

Sussman, Herbert, *Masculinities: Manhood and Masculine Poetics in Early Victorian Literature and Art* (Cambridge: Cambridge University Press, 1995).

Tosh, John, *A Man's Place: Masculinity and the Middle-Class Home in Victorian England* (New Haven, CT: Yale University Press, 1999).

—— *Manliness and Masculinities in Nineteenth-Century Britain: Essays on Gender, Family and Empire* (Harlow: Pearson, 2004).

Vincent, David, *Bread, Knowledge and Freedom: A Study of Nineteenth-Century Working-Class Autobiography* (London: Europa, 1981).

Walkowitz, Judith R., *Prostitution and Victorian Society: Women, Class and the State* (New York: Cambridge University Press, 1980).

Wiener, Martin J., *Men of Blood: Violence, Manliness and Criminal Justice in Victorian England* (Cambridge: Cambridge University Press, 2004).

Woods, Robert and Nicola Shelton, *An Atlas of Victorian Morality* (Liverpool: Liverpool University Press, 1997).

Zwinger, Lynda, *Daughters, Fathers, and the Novel: The Sentimental Romance of Heterosexuality* (Madison: University of Wisconsin Press, 1991).

Index

Abrams, Lynn, 182
adoption, 10, 23
   in America, 165–77
The Adventures of Huckleberry Finn
   (1884), Mark Twain [Samuel L.
   Clemens, 1835–1910], 171
Advice to Young Men (1829) (William
   Cobbett, 1763–1835), 47
America, 8, 23, 99, 165–77
Anderson, Michael, 117, 122
anti-slavery, 18, 130
apprenticeship, 114–15, 117–22, 169–71
Armstrong, Chester, 21, 33, 37–9
Arnold, Thomas (1795–1842), 56
art, 2–5, 71–84
atheism, 33–5
autobiography, 1, 5, 37–9, 66–7, 85–6,
   101, 122, 126–37, 141–8, 155–7,
   178–9, 186

Balfour, Clara Lucas (1808–78), 135
Banks, J.A. and O., 94
Baptists, 18, 129, 132–3, 153
Barnardo, Dr Thomas (1845–1905), 168
Barringer, Tim, 79
Bella, Leslie, 97
Bennet, George, 159–61
Benson, Edward Frederic (1867–1940),
   56
Benson, Edward White (1829–96), 56,
   61
Benson, Mary, née Sidgwick
   (1841–1918), 56
Besant, Annie (1847–1933), 21, 33,
   35–9
Besant, Frank, Revd (1840–1917), 35–9
Beveridge, Annette (1842–1929), 183–4
birth control, 19–20, 36, 86
Blackstone, William (1723–80), 1, 23
Brace, Charles Loring (1823–90), 168–9,
   171–2
Bradlaugh, Charles (1833–91), 36–7
Bright, John (1811–89), 80, 128

brotherhood, 14–18, 63
   Christian, 18, 22, 154, 158, 161–2
Brown, Ford Madox (1821–93), 79
Burdett, Sir Francis (1770–1844), 50
Burnett, Frances Hodgson (1849–1924),
   172–3
Butler, Samuel (1835–1902), 5

Caine, Barbara, 19
Calvinism, 18, 133, 134
Carl Krinken or the Christmas Stocking
   (1854), 99
Carlyle, Thomas (1795–1881), 79, 86
Carnes, Mark, 174
Carpenter, Mary (1807–77), 134
Cash, S.J., 102–3
census, 86, 87, 116–18, 121–2
Chartism, 11, 101, 130–1
child
   artistic representation of, 2–3, 71–84
   author as, 6
   of British in India, 172, 178–90
   death of, 138–49
   discipline of, 4, 10, 18, 38–9, 56, 62,
      64–5, 89–90, 114–15, 119, 128,
      133
   emotional responses to, 85–6, 90–1,
      100–1, 138, 141, 143–6, 174–5
   illegitimate, 11, 127, 143
   and independence, 114–15
   literature for, 55–70, 133–4, 165–77
   motherless, 12, 71–84, 129, 133,
      146–7, 172–4
   neglect of, 10, 114, 135, 139
   play, 2–3, 71, 97–8, 101–2, 106
   as property of father, 9, 46
   'public children', 168–9
   and religion, 16–18, 31–42, 115,
      128–30, 133–4, 166–71
   siblings, caring for 8, 19, 75, 78
   slum, 168
   violence against, 9–10, 135, 139
   as ward of court, 33, 35–6

child (*cont.*):
  welfare, 10, 32, 135, 165–77
  see also adoption, education, labour, protection
childhood
  'Deity of Childhood', 166
  romantic idealization of, 16, 33, 108
Children's Aid Society, 168, 171
Children's Employment Commission, 114–15, 118–19
Chinn, Carl, 122, 146
Chitty, Susan, 57
Christianity
  and brotherhood, 18, 22, 130, 154, 162
  and family, 4, 13, 16–19, 21, 31–9, 114–15, 126–37, 153, 161, 166–71
  missionary, 153–64
  muscular, 79, 140
Christmas, 96–110
  feminization of, 97, 107–8
Church Missionary Society, 153
citizenship, 3, 10–11, 14–15, 18–20, 23, 43–54, 115, 121, 131–3, 135
Clark, Anna, 45, 113
coal industry, 113–25
Cobbe, Frances Power (1802–1904), 134
Cobbett, William (1763–1835), 46–7
colonialism, 3–4, 7, 22–3
  colonizer–colonized relationship, 153–64, 178–87
  see also imperialism, empire
conduct literature, 6–7, 13, 21, 47, 132, 153, 166
Contagious Diseases Act, 12, 132
Cott, Nancy, 166
Court of Chancery, 9, 33–7
Cromby, Charles, 102, 104
custody of children, 9, 10, 33–7, 171
Custody of Infants Act, [1839] 9, [1873] 36

Darwinism, 17, 60
daughters
  and fathers, 6, 12, 49, 55–7, 64–5, 71, 75, 78, 87, 90–3, 121, 126–37, 143–6, 166–9, 172–3, 182–3, 186–7
  and mothers, 12, 35–7, 127, 143–4
  without mothers, 35, 78, 87, 129, 133–4, 166–9, 172–3
  and sexual danger, 35–7, 49

Davidoff, Leonore, 16, 52, 153
Dawson, Graham, 184–5
death and bereavement, 19, 71–84, 87, 133, 138–49
Dickens, Charles, (1812–70), 14, 62, 96, 102, 172
divorce, 9, 34, 35, 37
domestic
  feminization of, 1, 6–7, 13, 145, 165–6
  masculine 'flight from', 7–8, 107, 126, 135, 184
  sphere, 4, 13, 16, 43, 50, 73, 78–80
  violence, 9, 101
domesticity, 1, 3–8, 13–17, 22, 32, 44, 50, 52, 94, 106–8, 153–4, 161–2, 165–75, 179, 184–5
  and middle-class hegemony, 1, 7–8, 13–17, 44, 71–84, 168–71
  working-class constructions, 3–5, 7–12, 15, 22, 44, 101, 113–14, 116, 121, 126–7, 131, 134–5, 146–7
  see also separate spheres
Doolittle, Megan, 6, 19
Dupree, Marguerite, 117

East India Company, 179, 180
education, 4, 21, 32, 34, 55–67, 114, 126–37, 170, 172, 178–9, 182, 184
  see also father, mother
elections, 46
Ellis, Sarah Stickney (1799–1872), 13–14, 132
empire
  and family, 4
  'of the father', 1, 8, 12, 20, 23, 153
  see also colonialism, imperialism
employers, 14–16
  of families, 113–14, 117–19
  as foster fathers, 166–71
Eurasians/Anglo-Indians, 179–82
evangelicalism, 16, 97, 108, 129, 153, 157, 161, 166

Faed, Thomas (1826–1900), 72, 75–80
family
  artistic representations of, 2–5, 49, 71–84
  commercialization of, 21, 108
  economy, 113, 122, 127–9, 134–5, 139–40, 142–3, 146–8

firm, 15, 114
ideology, 6–8, 11, 15, 75, 126–7, 134–5, 142, 178–9, 182
law, 1, 6, 8–12, 30, 33–7, 165, 171
as metaphor for nation, 2–5
middle-class and upper-class, 6–8, 33–7, 90, 96–7, 99, 178–89
and political representation, 3–5, 7–8, 11, 20, 31, 43–54, 128–9, 131–5
and poverty, 11–12, 32, 50, 75–6, 135, 140, 146–7, 169
shape, 1, 8, 19–20, 22
working-class, 2–5, 6–8, 14–15, 32, 37–9, 48, 72, 113–49
see also child, Christianity, daughter, domesticity, father, labour, mother, son
Farningham, Marianne (1843–1909), 132–5
Fasick, Laura, 58–9, 62
fathers
absent, 4, 62, 66, 74, 91, 98, 142–3, 174, 178–90
abusive, 5, 10, 32, 114
and accountability, 7, 20
adoptive, 10, 23, 165–77
affectionate, 47, 55, 74, 81, 130
American, 23, 25, 165–77
authority of, 3, 6–7, 9, 13, 15, 20, 22, 31, 52, 62–3, 102
and childcare, 6, 12, 14, 18, 22, 75–6, 78, 88, 126–35, 145
controlling 65
and daughters, 6, 12, 55, 90–2, 121, 126–37
death of, 146
declining status of, 6–8, 13, 74, 117, 126, 135, 166
deference to, 7, 126–7, 132–3, 135
and discipline, 4, 10, 18, 38–9, 56, 62, 64–5, 89–90, 114–15, 119, 128, 133, 153–4, 157
and domestic sphere, 4, 13, 73, 78, 80
and education, 4, 21, 32, 34, 55–67, 114, 128–30, 133–4
and emotional sensibility, 4, 16, 22, 86, 91, 100–1, 138–48, 174–5
'empire of the', 1, 8, 12, 20, 23, 153
as family representative, 3, 20, 31, 44–7, 128, 131–2, 135, 153
and 'feminine' side, 85, 87, 90, 94

fictional, 5–6, 13–16, 55–67, 85–95, 165–77
forefathers, 48, 154
grandfather, 19, 127
and the law, 1, 6, 8–12, 33–5, 171
missionary, 153–62
as mother, 71–84, 90
and patriotism, 3
playful, 1, 2–4, 5, 75, 78, 88–9, 97–8, 101, 106–8, 128–30, 145, 166
and marriage, 9–11, 21, 34, 39, 73
and remarriage 12, 129, 133
as replaceable, 146, 165
responsibilities of, 8–9, 11, 14, 16, 129, 135
rights of, 5, 7, 9, 17–18, 33–57, 132–5
sanctions against, 31
single, 12, 19, 22, 71–84, 87, 90–1, 94, 129, 133, 144, 146–7
soldier as, 2–5, 12
step, 37, 87, 169
surrogate, 10, 165–8, 184–5
as symbolic figure, 5–6, 13, 31
unnatural, 39
'Victorian', 1, 5, 19, 85, 94, 126
welfare of, 13, 132
see also child, labour, mother, son, widower, working-class father
fatherhood
and breadwinner 'ideal', 4, 8, 11–12, 15, 20–1, 32, 56, 75, 100, 108, 113–14, 122, 127, 131–3, 135, 146–8, 184
feminization of working-class, 74–6, 78, 80
and franchise, 10, 43–54, 80, 101, 115, 128, 131–3, 135
'of God', 4, 16–19, 153, 166
and householder status, 6–9, 45–6, 73, 128, 131–3
and independence, 10–11, 14, 32, 45–6, 82, 126–7
moral responsibilities, 21, 31–2, 34, 36, 114–15, 127–35, 167
protection, 3–4, 11, 18, 21, 31–9, 56, 153
psychoanalytic models of, 5–6, 19, 126
representation of father in, 5, 13–16, 23, 59–61, 66, 85–95, 165–77

fatherhood (*cont.*):
  and respectability, 3–6, 8, 12, 15, 23, 44–5, 51, 76–8, 80–2, 101, 114–15, 121, 127–8, 142
  see also Christmas, domesticity, fiction, masculinity, paternalism, paternity, patriarch
fertility, 19–20
Fildes, Sir Luke (1843–1927), 71–82
Foakes, Grace, 101
Foley, Alice (1891–1974), 139
Foley, Winifred (b.1914), 122
fostering, 10, 165–6, 168–71
Freud, Sigmund, 5, 19
friendly societies, 141
Frith, William Powell (1819–1909), 75

Galsworthy, John (1867–1933), 5
Gaskell, Elizabeth (1810–65), 14, 16
gender
  historiography of, 6, 43–4, 52, 113–14, 138, 141–2
  as a primary category of political inclusion and exclusion, 20
  see also fatherhood, masculinity, motherhood
Gillis, John, 7, 56, 96–7, 182
Gittins, Diane, 142
Goodrich, Samuel ['Peter Parley'] (1793–1860), 60, 166
Gosse, Edmund (1849–1928), 5, 56
Gosse, Philip (1810–88), 56
Gray, Robert, 15

Hall, Catherine, 16, 18, 44, 52, 185
Hamilton, Janet (1795–1873), 127–9, 134–5
Hardy, Frederick Daniel (1826–1911), 2–5, 14, 23
Hardy, Thomas (1752–1832), 48, 50
Harris, Jose, 101
Havelock, Major-General Sir Henry (1795–1857), 184–7
Haweis, Thomas (*c.*1734–1820), 155
Hawes, Christopher, 180–1
Holt, Marilyn Irvin, 168
home
  in afterlife, 17
  and Christmas, 97
  feminization of, 1, 6–7, 13, 145, 165–6
  and work divide, 6–7, 13, 135
  see also domestic, separate spheres
Hosgood, Christopher, 106–7
Hughes, Thomas (1822–96), 167

illegitimacy, 11
imperialism, 178–91
India, 178–91
  'Mutiny' (1857–8), 4, 181, 184
  and nationalism, 36, 186
industrial society
  and anxieties about fatherhood, 8, 12–16, 114–15
  and masculinity, 79
Ittman, Karl, 138, 142

Jalland, Pat, 139–40
James, Henry (1843–1916), 94

Kaye, Cecil (1868–1935), 178
Kaye, Mary Margaret (b. 1909), 178, 179, 187
Kaye, William, 178, 187
Keating, Peter, 76
Kestner, Joseph, 73, 75, 78, 80
Kingsley, Charles (1819–75), 21, 55–67
Kingsley, Fanny (née Grenfell) (1814–91), 57–8
Kingsley, Grenville, 55, 57, 59
Kingsley, Mary (Lucas Malet) (1852–1931), 55–8
Kingsley, Maurice, 55–8
Kingsley, Rose, 55, 58
kinship, 8–9, 19, 31, 35, 181
Kipling, Rudyard (1865–1936), 182, 187
Knibb, William (1803–45), 130

labour
  biblical emphasis on, 155
  child, 3, 8, 11, 32, 113–25, 127, 129, 134, 165–71
  family and division of, 2, 3, 6–8, 15, 22, 113–39, 143, 146–8
  fathers and family recruitment, 3, 117–22
  female, 8, 13, 116, 121–2, 126–37, 146
  and the home, 6–8, 12–16
  and masculinity, 2–5, 12–16, 74–81, 97
  movement, 113
  see also father, mother, provision

INDEX 197

law
  father and, 8–12, 33–5
  father as, 6
Lewisohn, Adolph (1849–1938), 165, 166
London Corresponding Society, 48
London Missionary Society, 153, 155, 157–9
Lord Lyndhurst's Act, 12
Lovett Richard (1851–1904), 159–60

Malthusianism, 86
Mangnall, Richmal (1769–1820), 59
Marcet, Jane Haldimand (1769–1858), 59–60
marriage
  companionate, 130–1, 135, 175
  and fatherhood, 9, 10–11, 21, 34, 39, 73
  in India, 179
  and occupation, 120–1
  remarriage, 12, 129, 133
  of soldiers, 3, 12
  in South Pacific, 156–7
  and married women's property rights, 9, 135
Marriage with Deceased Wife's Sister [Lord Lyndhurst's Act] (1835), 12
Martineau, Harriet (1802–76), 60
masculinity
  and authority, 20, 167, 185
  and cars, 102–3
  and 'civilizing' discourse, 153–64
  and domesticity, 7, 45, 63, 73–4, 76, 81, 86, 107, 147, 153–64, 175
  and effeminization, 74–8, 80, 90, 185–6
  and emotion, 62, 85–95, 101, 107, 129, 138–49, 174–5
  evangelical, 7, 16–19, 129, 153, 157–8, 161, 166
  hegemonic, 3–8, 75–6, 79, 81
  historiography of, 1–2, 6–8, 43–6, 58, 107–8, 113–14, 174–5
  homosocial, 7, 35, 75, 107–8, 128
  hyper-masculinity, 49, 59
  imperial, 3–4, 7, 178–89
  languages of, 15, 18–19, 48, 153–4, 161–2
  and marriage, 9, 31–54, 73
  muscular, 79, 140
  and 'new man', 6, 89
  public, 43, 45, 48, 52
  and racial difference, 153–64, 179–2, 185–6
  sexuality, 45, 58–9, 155–7, 159–60
  and work, 6–7, 13–16, 74, 79, 113–25, 135, 138–52
  see also fathers, fatherhood
McClelland, Keith, 44, 80, 128
migration, 116–17, 121–2, 131, 134, 166–71
Mill, James (1773–1836), 56
Mill, John Stuart (1806–73), 56, 132
missions
  'civilizing' discourse, 153–4, 156, 159–61
  class relationships within, 154–8
  gendered construction, 18–19, 153–4, 161–2
  female missionaries, 154
  see also colonialism, paternalism
modernism, 126
mother
  and child custody, 9, 31–7
  and childcare, 4, 7, 32, 55–67, 85–95, 165, 166
  as educator, 4, 21, 55–67, 127
  father as, 71–84
  and illegitimacy, 11, 127, 143
  inadequate, 168
  as irreplaceable, 133–4, 146, 165
  legal identity of, 1, 9, 34–37
  memoirs by, 126
  moral influence of, 1, 35–7, 74, 76, 114–15, 127–8, 133–4, 167–8
  neglectful, 114, 139
  rights of, 1, 9, 20, 57, 132
  stepmother, 12, 60, 129, 184–5
  widowed, 140, 165
  see also child (motherless), daughter, father, motherhood, son
motherhood
  craft of, 140
  and cult of domesticity, 1, 4, 74, 101, 165, 169
  historiography on, 6–7, 138, 142, 146, 169, 182
  social, 134
  see also mother
Motherless (1883), 77
Mutiny Act (1837), 12

National Society for the Prevention of Cruelty to Children, 10, 135
Nead, Lynda, 76
Nehru, Jawaharlal (1889–1964), 186–7
Nelson, Claudia, 6, 13, 19, 62, 73

Oliphant, Margaret (1828–97), 57
orphans, 10, 17, 127, 168, 169, 181

paterfamilias, 1, 5–7, 13–14, 16, 73, 75, 126, 169
paternalism
  and 'Fatherhood of God', 16–19
  imperial, 22–3, 178–87
  industrial (and class), 12–16, 18, 102, 113–14, 165–6, 169–71
  missionary, 18–23, 153–64
  paternal metaphor, 1, 8, 12–18, 153
  in social movements, 11–12, 15, 132
paternity (biological), 3, 8–9, 19–21
  exemption from paternal duty, 12
  and illegitimacy, 11
  race and denial of paternity, 23, 180–2
  rights of overridden, 10–11, 33–5, 169
patriarch
  authority of, 1, 7, 11, 43, 45–6, 52, 80, 82, 94, 96–7, 100, 108, 113, 128, 133–4, 142, 145, 154–5, 157–9, 161, 166–7, 185–6
patriarchy, 7, 22, 36, 38, 43, 45, 52, 75, 80, 133, 145, 166–7
  challenges to, 7
  and colonial challenges, 154–5, 157–9, 161, 185–6
  contradictions in, 7, 97, 108, 154
  and 'Fatherhood of God', 16–19, 128, 133–4, 153, 166
  and gift relationship, 96–7, 100, 108
  and intimacy, 145
  limits to 75
  and respectability, 82
  as rule of householder, 20, 36, 43, 45, 52
  as rule of father, 52
  in working class, 79, 113–14, 127–8, 133–4, 142
patriotism, 3
periodicals, 13, 126
Pettigrew, Elsie (b. 1910), 147

philanthropy, 32, 78, 98, 102, 106, 108, 114, 128, 130, 140, 153–4, 161
  female, 18, 114
political economy, 86
politics, 3–6, 11–12, 20, 43–54, 80, 115, 128, 130–5
Poor Laws, 11–12, 34–5, 140, 146
Presbyterian, 127
prostitution, 12, 132
provision, 4, 8, 11, 15, 21, 32, 100, 113–14, 122, 127, 132, 135, 138, 140, 142, 146–7, 184
  emotional element of, 138–44, 174–5

race, 23, 44, 182, 185
Rathbone, Eleanor (1872–1946), 139, 147
realism, 72, 82
Redgrave, Richard (1804–88), 72
  The Sempstress (1844), 72
Reform Act, [1832] 20, 44–6, 51–2; [1867] 44, 52, 80, 131, 135
Rendall, Jane, 44
residuum, 80
Roberts, David, 98
Roberts, Elizabeth, 142
Roebuck, John Arthur (1802–79), 44
Roper, Michael, 43
Rose, Sonya, 15, 113
Rosen, David, 58
Rotundo, Anthony, 169
Ruskin, Margaret (1781–1871), 57

Seccombe, Wally, 8
secularization, 2, 7, 17
self-improvement, 126–9, 131–2
self-interest, 12–13, 132
Sennet, Richard, 174
sentimentality, 66
separate spheres, 13, 15, 21, 52, 73, 116
  limitations of as a concept, 6, 21, 116
  see also domesticity
separation agreement, 35–6
servants, 8, 122, 127, 185
sexuality, 12, 37, 45, 58–9, 155–7, 159–60
Shelley, Mary (1797–1851), 33
Shelley, Percy Bysshe (1792–1822), 21, 33–9
Smelser, Neil, 122
Smiles, Samuel (1812–1904), 86

Smith, Mary (1822–89), 129–32, 134–5
Society for the Protection of Women and Children, 10
soldiers, 2–5, 12, 50
sons
   and fathers, 4, 6, 7, 15, 33, 35–6, 47, 50, 55–7, 59, 62–5, 75, 85, 87–9, 91–3, 113–25, 130, 145, 159–60, 178, 184, 186–7
   and mothers, 33, 35–6, 57, 59, 62, 64
   see also paternalism for father–son metaphor
Stark, Herbert, 181
Steedman, Carolyn, 123
stepmothers, 87, 129, 133
Stocks, Arthur (1846–89), 71–84
Strachey, Richard (1817–1908), 19
Stratton-Porter, Gene, 172–3
Sunday schools, 17, 114–15, 132–4, 154

Talbot, Adelbert, 183–4, 187
Talbot, Guendolen, 183
temperance, 9–10, 128, 131–2
Tosh, John, 1, 7–8, 21, 35, 43, 56, 73, 79, 97, 99, 107, 126, 130, 166, 184
Towey, Alice, 101
trade unions, 114, 121–2, 141, 143
Trevelyan, Sir George (1838–1928), 183–6
   The Competition Wallah (1864), 183, 186
Trollope, Anthony (1815–82), 21, 23, 85–95
Trowbridge, J.T., 169–71
Tyerman, Daniel (1773–1828), 159, 160

unitarian, 18
utilitarianism, 86

Vason, George (1772–1838), 154–8, 161–2
Vincent, David, 141
violence, 9–10, 101, 135

wards of court, 35, 36
Warner, Susan (1819–85), 166–7, 169, 173
Wesleyans, 153
Westbrook, Harriet (1795–1816), 33, 39
widows, 139–40, 146, 165–6
widowers, 12, 19, 22, 71–84, 87, 90–1, 94, 129, 133, 144, 146–7
The Widower, 72
Wiener, Martin, 10
Wilkes, John (1725–97), 49
Wilkes, Mary, known as Polly (b. 1750), 49
Wilkie, David (1785–1841), 71–2
Wodehouse, Thomas, 2nd Lord Newton (1857–1942), 98–9
Wolf, Simon (1826–1923), 165–6
women
   'new women', 7
   as target for conduct literature, 7
   violence against, 9–10
   'woman's mission', 18, 162
   women's rights, 7, 132–5
   see also daughter, labour, mother
Wood, Charles, 1st Viscount Halifax (1800–85), 97–8
Wood, Charles Lindley (1839–1934), 98
Wood, Edward, 1st Earl of Halifax (1881–1959), 98
Woolf, Virginia (1882–1941), 5
working-class father
   constraints on, 75, 79, 127–8
   and class pride, 48, 114, 131, 142
   and criminal law, 9–10
   object of middle-class hegemony, 5, 9–10, 14, 73–82, 114, 126, 129
   and Poor Law, 11–12
   see also labour
workhouse, 10, 11, 102, 147, 158

Zelizer, Viviana, 173
Zoffany, Johan Joseph (1733–1810), 49

Lightning Source UK Ltd.
Milton Keynes UK
UKHW022257140619
344284UK00016B/397/P